THE REMARKABLE STORY OF **BRIAN CLOUGH'S**
EUROPEAN CUP-WINNING TEAM

I BELIEVE IN MIRACLES

DANIEL TAYLOR FOREWORD BY
JOSÉ MOURINHO

headline

First published in hardback in 2015
by HEADLINE PUBLISHING GROUP

First published in paperback in 2016 by HEADLINE PUBLISHING GROUP

1

Cataloguing in Publication Data is available from the British Library

Hardback ISBN 978 1 4722 3358 5
Paperback ISBN 978 1 4722 3359 2

Typeset in Cronos Pro by Palimpsest Book Production Limited, Falkirk, Stirlingshire

Printed and bound in Great Britain by
Clays Ltd, St Ives plc

Headline's policy is to use papers that are natural, renewable and recyclable
products and made from wood grown in sustainable forests. The logging and
manufacturing processes are expected to conform to the environmental regulations
of the country of origin.

HEADLINE PUBLISHING GROUP
An Hachette UK Company
Carmelite House
50 Victoria Embankment
London EC4Y 0DZ

www.headline.co.uk
www.hachette.co.uk

Daniel Taylor grew up watching Nottingham Forest from the terraces of the City Ground before moving into the pressbox, and is currently the chief football writer for the *Guardian* and the *Observer*. This is his fourth book and his second on his specialist subject – Clough and Forest. Taylor grew up in Nottinghamshire and started his career at the *Newark Advertiser*. He was appointed by the *Guardian* in 2000 and now lives in Manchester.

Jonny Owen was born and bred in Wales' most famous footballing town, Merthyr Tydfil. As well as acting in some of the UK's biggest TV shows and writing and starting in the Universal movie *Svengali*, he's also written about football for the *Guardian*, *The Times* and the the *Western Mail*. A little slower than he once was, he still trots out for a local five-a-side team and is currently working and living in Nottingham and London.

9 40255225

Contents

Foreword

by José Mourinho

'I like the look of Mourinho, there is a touch of the young Clough about him.' *Brian Clough*

In 1996, when the European Championship was held in England, I had just started working at Barcelona with Bobby Robson. I came over to England to watch the tournament, mostly to follow the Barcelona players, and one of the games on my list was Portugal against Turkey at the City Ground in Nottingham. I was curious about this city. I had never been to Nottingham before, but I had grown up as kid hearing all the stories about Robin Hood, the Sheriff of Nottingham and Sherwood Forest, reading all the books and watching all the movies. And more than anything, I knew about Brian Clough and Nottingham Forest.

I was sixteen when they won the European Cup in 1979 and seventeen the following year when they did it again. Like a lot of boys of that age, I was fanatical about football. But it was a lot different back then. There was no Internet in those days and, growing up in Portugal, the only live matches involving English teams were the FA Cup finals and if they were involved in the European Cup finals.

Even so, I knew all about this team. I knew who Brian Clough was, what he did for that team and the size of the achievement. I knew every player in their team, who the best players were and that their manager stood out even in a generation when there were so many greats of his profession. This was the era of Rinus Michels, Stefan Kovacs, Udo Lattek and so many others who did amazing things.

So I travelled to Nottingham with curiosity to see the city because I knew about this place, with Nottingham Forest and Robin Hood. I got the train in the morning from London to Nottingham and I stayed there all day. I went early so I could have a look around, and when I got off the train I walked into the city centre. I walked to Nottingham Castle and I saw the statue of Robin Hood. And then I walked all the way to the stadium. Nobody knew me at the time, so it was okay. It was a long time before I was thinking about winning European Cups myself. I walked all the way and when I saw the stadium I thought: 'Are you kidding me – this club won the European Cup? Twice?'

It was a nice stadium and a nice city, but it was a small place. It was the size of the stadium that really took me aback. A small stadium, a small crowd – I looked around and tried to take it in. There are some places in football where you go to watch a match and immediately you can feel it is a club with an important history. You go to Manchester United, or Milan, or Madrid and they might not play well, or it might not be their best team playing, but you can smell the history. You go to Nottingham and this small ground – and these guys won two European Cups?

Let me say this: I don't generally believe in miracles. I agree with the title of this book, and Jonny Owen's film, and I understand the meaning of it. But I also believe it's only talent that can make miracles. I believe talent can make incredible things and in this story there must have been a lot of talent to be called a miracle. There are certain things in the history of football that will stay there forever and this is one of them. Brian Clough and Nottingham Forest did things that history can never delete.

My memories of that team? I remember them as well as I remember the Ajax of that time or the Bayern Munich of that time. When I was managing Porto, I played a UEFA Cup final against Martin O'Neill, then the manager at Celtic, so he is an easy one for me to connect with first of all. I remember John Robertson scoring the winning goal against Hamburg in 1980. I remember Trevor Francis, Tony Woodcock, Garry Birtles, Archie Gemmill. Viv Anderson has gone down in history as the first black footballer to play for England, but I remember him more because of the kind of full-back he was. Forest were ahead of their time because they and Ajax were the first teams whose full-backs went forward. Anderson was the first of that generation.

And then, of course, there was Brian Clough. A lot of people say we have similarities and there are certainly coincidences. Clough won his first European Cup on German soil and I did the same with Porto. For his second European Cup, it was not just that he won in the Bernabeu, as I did with Inter Milan, but we both beat German opposition. His team beat Hamburg, mine beat Bayern Munich. It is also another coincidence that Nottingham and Porto are the smallest cities to have won the European Cup, beating what I call the 'sharks'.

The sharks are the teams who are always usually there in the final stages of the European competitions. They are the favourites. For an outsider such as Nottingham Forest – and

I don't think they were even considered an outsider – to win the European Cup not once but twice is something unbelievable to me.

We all probably remember Clough's best quotes. 'I wouldn't say I am the best football manager there is,' he used to say, 'but I am in the top one.' I love that line. He had all that self-esteem and big self-belief. He was very confident about himself, and from what I know about him he was very comfortable with the attention.

I remember him talking about the football pundits on television and saying: 'There are certain people who go on about tactics and they couldn't even win a game of dominos' – and I wonder what he would think about the way some of today's pundits earn more than some Premier League managers.

I also enjoyed watching that famous interview of him with John Motson from the BBC – you can find it on YouTube – where he sat down with a face like he was the Prime Minister. There is all that self-esteem again. But there is sarcasm, too, and he is very, very funny. He doesn't care what people think and you can see he is enjoying himself. He never laughed, he never looked like he was joking. But he had this super profile in front of the television cameras. And then 'ping, ping, ping' – he starts taking aim. And the interviewer doesn't stand a chance. 'Ping, ping, ping!'

He was certainly a very charismatic man, but let's not overlook that on the football side he was also brilliant at what he did. It sometimes feels to me like people focus too much on a manager's personality, and they forget it needs more than personality to win titles. What wins titles is the other part: football knowledge and methodology.

Maybe because Brian Clough was such a huge personality, with so much charisma, everyone remembers his quotes and the stories and a few people forget his talents. The guys who played for him can speak about that better than me. I'm sure they can tell the world that it is not possible to do what he did, winning all those trophies, just because he was a guy with charisma. I could go into London and find 100 people with charisma in a single day – but none of them would be a top manager. So I think maybe he deserves the highest praise too about the football side.

As a kid, I knew about him because he was the manager who kept winning the European Cup. It's only since I came to England that people started telling me: 'Oh, you have some things in common with him.' But people tend to speak about him because of what he might have said in an interview, rather than his methodology.

I understand why because he came out with some great quotes. For example, when Sven-Goran Eriksson was appointed the manager of England it was Clough who pointed out 'the good thing is that he speaks better English than some of the players.' This sense of humour, as well as the so-called mind games, was a big part of his character. But there was another part, which was him just as a football man. He didn't win two European Cups with Nottingham Forest just because of his charisma.

I feel like I am in this position myself sometimes. I can go into a big match as Chelsea manager and, if we win, people say it is because I said something fantastic in the press conference beforehand. No, it wasn't because of the press conference that we won. It was the choice of the players, playing the right players, adapting play to the qualities of the players. Clough would have known all about that.

What he also had was a big personality and no doubt that helped when everyone was saying Nottingham Forest would collapse. As a manager in that position, you have to convince your players they can do it, no matter what everyone else thinks. At the same time you have to enjoy it. You have to go to the big stage and show them, 'Hey, this is no problem for me,' so the players will think it is no problem for them too. Clough was brilliant at this. But you can only be brilliant under that kind of pressure if you have a certain personality. It's not something you can copy.

When you get to the quarter-finals of the European Cup, you know all the sharks are coming. That's when it needs that special personality to be able to cope. Porto went into the Champions League, a lot like Nottingham Forest, with all the big teams – the sharks. I remember my press conference before we knocked out Manchester United at Old Trafford. I was very big-headed, very confident, very aggressive, because I knew my players were waiting to see if I would be different at Old Trafford than if Porto played, say, Braga. I had to show them.

In my first season at Chelsea, in 2004–05, everybody said we would collapse, just like people said Nottingham Forest would. We will collapse at Christmas, they said. We will collapse at Easter, we will collapse in the final three weeks of the season, we will collapse when Manchester United put pressure on us. We never collapsed. This is the kind of pressure that is put on teams at the top and this is when a manager's personality is very important. If you don't enjoy it, you collapse. You let the team collapse. You cannot lead your team to trophies and championships if you cannot take the pressure. But if you enjoy it, you can make your team even better and even stronger. Brian Clough looks to me like he enjoyed it.

History cannot delete what he and Nottingham Forest did – their results, the cups, the achievements, absolutely unbelievable achievements. I have huge respect for what they did. And I will tell you something else. I think if Brian Clough was around today, we would get on.

'When I sit in my garden and close my eyes, I still see that moment in Munich when John Robertson suddenly took control and made his move by the left touchline. The anticipation, that strange sense that something special is about to happen, caused Peter Taylor to stiffen and grab my arm. Robertson is not far from the corner flag. There are half a dozen or more Malmo players in the box, Trevor Francis is hurtling towards the far post and Robbo sends in the perfect cross. One-nil, pass me the European Cup. Thank you very much.'

Brian Clough

Chapter One
Nowheresville

'Possibly the worst result in our history.' *John Mounteney, Notts County director*

Duncan McKenzie was soaking in the bath when the doorbell chimed and the first strains of 'Jingle Bells' started drifting in from outside. It was his son who shouted up the stairs that Brian Clough and the Nottingham Forest players were singing Christmas carols at the front door.

'Very funny,' McKenzie shouted back. 'Give them fifty pence and tell them to go away.' Except the collection of male voices then moved on to 'Ding Dong Merrily on High,' and when McKenzie pulled on a towel and went downstairs he realised it wasn't a joke. McKenzie was an ex-Forest player and had briefly been with Clough when he was managing Leeds United. 'Right lads,' Clough shouted, after insisting his former player had poured everyone a Christmas drink, and off they went again.

Clough certainly kept it interesting during the years when he appeared to hold the keys to the football universe, and it is probably safe to assume they do it very differently on the managerial courses that anyone wanting to get into the business is required to go through these days.

On one occasion, for reasons that were never fully explained, Clough abandoned training after the first five minutes and, eyes twinkling, sent his players into a nearby meadow to look for wild mushrooms. Larry Lloyd shouted across that he had found some of the magic variety and Clough wasn't fazed in the slightest. 'Chuck them in as well,' he shouted back.

Clough once ordered the team coach to pull over at the side of the road, en route to the airport for a mid-season trip to Kuwait, after hearing Garry Birtles grumbling about it at the back of the bus. Birtles was told to fetch his suitcase and get off. Clough then hailed down a passing car, persuaded the bewildered motorist to drive the player back to Nottingham and threw the case in the back seat.

He fined another player for making a bad pass, and his way of awarding John McGovern the captaincy was to throw the ball at his midriff with enough force it would have winded him if the player had not had quick reflexes. 'I caught it just in time,' McGovern recalls. 'He said: "You're good at catching the ball, so you might as well lead the team out" and that was it. It remained that way for seven years.' McGovern was lucky. Clough would often throw the ball at players, even the opposition sometimes if the opportunity arose in front of his dugout. The usual tactic was to 'aim for the bollocks'.

His players have hoarded these stories like personal souvenirs and it is always Clough who seems to come out on top with the beautifully delivered pearl of wisdom, one of his lacerating putdowns or his unerring ability to wrong-foot whoever is in his company. McGovern tells his favourite ones with the best impersonation since Mike Yarwood used to send up Clough as 'the great Chatsby' on Saturday night television. 'Hey, young man, listen up and you might just learn something,' with a wagging finger for added emphasis. Those years, McGovern says, were 'humorous, great fun and certainly didn't feel like work' and that is worth keeping in mind when it comes to the misconception that Clough's success was based around a culture of fear. His players have always disliked that theory; even the ones who regularly wanted to drop a flowerpot on his head.

Those players spent a lot of time trying to fathom out Clough's peculiar, precious magic, but none of them ever really managed it. Clough could never be pigeonholed. He had a large and colourful palette of moods and trying to second-guess him became a sport in itself. But it was impossible. He was an enigma. As soon as his players thought they had worked him out, he would always do something to unravel all their conceptions.

Tony Woodcock suffered more than most during Clough's early days at Forest, but he also tells a story about the time he was getting married and asked his boss for permission to take a day off training. Forest had lost the previous week and Woodcock was unsure how Clough would react. 'Leave it with me, son,' Clough said. He had a friend in Jersey with a hotel and sent the newlyweds away for the week, flights and all, for their honeymoon.

Chic Thomson, the goalkeeper in Forest's 1959 FA Cup-winning team, changed his mind about the man who called himself Old Big 'Ead when he found him helping out at a residential care home in the city. Thomson had always thought Clough was in danger of drowning in his own ego. His opinion changed when he saw Clough on his hands and knees, sleeves rolled up, mopping the toilet floors.

Then there was the time Clough heard that one of his former players at Derby County had got himself into such dire financial problems that he had been forced to put all his medals and other football possessions up for sale. Clough rang him up to tick him off for being so careless. Then he went to the auction, bought everything and immediately gave it all back.

The people who knew Clough best remember a man who could be fiercely loyal to those he thought deserved it and capable of great acts of kindness. Like the time, for example, when he sent a festive hamper to Frank O'Farrell's family shortly before Christmas in 1972. O'Farrell had just been sacked as manager of Manchester United and a reporter later asked Clough if it was true. 'That's private,' Clough said, which suggested that it was.

When Terry Curran joined Forest a few years later, he could not settle in Nottingham in his first few months and kept going home to Doncaster in his spare time. Clough got wind of it and took Curran's car keys off him one day. When Curran finished training he nervously asked for them back, anticipating one of those lectures when Clough's voice could have the soothing properties of a pneumatic drill. Clough threw him the keys to a brand-new Triumph Spitfire that was waiting outside. 'You drive more miles than James Hunt,' he told Curran. 'You need a proper car if you're going up and down that bloody motorway.'

Clough's tongue could be the hardest part of his body, capable of inflicting the worst kind of verbal buffetings, while there were other moments when he gave the impression he could charm the birds down from the eaves. He became a statesmanlike figure in Nottingham, a preacher and prophet who was held in so much reverence the city's hospice turned to him when one of its patients was starving herself to death. Clough spoke to the woman for half an hour, putting himself across so beautifully she promised to start eating again. She said later that she had 'never felt such tenderness,' and it was the same again when a young man was threatening to jump off Trent Bridge, one of Nottingham's notorious suicide spots, and the two police constables at the scene were struggling to talk him out of it.

Clough had been driving past when he saw the crowd gathering. He stopped his car and spoke to the man, named Stephen, for as long as it took to persuade him to come down. 'It's not just yourself you'd be throwing into that mucky old river,' Clough told him. 'I'm not jumping after you but one of these poor policemen might have to. And you can't do that to your mam, can you? Remember, Stephen, never let your mam down.' Clough received a citizen-of-the-month award from the Chief Constable of Nottinghamshire but, for all the famous braggadocio, he doesn't refer to it in any of his books and was reluctant to pose for photographs.

His players remember the time they played at Sunderland and he noticed two young boys, almost urchin-like in appearance, trying to get autographs outside Roker Park and out way too late for his liking. Clough invited them on to Forest's bus to find out where they lived before Albert, the driver, was instructed to get out his map and squeeze his vehicle through several rows of terraced streets to find the right place. That was the point the entire team disembarked while Clough knocked on the door to make sure his two young passengers, now armed with a full book of signatures, got in safely.

Albert, incidentally, was possibly the only bus driver in professional football who had the manager's permission to chug his way through twenty Silk Cut on every trip. Yet Clough was also the man, before a pre-season game against Barcelona in Camp Nou, who had the temerity to remove a cigarette from the mouth of Cesar Luis Menotti, drop it on the floor and nonchalantly stomp it out with his shoe. 'Terrible habit, and you should know better,' he explained to the man who had led Argentina to the 1978 World Cup. Menotti, known as *El Flaco*, was one of football's famous chain-smokers, someone whose long, gaunt face somehow seemed incomplete without a little white stick drooping from his lips. He nodded obediently, waited for Clough to disappear then sparked up once more. Clough came back and did exactly the same again.

Everyone who has spent any time with Clough has a story of his unorthodoxy, the sense of mischief and irascibility, but there were not many people in the world who ever properly worked him out. 'Was Brian Clough a genius, or was he off his head?' Stan Bowles once asked. The one-liners have become legendary and that repartee, the non sequiturs and acidic turn of phrase can make you pine for more interesting times in these bland days when modern managers are trained to see nothing and say even less. Clough did not need to surround himself with an army of puffed-up PR advisers or press-release writers. He handled it all himself, disarming his audience with long, impassioned homilies about football, politics or any other subject. He talked in plain English, free of clichés and banalities. He was a natural in front of the camera – telegenic in a way no other manager

6

had ever been – and, unusually, he never spoke better or with more authority than when he was under pressure.

Yet it wasn't always fun. Clough could be hostile, dictatorial and unforgivably rude. He had a temper that could go off like a car alarm, and there were so many different layers to his personality that his players were always on their toes, never quite sure what to expect. 'A pickle of a man,' his friend Sir Michael Parkinson once said. 'He was lovable and impossible, wise and silly, attractive and appalling.' Sometimes, indeed, all in the same conversation. As the psychiatrist said of Basil Fawlty, there was enough material there for an entire conference.

When Peter Shilton signed for Forest, it was one of the first times an agent had been used to complete a football transfer. Shilton actually had two, Jon Holmes and Jeff Pointon, carrying business cards for a company called Pointon & York and wearing pinstripe suits as they arrived at the ground with their leather briefcases. 'Clough was in his green rugby top, shorts and scruffy trainers and had a squash racket in his hand,' Shilton says. 'My two advisers went in first and suddenly I saw them go sprawling across the floor. Clough was hiding behind the door and tripping them up with his racket. I've no idea why.'

Clough must have been going through a tripping-up phase at the time. Phil Thompson played in the formidable Liverpool side that Forest knocked off their perch long before Sir Alex Ferguson coined the phrase with Manchester United. He remembers following Clough once into the players' tunnel at Anfield. 'Alan Hansen was a quiet lad in those days. Clough was just behind him and kept clipping his heels. Alan kept

7

looking round but it didn't stop Clough. "What the fuck are you doing?" I started saying. He never flinched, turned towards their dressing room and disappeared without even a glance back.'

Jimmy Case, one of Liverpool's legendary hard men, got a passing kick up the backside as he left the pitch at half-time of another match, as retribution for a succession of over-the-top challenges on the pitch. Case was one of those Liverpool players who could lose his temper in a game of Pooh Sticks and nothing wound them up more than Forest's success. Clough did, in fairness, apologise for that one.

At Forest, there were players who could not decide if they liked him, hated him or maybe a bit of both, but they all knew he was special. Larry Lloyd often wanted to throttle him but listen to the old centre-half now and he reminisces about 'old Cloughie' with the dewy-eyed affection that is usually reserved for a favourite uncle. Martin O'Neill is the same. All they really craved was Clough's approval when, unfortunately for them, it didn't come easily. Clough knew who to praise and who to needle. He was a master of mind games and reverse psychology before the terms were even invented.

The only player Clough doted on was the podgy little Scot he once described as 'the Picasso of our game'. When Clough walked into Forest's dressing room for the first time, John Robertson had a chip-fat grin, a slapdash attitude and a packet of Polos strategically hidden in his back pocket to help cover up his fag-breath. Robertson's career was drifting and it took a while for the chemistry between him and Clough to work. Yet he has never forgotten Clough's first day and the instinctive feeling that something better might be on the way. It wasn't anything Clough said that resonated. It was the aura. It was the moment the dressing-room door almost flew off its hinges. It was the way, before uttering a single word, that in one swift movement Clough was already taking off his jacket and flinging it at a wall peg, as if he had been there years. Clough being Clough, it landed plum on the hook. 'It was like a whirlwind coming in,' Robertson says, with the awe still apparent in his voice. 'I'd never seen anyone in my life with so much charisma. All I could think was: "Jesus, this guy means business." Right from the very first minute.'

The date was 6 January 1975. Margaret Thatcher was a few weeks away from taking over as leader of the Conservative Party. *Monty Python and the Holy Grail* was trying to make it past the film censors and Mud were number one in the pop charts with 'Lonely This Christmas'. *The Sweeney* had just premiered on ITV, Abba had won the Eurovision Song Contest and Ray Reardon was the world snooker champion. Malcolm Forbes was almost killing himself trying to fly a hot-air balloon across the Atlantic. A thousand Led Zeppelin fans were rioting in Boston. Charlie Chaplin had just been awarded a knighthood and that evening the largest television audience in the country would see Bet Lynch drowning her sorrows at the bar of the Rovers Return because bin-man Eddie Yeats had stood her up. Nottingham's Broadmarsh shopping centre was about to open its doors for the first time and it wasn't just because of Clough that the city's sporting scene was about to change dramatically. Nobody really paid much attention at the time but a young police cadet called Christopher Dean and a newsagent's daughter by the name of Jayne Torvill, aged sixteen and seventeen, had just skated together for the first time.

That was the season, 1974–75, when Manchester United could be found grubbing around for points in the Second Division and George Best's career took an eccentric turn towards Dunstable Town. Bob Paisley had taken over from Bill Shankly as Liverpool manager and Don Revie had been placed in charge of the England team. Clough had replaced Revie at Leeds but had been sacked after forty-four wild and acrimonious days. Derby, Forest's arch-rivals, were on the way to their second league championship in three years and not many people had been taking a great deal of notice in the tatty, unfashionable club by the banks of the River Trent. Forest, to use Clough's phrase, were 'in the shit'.

Or to put it another way: thirteenth in the Second Division. Forest were five points off the relegation quicksands when Clough arrived. The stench of disillusionment had been years in the making and the City Ground was nothing like the shiny, photogenic stadium that reflects off the Trent now. Three quarters of the ground were made up of rough, hard-faced terraces. A spindly floodlight rose from each corner and the rows of benches at the back of the old East Stand were cold and hard enough that many spectators brought their own cushions. The wooden boards were divided into individual seats by hand-painted lines. Nobody, unfortunately, had used a tape measure, meaning there was a haphazard Laurel and Hardy pattern to the different sizes.

One end was completely uncovered and had an electronic

scoreboard, owned by the local Shipstone's brewery, that was often faulty but on the better days showed 'Ivor Thirst' celebrating goals by waving a rattle. At the opposite side, the Trent End, the sloping metal roof offered some protection but was so low that a thick, uncompromising fog would sometimes drift in from the river, making it impossible to see from one goalmouth to the other. Clough quite liked the way the team used to run out to the theme song from *The Adventures of Robin Hood*, but the players used to cringe when the chorus of 'Robin Hood riding through the glen . . . Robin Hood with his merry men' started echoing round the ground. Peter Cormack, who played for Forest in the early 1970s, remembers 'the opposition players used to rip the piss out of us something rotten as we were leaving the changing rooms.'

To a younger generation, football in that era must sound like a bizarre age. But life itself was very different back then. The average wage was £70 a week. Only one in two households had a phone. There were three television channels to choose from, rather than the hundreds we have now, and nobody had a computer, never mind iPads, smartphones, TomToms or Kindles. Tweeting was something birds did, not humans, and trolls existed only in fairy tales, usually living in a cave. And, in football, there was little to suggest that one day it would be a sport for millionaires' row, the haves and have-yachts, the super-rich and the glitterati, where sometimes it feels like money is how they keep the score.

Footballers drove sensible cars and lived in what seem now to be inconceivably modest suburban semis. They had equally inconceivably big hair, flared trousers and kipper ties, and played in rough, grimy stadiums filled with cigarette smoke, where there was always the possibility a brick or punch might be thrown. There were no all-seater stadia, no cuddly mascots, no Michelin-starred chefs in the kitchens, no executive boxes serving vol-au-vents and vino behind the tinted windows. Clough once described the dressing rooms at Chelsea as being 'a pigsty' and caused them so much embarrassment one of their supporters offered to decorate the place, free of charge. Stamford Bridge was unrecognisable from the giant fruit machine being played by Roman Abramovich and José Mourinho forty years later.

Forest were the second oldest of all the English league clubs, formed in 1865, but their only trophy since the war was in the era of *Pathé News* coverage. The ground was dank and inhospitable in most parts, with only the Main Stand giving the place some modernity, and the training pitch was a rough patch of grass and concrete beside the Trent rather than the gleaming buildings with state-of-the-art gymnasiums and Olympic-sized swimming pools every club worth their salt has these days. It was liable to flooding and there was no shelter or fencing, which meant anyone could wander in, long before the days when dog-walkers bothered with poop bags. There were no changing rooms, other than those back at the City Ground, and a misplaced punt would often put the ball in the river or among the groups of anglers, their rods and tins of maggots.

There was also something about the club's administrative set-up that left the distinct sense the people in charge were desperately out of touch. Forest didn't have directors in the ordinary sense. Instead, they had a nine-man committee of local worthies and businessmen elected by the club's 200 members, much like a golf society or branch of the Round Table. Membership was a couple of pounds a week to get a seat and the privilege of a vote that meant an input into the running of the place. Yet there wasn't even a waiting list when Clough arrived, and it wasn't difficult to understand why some of his contacts had tried to warn him off. Brian Appleby, one of the committee members, summed it up best. Forest, he said, were the 'most unprogressive club in the country'.

Clough, of course, always backed himself to bring light to even the darkest corners. His time at Leeds counted as an ugly cross on his managerial record and his previous job, a jarring nine-month stint at Brighton and Hove Albion, hadn't been too much fun either, featuring the humiliation of an 8–2 home defeat against Bristol Rovers and a 4–0 thrashing against non-league Walton & Hersham in the FA Cup. Clough was always an awkward fit for a club in the Third Division. 'It was like asking Lester Piggott to win the Derby on a Skegness donkey,' he said, 'and then telling him he was rubbish when he didn't do it.'

But there was still a glint of superiority in his eye. Clough had taken a plodding Derby side from the depths of the Second Division to promotion and, in 1972, the First Division championship. In his pomp he gave the impression his person-ality was a juggernaut that could drive him wherever he wanted. He was, as O'Neill put it, 'on *Parkinson* just about

13

every other week'. He had sparred verbally with Muhammad Ali live on television. Clough, to nobody's surprise, made absolutely certain to have the last word and he still had that aura of invincibility, even though he had been out of work for four months. On the day of his appointment at Forest, a cartoon in the *Daily Express* showed him walking on water. Clough was crossing the Trent to begin his new job. His feet were kicking up spray. His chest was puffed out. It did not seem to bother him in the slightest that he was frightening the ducks.

To the players, he was mesmerising. 'It was like getting on a train,' O'Neill says, 'and never getting off.' Yet there was a time when O'Neill had wondered whether that train would even get out of the station and whether Clough was 'so hot, so hard to handle' that Forest would find an excuse not to go through with it. Clough wound up people for the hell of it. He was the loosest cannon on the managerial deck and his eccentricities did not stop at occasionally planting a kiss on a television interviewer's cheek, disappearing in the middle of the season for a week's holiday or, as happened at Brighton, excusing himself from one match to fly to New York for Ali versus Joe Frazier.

Clough had a reputation for being able to argue any point, sometimes when he didn't even have a shadow of a leg to stand on. He could be temperamental, erratic, abrasive and, for a prospective employer, a challenge, to say the least. He had left Derby because his relationship with the chairman, Sam Longson, had completely unravelled and he had blown through Leeds in the only way he knew: full of arrogance, openly confrontational, unconcerned about who he might offend. Clough went by his own rules, breaking authority wherever he went, and Forest's chairman, Jim Willmer, could imagine the hassle it would bring. 'We don't want success at any price,' he told Appleby. 'Bring him in and we'll live to regret it.'

Four committee members threatened to resign when they discovered what was being proposed and plenty of others didn't like the idea of anyone, let alone an ex-Derby manager, threatening their culture of nineteenth-hole chumminess. Yet Forest were desperate. Clough knew the secrets of how to recast and inspire a football team and, ultimately, the pro-Clough lobby outnumbered the opposition. Ivor Thirst was in danger of dying from dehydration. A mutiny was building on the terraces and the team were crying out for someone with the personality to offer something better. Clough was there, according to Appleby, to give a 'transfusion of life to a dying club'.

Forest had been relegated in the year Clough took Derby to the league title and were so hopeless that season, under the management of Matt Gillies, that one training session was arranged against invisible opponents – no opposing players or even any cardboard cutouts – in a desperate attempt to boost confidence when the goals started going in. It had the opposite effect. Forest finished second from bottom, in the face of regular 'Gillies Out' protests, and recorded the lowest points total in their history. They also lost twice to Derby, including a 4–0 thrashing at the Baseball Ground, and there was another moment of tragicomedy when the players complained Gillies was working them too hard in training on Thursdays, only forty-eight hours before games, and it was leaving them worn out on Saturdays. 'We can't swap it around,' the coach, Bob McKinlay, explained. 'The manager likes to play golf on Wednesdays.'

That side ended up with more home defeats than any other team in the league and the players could probably be forgiven for suspecting Gillies had his priorities mixed up. Tommy Gemmell had played for Jock Stein at Celtic and scored in the 1970 European Cup final. 'We're breathing out of our arses on a Saturday because Mattie plays fucking golf every Wednesday,' he complained, walking off in disgust one day. 'Big Jock wouldn't organise training around golf. Wait until I tell him, he'll not fucking believe me.'

The following season, 1972–73, Forest finished fourteenth in the Second Division, with Dave Mackay taking over from Gillies, while Clough led Derby to the semi-finals of the European Cup where they were nobbled only by some highly suspicious refereeing. Clough was brilliant for Derby. Everybody knew it, especially himself, so when he walked out in October 1973 and Mackay abandoned Forest to take over at Derby, a petition was raised in Nottingham demanding Clough was redirected towards the City Ground. Fans chanted: 'We want Clough.' Banners called for the committee to resign and letters appeared in the local newspaper from disgruntled supporters threatening to stay away unless it happened. Clough, they argued, was the only man who could do the job properly.

It got them nowhere and at the next home game the club's secretary, Ken Smales, took them to task in the match programme. 'It must be pointed out that many anti-BC letters have been received by the club, so his appointment here would not necessarily have received the unanimous support

I BELIEVE IN MIRACLES

the press would have us believe,' Smales, a straight-talking Yorkshireman, wrote, putting 'anti-BC' in bold for extra emphasis. 'More disturbing, though, is the attitude that has crept into modern-day football life when the threat to withdraw support on the slightest pretext is prevalent. The chanting of "committee out" by fifty or so supporters last Saturday because their particular favourite was not appointed is another sign of the times.'

Allan Brown, a 47-year-old Scot, was appointed a couple of days later and that epitomised Forest's low-level ambitions. While Clough had been expertly piecing together a championship-winning team of style and substance at Derby, Brown had been managing Bury among the puddles and potholes of the Fourth Division. Before then, he had an unremarkable spell at Torquay, a promotion season at Luton Town and three years as player-manager at Wigan Athletic, then playing in the Cheshire League.

Brown had been an inside-forward in the great Blackpool side of Stan Mortensen and Stanley Matthews, as well as being part of the Luton team that lost to Forest in the 1959 FA Cup final, but his management record was bland and he got off on the wrong foot with his players from the first day.

'If you are late I will fine you 20p,' he announced, 'and if you're late a second time it will be 40p.'

Twenty pence in 1973 was the equivalent of a loaf of bread and pint of milk and there was an awkward silence while the players worked out if he was pulling their legs or if that was genuinely the new disciplinary code. It turned out he was serious. Neil Martin, the team's experienced striker, eventually broke the silence. 'Here's a pound,' he said, pulling a handful of coins out of his pocket. 'I'll see you next week.'

Brown had already managed to call John Robertson by the wrong name – 'How are you, Jimmy?' – and his lack of authority was probably summed up by a story over Easter when the team had back-to-back games. Forest lost the first one at Bristol City and then had a marathon bus journey to play Carlisle at Brunton Park the following afternoon. They were beaten again, and on the way back the players stocked up with as many bottles of beer as they could carry and were so sloshed by the time they reached Charnock Richard services on the M6 they started rolling their empties down the aisle of the bus, seeing if they could skittle them all the way to Brown's seat at the front. The consensus from the back of the bus – where they mimicked 'twenty pee' in Brown's Fife accent – was that the manager was 'weak as piss'. Brown, trying to reassert some control, later told them he had heard more noise from them on that journey than in the previous six months.

In fairness to Brown, his team did finish seventh at the end of the 1973–74 season, without seriously threatening promotion, and were winning 3–1 in an FA Cup quarter-final at Newcastle until a pitch invasion created so much mayhem that when the game restarted Forest capitulated to three late goals. The club's complaint was upheld by the Football Association but Newcastle eventually went through after two replays – both staged, to Forest's intense irritation, at Goodison Park, home of Everton – and, that apart, there hadn't been a great deal of excitement for Forest since the 1966–67 campaign, when the pipe-smoking Johnny Carey assembled a side that finished as runners-up to Manchester United and reached the FA Cup semi-finals. The next six finishes sum up the club that Forest had become: eleventh, eighteenth, fifteenth, sixteenth, twenty-first and, in the Second Division, fourteenth.

Ian Storey-Moore, the star player from Carey's 'fizz-it-about' team and described by the *Sunday Telegraph* as 'probably the most talented ball player in the country when Georgie Best is not on full song', had left to join United and the Holy Trinity of Charlton, Best and Law. Duncan McKenzie then took over as the crowd's favourite – '*We all agree, Duncan McKenzie is magic*,' chorused the Trent End. '*Is magic . . is magic . . is magic*' – and became so revered one match report noted that the churchgoers outside the ground, holding up posters proclaiming 'be prepared to meet thy God', would have seen the next best thing if they had bought a ticket to enter the ground. McKenzie – the man who could leap over Minis and throw a golf ball the length of the pitch – was a brilliant wearer of Forest's colours but a player with his flamboyance, scoring twenty-six goals in the 1973–74 season, was never going to stick about at a club scuffling around in the Second Division. McKenzie fell out with Brown and effectively went on strike, training with Borrowash Victoria and contemplating opening a newsagent's, before taking a phone call one night and hearing a familiar voice at the other end of the line.

'Duncan, Brian Clough here. Now then, don't piss me about, young man, I have half a chance of signing you. Are you going to that Dave Mackay at Derby County, because I know you've been tapped up, or would you like to join me at Leeds United?'

McKenzie went to Leeds for £250,000 and that didn't leave

a great deal in Nottingham when Clough turned up midway through the season to take over from Brown. Sir Walter Winterbottom once said that every football manager would like to work at Forest. Clough wasn't so sure after his first look. There were six centre-halves on the books and, according to Clough, 'not one of them could be relied upon to head the ball.' There was no obvious goal-scorer and 'nobody who could play left-back to save his life'. One of the players was using a Shipstone's Brown Ales beer mat as a tax disc. Several were overweight and Clough was closer to the mark than he realised when he announced on his first day he had 'rejoined the rat race'. Forest's location by the river made the ground a haven for rodents. The club's solution was to adopt a cat, Ginger, to keep the numbers down, even if it meant various mouse parts and half-eaten corpses being strewn across the pitch. The committee figured it was cheaper than bringing in pest-control.

Brown had been sacked after the ignominy of losing 2–0 at home to Notts County, a result that left Forest's near-neighbours at the top of the city's football ladder for the first time since the 1950s. The ground that day was half-empty and in the previous game the attendance was down to 8,480 for a numbing goalless draw against mid-table Blackpool. Earlier in the season, a club that regularly played in front of 40,000-plus in the late-1960s drew a crowd of only 7,957 for a game against Millwall.

Nottingham, to quote Lawrie McMenemy, had become a 'football village'. There was the castle, Nottingham had the oldest pub in the country and its lace was among the finest in the world. There was Robin Hood, of course, and DH Lawrence.

Alan Sillitoe had put Nottingham on the map with his first novel *Saturday Night & Sunday Morning* and the Raleigh factory where he used to work on Triumph Road was still turning out bikes. Paul Smith had opened his first store in Byard Lane and red-blooded men from all over the country flocked to the city to investigate the alleged ratio of five females to every male. Yet Nottingham was a sporting black hole and Forest had become a club of pub-quiz trivia and not much more. They were the first team, in 1874, to use shin guards, even if they were worn outside their socks. They were the first to let the referee use a whistle (1878), the first to play under lights (1889), the first to use goal-nets (1894) and, though it wasn't something they boasted about, the first to lose a player to injury because he was bitten by a rat, as happened to the unfortunate LO Lindley before an FA Cup tie against Aston Villa (1881).

Otherwise, the official history of the club conveys rather neatly the bland existence of the previous ninety years. 'The club's trophy cabinet had not exactly kept an army of cleaners occupied,' it notes. 'There were two FA Cups – in 1898 and 1959 – and that really was that.'

Clough did not walk across the Trent on that first day. Instead, he arrived in the pale-blue Mercedes he had been given as part of his settlement from Leeds – or as Clough called it, the 'fuck-you money'. There was plenty of it too, but his reputation had taken a battering in the process. Glory at Derby had been followed by ignominy and rancour at Brighton and Leeds.

The players at Leeds had passed a vote of no confidence in him and the people closest to Clough suspected it had hurt and chastened him more than he let on.

Clough had spent his period of unemployment choosing not to watch football, making himself available only to a select few. He changed his number even though he was already ex-directory and he contemplated turning his back on football sine die. He was intrigued how far someone with his personality could make it in politics. His wife, Barbara, thought his talents might be better suited for teaching and encouraged him to get the necessary qualifications. Yet the old urges kept coming back. Clough might have been the Hollywood actor who had taken a wrong turn and ended up on Skid Row, but Forest had given him the chance to return to the game that had filled so much of his life. And, on the bright side, at least his new set of players looked at him differently from the ones at Leeds. It was awe and wonder, rather than disdain and contempt.

In the offices at the City Ground, they quickly felt the impact of Hurricane Clough. Paul White, the assistant secretary, remembers there were none of the usual introductions, just a message to do something about the scrum of journalists who were outside. 'He said: "Get this fucking rabble into the guest room or whatever you have here, give them a cup of tea and I'll speak to them after training." Then he was off to the training ground. End of discussion.'

The players were waiting for Clough in the dressing rooms of a stand that six years earlier had been wrecked by fire. Sammy Chapman was the club's longest-serving player and the first one Clough sized up. 'Bloody hell, Sam,' he exclaimed, rubbing his hands together. 'It's cold enough to freeze the balls off a brass monkey, isn't it?'

There was a nod of recognition to Barry Butlin, one of his former players at Derby, but no proper introductions other than a 'Gentlemen' – a regular Clough-ism – and then the new manager was straight into business.

In his pocket, he said, he had the names of the players he would take to his first game, an FA Cup third-round replay at Tottenham Hotspur, then seventeenth in the First Division. The list would be pinned to the wall, but first the players were going out on the training ground so he could have a look at them. 'And nobody in tracksuit bottoms, because no bugger wears tracksuit bottoms during matches, so why bother now?'

Oh, and one last thing. 'Is young O'Neill in here?'

Martin O'Neill – a 22-year-old midfielder signed from Distillery during the Gillies era – had fallen out with Brown and was on the transfer list. He raised his hand tentatively.

'You're coming with us, son.'

Clough had made it clear in a matter of minutes that everything was going to be different on his watch. His swagger, his energy, the speed at which he moved; it was the antithesis to Brown's weak grip and twenty-pence fines. But there was also no doubt he had joined a club of profound desperation. Forest were in Nowheresville, with plummeting crowds and a dwindling team in genuine danger of dropping down another division.

O'Neill's memory is of a club 'firmly entrenched in the mire' and wondering if some of his older team-mates had started to give up. 'The side that had been in the semi-finals of the FA

Cup and came close to winning the league had disintegrated. Some of the older players had lost enthusiasm for it. The team were struggling. The crowd was restless and disgruntled. We were languishing in the Second Division and there was no real sign we were going to come back up again.'

Viv Anderson remembers 'a provincial club bumbling along'. Anderson had been rejected by Manchester United's youth system and was working as an apprentice printer until Forest, his hometown club, decided he was worth a look. He, like O'Neill, had wondered whether Forest would dare appoint someone with Clough's personality, and their conclusion was that it would be totally out of character. Anderson was only eighteen, a young and impressionable right-back, but even at that age he had the distinct feeling the people running the club were 'content with mediocrity'.

Clough's first programme notes made it clear that he was of a similar mind. 'When I was first asked to write this article, my initial reaction was to say no because a football manager's job is not about writing notes for a match programme,' they began. 'But it is the first opportunity I've had to introduce myself so I'm here for the first – and last – time this season.'

On the opposite page there was a photograph of chairman Jim Willmer, wearing a tweed jacket and a Bobby Charlton-style combover, and his own column. Clough, he wrote, was 'an energetic young man with an exciting background who, I am certain, loves this great game of soccer'.

The problem was the 'energetic young man' was already taking aim in precisely the way Willmer and the other committee members had feared. Clough described signing McKenzie for Leeds as taking 'the last pearl from Forest's oyster', but he sympathised with the player for tiring of a club that had so little ambition. 'This club has gone places in the past but so much has gone wrong, too many bad decisions have been made and not enough work put in. One of the greatest tragedies to my mind is the way quality players have been allowed to leave over the last five or six years. None of that would have happened had I been here.' Forest, he estimated, must have lost close on a million pounds' worth of talent without bringing in adequate replacements, McKenzie just being one example. 'Nobody knows why he made his stand against Forest better than me. He must have been frustrated with what was happening and I can imagine his feelings were similar to yours. You had run out of patience because of what had gone wrong in the past and run out of hope for the future.'

Clough might as well have taken out a full-page advert and left it at three words: blame the committee. Nor did he sound hugely enthused by the team's chances. 'I know from the reaction there has already been to my arrival that something special is expected of me. But if you want wild promises of First Division football, big signings and glamour in the near future . . . forget it!'

Clough was never one to sugar-coat the truth. He also had a ghost-written newspaper column on the day of his appointment. The fee, he said, would pay for the club to get a new oven because the 'old one was knackered', following it up with a joke about whether he should play it in attack.

But it was a strained kind of humour and, for someone with Clough's thirst for success, a numbing way to lead his life. Leeds had taken on Jimmy Armfield as their new manager and climbed eight places up the First Division table since Clough walked out of a side door at Elland Road, draped an arm incongruously around the chairman Manny Cussins and, looking unnaturally relaxed for a man in that position, announced that his brief and chaotic spell at the club was over.

Derby, the club Clough had never really wanted to leave, were three points from the top of the league with a game in hand. Mackay had inherited a side featuring Colin Todd, Roy McFarland and Kevin Hector and was showing he could handle what the *Guardian* had described as 'a black comedy entitled Can the Rams ever forget Brian Clough and find True Happiness playing Somebody Else's Football?' Derby had finished third in their first season of playing somebody else's football and Mackay was in the process of re-establishing them as the best team in the country.

Clough looked for all the world like a man who meant business. He had worked a football miracle at Derby. He had been convinced at Leeds that he could persuade a dressing room of battle-hardened players to stop despising him, and his inability to leave a lasting impression on Brighton hadn't left the tiniest scuff on his formidable ego. There were even times in his first managerial job at Hartlepools United, with their famously leaking roof and superfluous 's', when he probably thought they would end up winning the European Cup.

Yet Clough did admit later that he was startled by what he found at Forest and that he had never expected it to be so bad. 'It was like entering a desert – a barren place devoid of life, lacking in colour with not even a green leaf to give hope. And, like a desert, there didn't seem to be any end to it all. I didn't realise how bitter the supporters were, how short of genuine talent the playing staff was, or how bad the finances were.' Clough kept it quiet at first but it did cross his mind, driving home on that first day, that he might have 'dropped a bollock' and if he was the kind of man who took other people's advice he would probably never have been there in the first place.

Mackay – the man Clough regarded as his finest ever signing at Derby – had not been at Forest long as manager. But it was long enough to see for himself the desolation and the lack of ambition of the people running the place. He had told Clough to steer clear and find another club.

'You'll never achieve anything there,' Mackay said.

Chapter Two
Rome Wasn't Built In A Day

'What's going to happen to Brian Clough now? Who's going to touch you with a bargepole?' *Austin Mitchell, Yorkshire TV*

Brian Clough always knew that knocking Tottenham Hotspur out of the FA Cup in his first game was a deception. It didn't fool him either when Forest won their next match away at Fulham. Clough knew they would find their true level once his honeymoon period was over and his suspicion was that it probably would not be very high. 'Nottingham Forest have one thing going for them right now,' he said, with all that renowned modesty. 'Me.'

True enough, Forest did not win any of their next fifteen games until they came up against a desperate Sheffield Wednesday side who were bottom of the league on April Fool's Day and George Lyall soothed the crowd's nerves with a penalty for the only goal. Even then, the headline in the *Nottingham Evening Post* was: 'Dismal Show'. The run was significantly worse than anything the club had encountered while Allan Brown was manager. There was only one more win all season, on the final day against West Bromwich Albion, and there was a real threat at one point that Forest's toes could be tagged for the relegation morgue.

They finished sixteenth, three places worse than when Clough arrived, and before the season was over a letter appeared in the *Evening Post* from someone purporting to be sick of the mediocrity and announcing he was switching allegiances so his scarf 'would be black and white from now on rather than red and white'. It turned out to be a mischievous Notts County fan, but nobody knew it at the time, and that season was the first in twenty years that Forest finished below their neighbours from Meadow Lane. County had been in the Fourth Division four years earlier and, for Forest, the embarrassment was considerable. The County chairman, Jack Dunnett, got himself into trouble once for saying that 'most people who can remember when County were a great club were dead.'

Had Clough, to use his own words, dropped a bollock? He had never shied away from hard work but the glories he craved felt an awfully long way away, and it can be overlooked sometimes just how long it took before a somnolent club began to stir. Ken Smales talked later about Clough regularly 'coming into the office in an extreme state of depression' and one particular day when the staff found him slumped in his chair, complaining that he had just witnessed the worst training session he could ever remember. Clough looked close to broken. 'My God,' he said, 'just think, I have to depend on some of those players and they can't even pass a ball, let alone control it.'

Clough used to watch some matches from the Main Stand during those early months, wrapped up against the cold after a bout of pneumonia, and Forest were so comically poor at times he would give the spectators around him a loud running commentary about the team's deficiencies. The game against Wednesday was as wretched as it got and Clough spent a significant part of it roaring his disdain, making various derogatory remarks about the attempts of Paul Richardson, a central midfielder, to fill the problem left-back position and announcing to anyone who cared to listen that he had seen better football played by Nottingham Pork Butchers. He did at least keep the crowd vaguely amused, but it was a strange form of tragicomedy.

Forest lost their next game 4–2 at Bristol Rovers, another team in the relegation places, and when the players headed back to the dressing room Clough bent down in front of Richardson and started pulling at his laces. 'He started to take my shirt off and untie my boots,' Richardson says. 'When I asked him what he was doing, he said he was helping me because I was the only player who had tried a jot. I told him I'd been crap. He said he couldn't disagree, but at least I had tried.'

Clough could see there was some untapped talent at the club, but he also noticed there was an empty row of seats behind the part of the ground where the committee used to watch games. When he asked why those seats were kept free, the explanation shocked him. 'The committee wanted it that way,' Smales told him, 'because they were fed up of people spitting on them.'

There was quite a bit of flying saliva once the initial surge of optimism surrounding the Tottenham game – 'Utopia,' Clough had called it – wore off, and it was the same again the following season, 1975–76, when there was a gradual improvement but the team never challenged seriously for promotion and suffered some calamitous results before a late run lifted them to eighth.

31

It certainly wasn't a straightforward process getting Forest back on an upward curve and the club were entangled in a relegation battle when Clough started the process of bringing in some new faces – or some old ones, to be more accurate – in the first few weeks after his appointment. John McGovern and John O'Hare had been expecting the call. The other players had too. 'Put it this way,' Martin O'Neill says, 'we weren't the slightest bit surprised.' It was the fourth time Clough had signed McGovern. O'Hare was another Clough favourite and had known him virtually all his career. Both players had been with him during the exhilarating highs at Derby and both had experienced the excruciating lows at Leeds, where they were tainted as Clough's men and discovered very quickly what a hard-faced, unforgiving club Leeds could be.

For McGovern in particular it had been a joyless experience, leaving his partner, Ann, in tears during one game when she sat in the main stand at Elland Road and heard the venom being spouted in his direction.

On McGovern's first day at Leeds, the club's legendary hard-man, Norman Hunter, shook his hand and didn't let go. The grip was tight enough to shell a conker. 'Last time you played here you dumped me on the halfway line,' he told the new signing, with a slightly sinister smile and one last squeeze. 'Good luck.'

McGovern suspected he was 'in the shit' but it was even worse than he had imagined. 'I was actually booed by the crowd before I had kicked a ball. But the players had it in for me too. They sold me short passes. When I passed it to them they slowed down and let the ball run out of play to make it look like a bad pass. I didn't stand a chance. When you're getting stitched up by your so-called team-mates, that does make things difficult for you.'

At one point Johnny Giles played what should have been a straightforward pass so it was sixty-forty in favour of McGovern's nearest opponent and the new signing was crunched by the resulting tackle. Soon afterwards, the same happened again and McGovern was flattened a second time. Giles was one of the more sophisticated players of his era, capable of pinpointing thirty- or forty-yard passes all over the pitch. 'I had always found him a difficult opponent to play against,' McGovern says. 'I found him even more difficult to play with.'

McGovern left Leeds with a grudge that has festered ever since, whereas O'Hare was also unwanted at Elland Road but never had quite it as bad. O'Hare already knew Billy Bremner, Eddie Gray, Joe Jordan and Gordon McQueen from playing for Scotland and had their respect. He found it difficult seeing, close-up, the dressing-room mutiny that edged Clough towards the guillotine, but he could sympathise, to a degree, with the players. 'Clough really did say some things to them that were unnecessary. He told them they were cheats, so you can understand why the Leeds players didn't take to him. "Was he like this at Derby?" they would ask me. They were the best team in Britain at that time but Clough wanted to change everything and he didn't care who he upset.'

With Don Revie in charge, Leeds used to keep a dossier on all their opponents so they would know the strengths and weaknesses of whoever they were playing. 'Somebody brought it in one day and Clough just ripped it up in front of everyone and threw it in the bin,' O'Hare says. 'He said: "It's what we do that matters." The Leeds players were used to the Revie style of management where everything was meticulously looked after. Clough wasn't like that at all. He was spontaneous, off the cuff, completely not what they were used to. The biggest issue, though, was what he had said about them all. He didn't like Leeds and he didn't like Revie. There was a real animosity there, so why Leeds ever gave him the job I'll never know.'

It was a mystery to everyone, bearing in mind Clough was on record saying Leeds should be relegated for bringing the sport into disrepute and insisting the players should throw away their championship medals because they had not been won fairly. Clough thought Leeds represented the worst traits of his industry, and never tired of saying so. And the rivalry with Revie was personal. Clough thought Revie had a heart of gold: yellow and hard. Revie, in turn, regarded him as a sworn enemy. Clough, he said, was 'the last man I would like to be stranded on a desert island with' and when Revie left to become England manager the Leeds players had irreparable grievances with the man taking his place. It was, Clough said, the equivalent of 'Brezhnev becoming Prime Minister of Britain with a Tory government'. Leeds won only one of Clough's six league games and were nineteenth in the table, with four points, when the players called the vote of no confidence. It was the club's worst start in fifteen years.

'Ultimately, the players got him the sack,' O'Hare says. 'I was in the meeting when they decided they wanted to get rid of him. They just couldn't forgive him and it had reached the point where the vice-chairman Sam Bolton ended up telling them: "Okay, we'll get it sorted." The general opinion was that Clough didn't know anything about the game. To me, he obviously did because he had been so successful at Derby, but the Leeds players thought he knew nothing and that Johnny Giles should be player-manager. Then Billy Bremner went home, thought about it overnight and thought he might like the job. So Johnny Giles wouldn't take the job and that became another issue. All they could really agree on was that they didn't want Brian Clough.'

O'Hare's loyalties remained with the man who had gone on television on the night of his sacking, sitting beside Revie for a one-off special, *Goodbye Mr Clough*, smiling into the camera and generally looking like a man who was about to be appointed the Emperor of Leeds rather than one who had just been fired, as he put it, without 'enough time to find out where the local butcher's shop is'.

Clough never looked better than he did that night: straight-backed, immaculately coiffured hair, slim and dapper in a crisp pale-grey suit, and almost hooting with joy when Revie complained about the way 'Brian' referred to him in the news-papers only by his surname. Revie was flint-faced and full of froideur, groping around for the right words, with the dark, brooding countenance of a senior officer from the Serious Crime Squad. Arthur Hopcraft, one of the doyens of sports writing, described Revie as someone with 'an outdoors face as though he lived permanently in a keen wind'. He seemed to be avoiding eye contact, struggling to conceal his resent-ment, whereas Clough actually looked like he was enjoying himself, leaning in at one point so they were almost touching knees, even getting in a wonderfully patronising 'good lad.'

Revie: 'Why did you come from Brighton to Leeds when

you criticised us so much, and said we should be in the Second Division, and that we should do this and we should do that? Why did you take the job?'

Clough: 'I thought it was the best job in the country . . . I didn't know the players, Don. I didn't know them intimately like you. But I knew you were the league champions. I wanted to have a crack at the European Cup and I wanted to do something you hadn't done. I wanted to win the league but I wanted to do it better than you.'

Revie: 'But there is no way to win it better. We lost only four matches.'

Clough: 'Well, I could lose only three.'

Revie: 'No, no, no.'

They cleared the schedules that night to show it straight after *News at Ten* and Clough's slick delivery and presentation – 'Leeds had to get someone who was slightly special,' he noted, 'now, I don't want to sound blasé or conceited . . .' – made him the Kennedy to Revie's Nixon. But that didn't surprise O'Hare in the slightest. He had known Clough since they were at the opposite ends of their playing careers at Sunderland. He could remember Clough's aura as the club's record-breaking striker – 'brash and arrogant, even then' – and he was there on the day his future manager skidded on the frosty pitch at Roker Park, collided with the Bury goalkeeper Chris Harker and suffered the injury, the snapped cruciate ligaments, that destroyed his playing career. 'Boxing Day 1962,' O'Hare says. 'He had already scored twenty-four goals that season. He was an idol up in Sunderland.'

At twenty-eight, O'Hare was taking a 50 per cent pay cut to move to Forest, selling his house to finance the move, and giving up the English champions for a club that was flirting with the idea of dropping into the Third Division. He made his debut in a 1–1 draw at Oxford and soon established that even on the reasonably good days the team were 'pretty average'.

What really concerned him, though, was Clough's demeanour. 'Something had changed. The Leeds thing had knocked him. You might think it would be pretty difficult to knock this man's confidence but he was as low as I had ever seen him. To the Forest lads, he was brash enough but John McGovern and I had known him when he looked like he could take on the world. I'd never known him to be so subdued before. He just wasn't the man we remembered.'

To understand why, the best place to start is probably the interview Clough gave to David Frost in November 1974, after two months out of work. He looked a picture of vitality – engaging, lots to say, determined to put the best face on it – and, again, it was stunning television. But there were glimpses of hurt too. Clough had never been sacked before and the experience, he admitted, had 'hit me right between the eyes'. He said he had been turned off football so much that he would need a long time to recover and would not be going back 'for many, many months to come'.

Clough also made such a point of not mentioning Revie by name, opting instead for pointed references to 'the other guy', that Frost asked him to explain why.

'I'm loath to mention him, and if we can refrain from it we'll do so,' Clough said, with a knowing smile. 'I hate to mention him because he's a very talented man . . . and I don't like him. Don't ask me why, because that's exactly what it is.

He's a very, very talented man and his record is unsurpassable. I just don't happen to like him, and I don't like the way he goes about football either.'

Frost pushed him one more time. 'Why don't you want me to ask why you don't like him?'

'I can't tell you. It's impossible . . . we'd get closed down, David.'

That brought laughter from the studio audience but the experience at Leeds had clearly taken its toll and, though it wasn't something the other Forest players could relate to, McGovern also felt the spark had gone, or at least faded, in his first weeks back with Clough. 'I used to travel in with John O'Hare to training. There was one week when I turned round to John and said: "I think he's going through the motions." He had lost some of that fantastic energy. It was a strong thing to say but that's how it seemed, based on my experiences with him at Hartlepool and Derby, and my gut feeling was that I was right. Brian Clough was always top man, yet his change of mood was clearly visible.'

McGovern wondered where all the amazing self-confidence was being stored, but he was also glad to be out of his own misery at Leeds. That period was so deeply unpleasant for him that his mother, Joyce, went to see Clough one day to complain that her son was being used as the whipping boy. Clough had asked McGovern to take Bremner's place, but that brought another wave of animosity from the terraces, and the player was still getting it in the neck long after the man who had brought him to the club was fired. 'Brian lasted forty-four days at Leeds,' McGovern says. 'Unfortunately for me, I was still there when he left.'

He and O'Hare had to stick it out for another five months before Leeds cut their losses and let them go for a knockdown £70,000, little more than half of what they had cost the club from Derby. McGovern's only other offers came from Carlisle United and Norwich City, and Clough was operating from a position of strength when it came to the contract negotiations. 'His exact words were: "You should be paying me to get away from Leeds,"' McGovern recalls. 'My good lady had warned me beforehand. She said: "I know what you're like, he'll put down a contract and you'll be daft enough to sign it without even reading it. You won the league championship at Derby, you're not a young player anymore, so please don't take a drop in wages." I promised I wouldn't accept a penny less then went off to meet Clough at the Posthouse in Sandiacre. And the negotiations lasted all of, well, ten seconds. I took a £30 drop in wages and I hardly dared walk through the front door that night. But the money was irrelevant. I knew this guy was going to bring the best out of me. I knew he was going to bring the best out of all the other players. I knew what was going to come and, after Leeds, I would have crawled down the motorway to get there.'

McGovern was used in the centre of defence during his early stages in Nottingham but he was signed essentially to play at the base of midfield, where Clough wanted someone who could read the game, find a team-mate with the ball, make the occasional tackle and not try anything too fancy-dan. Ian Bowyer was on the left wing, George Lyall was on the right and O'Hare went into attack with Barry Butlin. O'Hare wasn't the fastest striker by any means, but he was full of competitive courage and fulfilled the role Clough thought essential of all centre-forwards: holding up the ball, even when tightly marked, taking the kicks from defenders and bringing others into play.

Clough said he had brought in O'Hare and McGovern to 'teach the others how to play football', but he actually liked to do that himself and on one of his first days he simply placed a ball on the palm of his hand, told his players he didn't know, or care, what had happened under the previous managers but that from now on they were to take care of it. Treat this ball as if it was your wife, he said. Caress it, cherish it.

Clough talked about the importance of building from the back and having a moral obligation to pass the ball on the deck. 'Planes were made for the clouds,' he told them, 'footballs weren't.' The priority was to use the ball better than their opponents because if they could keep the other side chasing it, using up priceless energy, they would eventually tire. Away from home, he wanted the team to drop further back, let the home side come at them and then spring them on the counter-attack. He wanted centre-halves who knew the basic tenets of defence – heading and tackling – and midfielders who understood the other side couldn't score if they didn't have the ball. He told his players to use the full width of the pitch, not to argue with referees in any circumstances and if anyone was fouled he expected them to get on with the game without any complaints – so no falling and no feigning. He wanted players to dress smartly, shave before games and give the club a good name. Get the ball, he said, and enjoy its company.

That all sounded well and good but putting it into practice was another matter. Counter-attacking football might be commonplace in today's game, but it wasn't de rigueur back then. Forest had sold all their best players – Storey-Moore, McKenzie, Cormack, Henry Newton, Terry Hennessey – and their replacements were mostly inadequate. Others had been at the club since relegation and, as such, were associated with failure. Sammy Chapman seemed to have been at Forest since time began. Paul Richardson had been on Forest's books since 1966. Liam O'Kane, a defender in his seventh season at the club, had come back from a broken leg. 'When do you tackle?' Clough growled at him one day. 'If you back off any further, you'll be in the bloody Trent.' The team lacked pace and creativity. They had an accident-prone defence and at least a dozen players Clough didn't trust. His analysis was brutal: 'Some of our players couldn't play, some couldn't kick the ball from A to B and several couldn't head it to save their lives.'

On a more positive note, Clough reckoned some of the younger players had half a chance if they could get rid of their bad habits. He liked the look of John Middleton, an eighteen-year-old goalkeeper who was tipped as a future England international and already in the first team. Clough had contemplated signing Viv Anderson when he was managing Leeds and he could see that Ian Bowyer understood the game and had something most of the others lacked: presence.

Bowyer had started his career as a striker at Manchester City and in 1970, at the age of eighteen, he came on as a substitute in both the League Cup final and the European Cup Winners'

Cup final. His problem at City was that he could never win over their notoriously hard-to-please supporters and eventually dropped into the Second Division for a couple of seasons at Orient before Mackay brought him to Forest.

In Eamon Dunphy's book, *Only a Game?*, the author writes about 'the good pro' – the guy who has your back, self-effacing, hard-working, totally reliable. 'If you are in the shit, having given your man that crucial extra yard or two, or you have lost your concentration for a minute, the good pro will often rescue you, leaving his man to get in a saving tackle or making what looks to the crowd like a simple interception. He is woven into the fabric of every good side and every great side too.' Bowyer was that type: future captain material, brought up on hard graft and discipline, driving an unpretentious Ford Capri – 'two-tone: brown and rust' – and already, at twenty-three, an important voice in the dressing room. He had a useful knack of scoring important goals and he was fearless in the tackle.

Clough saw something in Bowyer and one or two others, but it was obvious that changes had to be made and the exodus started in his first summer. At committee level, there was a feeling that Tommy Jackson, a Northern Ireland international, could become the new McKenzie. Clough didn't fancy him and when Manchester United picked up Jackson on a free transfer it caused a stir behind the scenes. 'I don't give a fuck if he has signed for Real Madrid,' was Clough's response. 'He can't play.'

Neil Martin had scored the goal that knocked Tottenham out of the FA Cup and was the only striker on the club's books to finish the season in double figures. Yet Clough had

O'Hare now and Martin left to join Brighton. Clough also packed off the winger Miah Dennehy and a reserve centre-half called Steve Baines. The list of 'dead wood' was extensive and there wasn't a great deal coming through the youth system. The FA Youth Cup had been in existence for twenty-three years at that stage – and Forest had the pitiful record of never progressing past its fourth round.

It wasn't just the youth set-up that made Clough think the club needed a complete rebuilding job. The training kit, Clough used to say, was 'like something you got from the Oxfam shop'. The practice ground was 'Siberia without a coat on'. One player, he reckoned, had to be taught how to take a throw-in. Another player asked Clough whether he should play the ball down the channel. 'The Channel is a stretch of water between England and France,' came the reply. 'Pass it to feet, or I will be throwing you in it.'

Clough's first appointment was Jimmy Gordon as the team's trainer, finding the man he regarded at Leeds as 'the only friend I had' working as a store-man for Rolls Royce in Derby after spending the previous two months on the dole. Gordon was old-school – tracksuit, whistle round his neck, Brylcreemed silver hair – and described by Clough as 'the fair-minded old pro whom I could trust with my life and my wallet, if I carried one'. Gordon's instructions were to take care of the training drills and get the players in shape before the manager started working on their minds. He had worked with Clough at Derby as well, and when Clough asked him what he thought of the Forest players the verdict was blunt and straight to the point. 'Very ordinary,' Gordon said.

One of them was John Cottam, a big, lumbering centre-half

who was in his seventh season at the club and, according to Clough, needed to lose at least half a stone. Clough had his own way of helping Cottam get rid of the excess cargo. He summoned the centre-half for a game of tennis when the team stayed at Bisham Abbey before the Tottenham cup tie. The game went on until darkness and Cottam was ordered to fetch every single ball to help him sweat off a few more pounds.

For Clough, turning the team around would need tenacity as well as vision. He started by trying to find another regular goal-scorer and persuaded the committee to pay £2,000 to sign Bert Bowery from Worksop Town. Bowery was nineteen and 'built like a brick shithouse', to quote Robertson, but there was a reason he was so cheap. Clough would say in later years that he was never any good at picking a decent centre-forward, and it certainly took him a long time at Forest before he realised the answer was right under his nose.

Tony Woodcock had been tipped as a sensation when Allan Brown gave him his debut, at the age of eighteen, in April 1974. Since then, however, he had lost his way, perhaps falling into the trap of believing he had already made it, and drifting to the edges. In football, it is known as a blip when a player temporarily loses form. Woodcock's had gone on half a year. The blip had become a slump and Woodcock can remember he was 'struggling even to get in the reserves' when Clough took over.

When he was included in the squad for the game at

Tottenham, he travelled down on the bus to Bisham Abbey wondering whether it was the break he needed to give his career some new momentum. Instead, it quickly became clear he was there to 'collect the balls, put down the cones, hand out the bibs and generally run all the errands'. Except it was worse than that. Perhaps Clough was trying to let everyone know that he was not afraid of bruising the players' egos and that things were going to be different from now on. Maybe he suspected Woodcock was a little too full of himself and needed bringing down a peg or two. Whatever it was, the getting-to-know-you exercise was a tough learning curve for the teenager.

Woodcock was not even among the substitutes at White Hart Lane, and on the day of the game Clough had another chore for him. 'We were having lunch,' Woodcock says, 'all the players were sitting at the same table when he turned to me and said: "Young man, here are the keys to my room, my shoes are waiting for you in front of the door and I want you to go to my room. Beside my bed I've left some polish for you. I want you to clean my shoes because I want to look my best this evening and we have to represent Nottingham Forest. So you need to make them look good."'

Woodcock's first reaction was a mix of horror and embarrassment, but he also knew his reputation among his peers, with all the senior players watching, might be ruined unless he stood up for himself and make it clear he was nobody's dogsbody.

'I looked up and down the table for some support and everyone's heads went down into their plates. George Lyall was the only one who looked up. He gave me a nod as if to say: "Do what he says, son." Nobody else said anything. So up I went.'

'Do a good job,' Clough called after him. 'I may be daft, but I'm not blind.'

Woodcock found the shoes lined up outside Clough's door. 'I polished them up and probably spat on them to give them a bit of extra shine. Then I went back downstairs and Clough was waiting. "Good lad," he said. "You'll go far." I didn't know whether he meant as a butler or a footballer but five minutes later Jimmy Gordon came over. "Don't worry," he said, "he did the same with Gordon McQueen at Leeds too – and he was a good player." That wasn't exactly a compliment either.'

Woodcock returned to the demoralising grind of reserve-team football, feeling increasingly sorry for himself and wondering how he could convince Clough to give him a crack at the first team. Fed up, he decided it was no use moping around any longer and that it was time to be a man, tackle Clough and show his new manager he was keen to make it work.

That moment arrived when Clough turned up in the laundry room one day while Woodcock was drying out his kit. Woodcock had visions of taking the number ten role and had prepared his speech. 'I think the problem for me here is that I've been playing on the left wing,' he told his manager. 'I don't really enjoy playing on the left wing and I reckon I can offer a lot more in a different position.'

Clough gave him a long, hard look. 'And where would you like to play?'

'The best thing all round would be if I went behind the striker, just in front of midfield. I'm pretty quick and I can score one or two goals.'

Woodcock remembers Clough's response going up in volume with every word. 'That tells me a couple of things about you, young man. One, you're too lazy to play in midfield and, two, you're not brave enough to play centre-forward. Now, get out.'

Bowyer had a bumpy introduction when Clough burst into the treatment room, announcing he was there to see 'the sick, the lame and the lazy', and then grilled his player about what was wrong, and how much training he had missed, before flouncing out.

Clough had an aversion to players being injured and did not care how unreasonable that might seem to others. Anderson did not even warrant a place on the bus for the first game of the new era – a punishment, many suspected, because the teenager had limped off with cramp in the previous match – and McGovern knew better than to expect sympathy when he suffered a groin strain during the dismal run of results, in the spring of 1975, that left Forest hovering perilously over the relegation places.

'I can't run,' McGovern shouted across to the dugout.

'It doesn't matter,' Clough shouted back. 'You never could.'

McGovern remembers it being pointless arguing. 'It was the manager at Nottingham Forest who told you when you were injured,' he says. 'Not the physio.'

Nobody was spared the whiplash of Clough's tongue, but one player undoubtedly felt it more than others. Clough might have brought Martin O'Neill back into the team but he suspected the 'O' in the player's surname must stand for obstinate. O'Neill had an education and a way with words that meant the other players called him 'Squire', but Clough wasn't impressed with the player's qualifications, or his inquiring mind, or particularly the way he would freely give his opinion when it was not always sought, often with the air of someone who thought he might know better. O'Neill was a popular member of the dressing room, with his sharp wit and passion for football, but he remembers that Allan Brown 'took an instant dislike to me' and he wondered sometimes if Clough was the same. 'You may have A-levels,' Clough would tell him, 'but you're thick as a footballer.' His nickname for O'Neill was the unflattering 'Clever Bollocks'.

John Robertson came from Uddington, the small town just south of Glasgow where the Celtic legend Jimmy Johnstone was raised, and he was a source of exasperation to Clough in different ways. Robertson liked a beer and more than the occasional cigarette judging by the nicotine stains on his fingers. He also appeared to live in a pair of orange-brown suede loafers that he refused to give up, even though he had spilt cooking fat on them on their first day.

Clough was on his back straight away, telling him he was living his life out of a frying pan and had better buck up his ideas if he wanted to be part of the new regime. But Robertson was young, easily led and living in digs with five other players of the same age, with Nottingham's nocturnal life waiting to be explored.

Robertson turned up to training one day with two black eyes after one of the locals had taken a dislike to him on a night out, and his explanation that he had been playing cricket and was hit by the ball was never going to wash with a manager as streetwise as Clough. His main drinking pal was Jimmy McCann, one of the fringe players, but one of his other mates was Dave Serella, a Gillies signing whose escapades included sneaking into the ground one night, climbing up one of the floodlights and swinging off it one-handed, gorilla-style, sixty feet up in the air. Another stunt was to climb over the side of Trent Bridge and dangle off a ledge above the treacherous currents.

Robertson had enough talent to make his debut at the age of seventeen, but it wasn't just Clough who had found it difficult getting him to knuckle down. When Gillies was manager, one of his coaches, a sergeant major-type called Tommy Cavanagh, gave Robertson such a hard time, telling him he needed to improve his appearance and stop coming in 'looking like shit', the target of all the opprobrium eventually snapped back.

'What do you want for seven quid a week – fucking Pele?'

Dave Mackay developed a soft spot for Robertson, despite fining him more than once for turning up late, but Brown didn't see anything special and tried to offload him to Partick Thistle. The deal fell through and Robertson, like O'Neill, was stuck with a manager he knew didn't want him. 'We just didn't get on,' Robertson says. 'He didn't like me and he couldn't even get my name right. That wasn't a great start and it didn't get much better from there. I was feeling neglected by the time Clough arrived, like the world was against me. Clough thought I was a wastrel. I didn't think I was quite that bad, but it's fair to say I wasn't taking football seriously enough. I'd started letting myself go. But I'm not going to put all the blame on Brown, because the truth is I wasn't helping myself very much.'

Robertson did at least have an ally in John Lawson, the Forest correspondent on the *Evening Post*. The team's reward for beating Spurs was a fourth-round tie against Fulham but Richardson was suspended and that left a space in midfield. 'At that stage,' Robertson recalls, 'Clough didn't know too much about the young players so he asked John Lawson to mark his card. John came up with my name and suggested I could play but might need a kick up the backside, so it was thanks to him really that I got in the team quicker than I probably would have done otherwise.'

There was nobody, though, to speak up for Woodcock as his first season under Clough became a personal ordeal. Woodcock's form had picked up in the reserves, but he still felt ostracised and unwanted. He had even been deployed as a makeshift left-back in one game, playing so well the referee came into the dressing room afterwards, grabbed him by the arm and asked him to sign his notebook. 'He told me he had seen a future England international,' Woodcock says. 'And yet I couldn't even get a place on the bench at Forest.'

His inability to impress Clough was bewildering to some of the older players. 'I could see this lad was a really good player,' O'Hare says. 'He was quick, sharp, he could score goals and he was terrific in the reserves. Whether Clough couldn't see it, or whether he was just waiting for him to change, attitude-wise, I'm not sure. But Tony didn't have a bad attitude, so I really don't know what the problem was. I just don't think Clough really liked him, or rated him, that much.'

One night, the reserves had a game at the City Ground and Woodcock was back on the left wing. In the first half, he suddenly became aware Clough was in the crowd. 'I thought I was doing okay when I heard this voice bellowing out: "Woodcock, get your foot on it!" That was Clough's big thing about forwards. He didn't like us flicking the ball on. He wanted us to be brave enough and tough enough to hold it up and bring others into play. But as soon as I heard that voice, I was a bag of nerves. I was terrible, couldn't trap a bag of cement.'

Woodcock was a mild-mannered boy-next-door type – 'so quiet,' according to Viv Anderson, 'you sometimes had to shake him to make sure he was awake' – and it was not his way to go looking for confrontation. But there was a story about when he signed professional terms that showed he was not a soft touch. At Forest there was a set policy that a first-year pro earned £30 a week and it went up by a fiver the following year. Woodcock thought he deserved to start on more and told the youth-team coach Bert Johnson he wanted £35. The club said no but Woodcock dug in his heels – and he won.

Clough was a different monster entirely, but when Woodcock saw him a few days after that reserve game he decided he had to let him know he was unhappy.

They were in the car park of the City Ground and Clough seemed in a good mood.

'Something wrong, young man?'

'Well, I thought I was doing all right for the reserves the other night, but suddenly you turned up and started bellowing from the stand. It was echoing throughout the whole stadium and it didn't put me at ease. That sort of thing just doesn't work with me.'

51

There were not too many occasions in Clough's managerial life when a teenage reserve had asked him to keep the volume down and, for a split-second, he was almost wrong-footed.

'I thought it might make you play better,' Clough said.

'No, boss,' Woodcock persevered. 'Completely the opposite.'

Clough took a few moments to formulate his response. 'Well, you can't win them all, can you?' he glibly noted, and sauntered off to his car as if he didn't have a care in the world.

Woodcock's lack of opportunities was all the more mystifying when Forest, to use Clough's description, were 'crap'. The crowds had gone up – Clough's appointment alone meant £4,000-worth of season tickets were sold in twelve days – but Forest won only three out of their seventeen league games in his first season, and he estimated it would take £500,000 to build a promotion team. The club's 200 members were asked to raise £25,000, but as his first season stuttered to its close only twenty-one had contributed and they had barely scraped together £3,000. Forest were skint – not bucket-collection skint, but they announced debts that summer of £77,618 and even held a cheese and wise event for local businesses to help bring in a few quid. 'Can you head the ball?' Clough asked one of the visitors, a boy of seventeen. 'If you can, I'll sign you because we've got no bugger who can head the ball properly at this club.'

It was obvious Clough had to be shrewd in the transfer market and that was around the time he took a call from Doug

Weatherall, a journalist friend in the north-east, asking him if he knew that Newcastle were about to let their captain Frank Clark go on a free transfer. Clark was approaching thirty-two, with a reputation for being injury-prone, and facing that period every footballer of a certain age has to go through when insecurity appears on the horizon.

He was in Doncaster talking to their manager Stan Anderson and the only other interest had come from Darlington and Hartlepools, both Fourth Division clubs. Clough saw someone who could be an organiser of defence and arranged to meet him at Scotch Corner on the A1. 'My car broke down on the way,' Clark says. 'That was probably the only time I was ever late to meet Brian, but fortunately he waited and we managed to get it sorted. He talked about his plans. He admitted they didn't have a very good team and that he desperately needed someone to play left-back, and he said I was the cheapest available – which made me feel great. But I knew Brian anyway. I'd played against him and I actually played in his testimonial match after he packed the game in. I knew all about his style – and I didn't have too many options.'

That solved the left-back issue, and when Clough took the team on a summer tour to Northern Ireland he decided to try Robertson on the same side of the pitch. Robertson wasn't keen at first. Yet Clough did not have many wide players on that tour who were fit and the experiment went well. Forest beat Coleraine 3–2 with a Bowyer hat-trick – and Robertson set up all three.

A recognisable Clough team was slowly taking shape. Clough left that trip with a new left-winger and, in mid-

August, Terry Curran arrived from Doncaster to add the pace that Robertson didn't have on the opposite flank. Yet it was still a work in progress and Clough's first full season in charge was, for long spells, joyless.

Forest lost again to Notts County inside the first month, this time to a goal in the eighty-ninth minute. There were more defeats against Hull, Charlton, Bolton and Bristol Rovers and then, two weeks before Christmas, Forest were at home to a dire Portsmouth side that had lost nine games on the bounce and were marooned at the bottom of the league.

Portsmouth had not won since the opening weekend of the season, taking eight points out of their first twenty matches. Forest lost 1–0 and the performance was so wretched it finished with the supporters behind Clough's dugout shouting that he was past it. And that was not even the nadir of Clough's winter. Three weeks later, Forest played Peterborough, a Division Three club, in the third round of the FA Cup. A team featuring Clark, McGovern, Bowyer, O'Hare and Robertson were held to a goalless draw at the City Ground. Peterborough won the replay 1–0 at London Road and Forest, once again, looked like a side whose bad days had all come at once. A tired, depressed side with low morale and a tendency to slip into basic ineptitude. A side that conceded all manner of goals – lucky ones, bad ones, great ones. A side that accepted their fate as soon as anything went against them.

Clough had been there a year and his team were in a worse position than when he started. He had won eleven out of forty-one league games. Brown had won fifteen at the same stage and, astonishing as it sounds, Clough was probably fortunate it was not the era of knee-jerk chairmen, cut-throat media and irritable Internet bloggers, for there was little doubt the bloodhounds would have been on his scent if those results had happened in the modern game. Liam O'Kane is convinced of it. 'In today's game, managers get sacked very quickly. I've no doubt Brian would have gone the same way in his first couple of seasons.'

By mid-January, Forest had slipped to fifteenth in the league and the *Evening Post's* John Lawson, who had been taken in as one of Clough's confidants, was predicting another relegation battle. New players were desperately needed and when O'Kane suffered another serious injury, this time one that ended his career, Clough set about trying to arrange a loan deal for a blond defender named Colin Barrett from Manchester City.

Barrett had lost his place at City but wasn't keen at first and sent a thanks-but-no-thanks message via their manager, Tony Book, only to discover that the person making the offer wasn't used to taking no for an answer. 'The next thing I knew, Brian Clough was on the phone to me: "Colin, I hear you don't want to sign for me." I told him it wasn't that I didn't want to sign for him, I just didn't want to come on loan. "I want to see you outside Leek Football Club," he said, "I'll be there in an hour," and then he put the phone down.'

Barrett was still unsure when he arrived but Clough was at his persuasive best. 'He said: "Where are you playing at the moment, Colin? Because you'd be better off playing in my first team on loan than Man City's reserves. I can get to know you and you can get to know me, you may not like me and I may not like you, but we can find out – so why don't you sign?" I drove home and got on the phone to my wife to say

I'd signed for a month on loan and had to report to the City Ground that Saturday for the first game.'

That was against Fulham and the new signing quickly learned that Clough did things differently from anyone he had worked with before. 'I met him in his office and he said: "Col, do you want a drink?" I said: "Hopefully I'm playing this afternoon, boss."'

'Oh, you're definitely playing,' Clough said, 'but if it makes you play better, have a drink.'

Forest won courtesy of an O'Hare goal. They also won the next home match against Sunderland and, finally, the team seemed to be getting a bit of momentum. The next game was against a York City side that had taken over from Portsmouth as the league's worst team and were on their way to back-to-back relegations to the Fourth Division. Forest's team at Bootham Crescent included McGovern, Robertson, Bowyer, O'Neill, Clark, Barrett and O'Hare. York: historic city, beautiful architecture, dreadful football team. York City 3 Nottingham Forest 2.

The late run of home wins continued against Orient, Oxford, Blackburn and Bristol Rovers, but Forest had never gone higher than eighth position and the season finished with Notts County, in fifth, looking down on them for a second successive year. County hadn't managed that since 1951, when Tommy Lawton wore the black and white stripes and a sixteen-year-old Clough was working for ICI in Middlesbrough.

A quarter of a century on, Clough was beginning to wonder how long it would be before he saw any significant improvement. There hadn't been a lot of laughter in his first eighteen months and Woodcock was pushing his luck when he turned up one day wearing several days' worth of stubble.

'I wanted to be different,' Woodcock explained, when the summons to Clough's office arrived.

Clough leaned in. 'Young man, if you want to be different at this club, you can go and score a hat-trick on Saturday. That would be different.'

Chapter Three
Not A Bad Little Club

'The best revenge is massive success.' *Frank Sinatra*

It isn't easy sometimes believing that Brian Clough could ever waver from his belief that he couldn't be quite sure where he ranked in the pantheon of great managers but it would be somewhere 'in the top one'. His bravado was a formidable weapon and it wasn't always clear whether he was sending himself up, or being deadly serious, when he reminded everyone in his company they were in the presence of greatness. The time, for example, when a colleague found him in his office, with his feet on the desk, listening to his favourite singer. 'Do you know Sinatra once met me?' Clough asked.

Clough was calling himself Old Big 'Ead long before he actually received his OBE. Even when he was setting out in management at Hartlepools, at the age of thirty and the youngest member of the profession, he was pronouncing himself 'better than the 500 or so managers who had been sacked since the war', adding that if they knew anything about the game they would never have been fired.

As for the time he did actually meet Sinatra, he was always slightly disappointed that the great man – or, at least, the other great man – did not make more of a fuss of him. He did, however, meet Roger Moore at the same event. Clough gave him a kiss on the cheek and when the James Bond of the era looked slightly taken aback he told him that he had been waiting to do that for years. 'Cloughie,' according to Michael Parkinson, 'was born with this innate sense of himself. The part of our brain that contains doubt and uncertainty – well, he didn't possess it.'

There has certainly not been another manager, before or since, to go on record saying that if he wanted a player's attention he did not even have to shout his name. Clough's belief was that he could sit silently in his dugout and, by sheer force of will, make any player he wanted turn to him. Anyone else would have been laughed out of town, but Clough had that rare quality that ensured his bravado was a source of wonder to other people. David Pleat's analogy in Pat Murphy's biography of Clough sums it up rather neatly. 'You know they're going to charge for Buckingham Palace? I reckon Cloughie could go up to the gates, persuade them to let him in every room for nothing and let him stroll around inside, inspecting every painting and every chair.' Clough being Clough, he might even have wandered on to the balcony to wave to the crowds below.

Yet it would be misleading to say he was always free of self-doubt and, after a season and a half at Forest, he could have been forgiven the odd flutter of insecurity. Clough was not really getting anywhere. His first eighteen months had been tough and it was not until Peter Taylor left his job as Brighton manager to join his side in the summer of 1976 that everything started to click again and Clough began to give the impression he was back in love with his work, walking on water and barely even making a ripple.

Without Taylor, something had been missing. It was gin without tonic, scotch without soda, a kiss without a squeeze. With him, the change was immediate. That was the point when Forest got what John O'Hare called 'the old Clough' back and John McGovern could announce to his team-mates that something special was about to happen, so watch this space. 'Clough was so invigorated I knew it was just a case from that point onwards of when we got promotion,' McGovern says. 'The other players said to me: "Don't you mean if we get promotion?" I said: "No, it's a case of when now."'

Taylor had been Clough's one consistent friend when they played in the same team at Middlesbrough. He had followed him to Hartlepool to become his assistant, giving up a better-paid job at Burton Albion in the process, and he was with Clough during the wild graph of highs and lows at Derby.

One photograph from the time sums up the Clough–Taylor dynamic from those years. They are in a wood-panelled room and Clough is sitting on a ledge in the kitchen with his feet up and his back against the wall. In the background there is a Bacardi bottle and four glasses of wine neatly lined up. Taylor, the older man by seven years, is sitting by a table with his back to Clough and looking into the semi-distance. But it is Clough's expression that makes the picture. His arms are folded, his feet crossed and his smile devoted. He is gazing down at the back of Taylor's head and it is almost adoration on his face, like he is seeing his kindred spirit.

Taylor was a neat fit for Forest given that he was brought up in the Meadows, the estate on the main walking route from the centre of Nottingham to the ground. Taylor was once on Forest's books as a goalkeeper and had stubbornly kept the accent that meant the team played at a place called 'Citeh Grand' and it was possible to call everyone 'duck', or even 'duckeh', and get away with it as Nottinghamshire's de facto term of endearment. More importantly, he was a wonderful judge of a player and a brilliant spotter of talent. Clough described the appointment as the 'best stroke of business this club has done for years' and it did not take long for the players to realise they now had two irresistible forces to deal with, rather than just one.

All of which brings us back to the player Frank Clark once described as a 'skilful tramp' and so 'away with the fairies' he barely knew what to say to him when he joined the club. Clough was still having trouble getting John Robertson to realise there was nothing worse in football than unful-filled talent. He had come to think the Scot was 'a scruffy, uninterested waste of time' and was starting to lose hope when the team flew out to their pre-season base in Augsburg and, on the first day, the players were sent out for a gentle warm-up. Robertson was nowhere to be seen. Clough found him shortly afterwards 'just standing there in the dressing room with his hands down his shorts, liter-ally scratching his balls'.

Taylor observed that session and his impression was that Robertson appeared to think it was possible to get fit and shed his excess pounds without 'moving out of a five-yard radius throughout the entire quarter of an hour'. Something had to be done and the next morning Clough told everyone to sit on the pitch in a semi-circle, because Taylor wanted to say a few words to introduce himself properly.

Taylor did not even let Robertson's backside touch the floor before starting the tirade. 'Not you,' he said. 'You're a disgrace – fuck off back to the hotel.' Robertson tried to protest but quickly realised he wasn't going to win this argument. 'It might save you some time,' Taylor shouted after him, 'if you started packing your bags now.'

Taylor later found Robertson beside the hotel pool with 'a spare tyre hanging over his shorts'. Taylor was a big, imposing man, standing at six foot two inches and he didn't mince his words. 'Everything is wrong with you as an athlete,' he said. 'I want you on the scales this minute. You're to go on a diet and extra training. I know about your associates and you're to break with them. You've fallen into the gutter, socially and professionally.'

Robertson was twenty-two, still living in digs, and had a chip on his shoulder that was starting to weigh him down like a rucksack filled with bricks. He didn't like what he was hearing and can remember that he briefly contemplated telling Taylor to 'fuck off back to Brighton'. Something held him back; probably because he knew deep down that what Taylor was telling him was true.

Taylor made it clear he had been brought in to decide who was kept on or shipped out, and he told Robertson to count himself lucky that Clough had not shown him the door already. The only reason, he added, was that they thought Robertson might actually have a chance if he could get his house in order. 'Which is why,' Taylor said, 'I'm sitting here discussing how to save you from the knacker's yard, instead of bombing you straight out.'

It was, in short, the biggest rollicking of Robertson's professional life and a kick up the backside that was delivered with sufficient force for the penny finally to drop. But what really stuck in Robertson's mind was a line at the end, once the tirade had stopped, when Taylor switched into good-cop mode to try another tactic. Suddenly, there was an arm around Robertson's shoulder. 'The thing is,' Taylor said, 'we think you can play.'

To Robertson, that 'we' meant Clough must rate him. 'Suddenly, after all the stick Peter Taylor had given me, there was a bit of compassion in his voice. "We think you can play" – that's what I wanted to hear. Nobody – not even Clough – had had a pop at me like that before, but it was exactly what I needed. I wasn't taking enough care of myself. I wasn't treating football seriously enough. I was in a phase that a lot of players get into, where they blame everything but them-selves for what's going wrong. That's why I say about Allan Brown, it wasn't all his fault. I realised after that rollicking that instead of being a spoilt little brat, I had to get on with my career and knuckle down.'

Taylor, in other words, had managed to do in one morning what Clough had been struggling to do in eighteen months. But that was just the start. Taylor's first mandate was to cast his eye over the playing staff and decide who to bin, and very quickly it became apparent to him that the squad was wholly inadequate. 'They're nice lads and no trouble,' he told Clough after watching Forest in two pre-season friendlies. 'But that was a feat by you to finish eighth in the Second

Division, because some of them are only Third Division players.'

A dozen were sold or released in the first season of new rule and it wasn't entirely painless for Clough. He had thought Middleton was a future England goalkeeper, but Taylor shook his head and said they would need someone else if they were promoted. Chapman was part of the furniture at the City Ground, but Taylor took one look and decided he was too old and accident-prone. 'He's shot,' came the verdict. 'We need to replace him fast.' Middleton and Chapman were not in the initial exodus, but as soon as Taylor arrived they were on borrowed time.

Clough let it happen, positively encouraging Taylor to take charge, sitting his partner in the manager's chair and entrusting him to find the right players. Their chemistry was brilliant and, straight away, they were back doing what they did best, putting together a football club, sparking off each other, squabbling, laughing, bouncing ideas back and forth. Taylor could be hard and standoffish but he, like Clough, had various layers to his personality and humour was a big part of it. 'He would have me on the floor, laughing and begging him to stop,' Clough once said. 'And I worked better with a smile on his face.'

Clough still gave the impression that if he saw Don Revie drowning twenty feet from shore he would throw a fifteen-foot rope. Yet the obsession with Leeds also seemed to fade, or at least was discussed less, once Taylor was on board. 'Clough obviously had a point to prove to Leeds and I think that was gnawing away at him in his first eighteen months,' O'Neill says. 'But it was a renaissance. Even without

Peter, you felt there was someone special working with you. Together, though, there was an extra vibrancy when his mate arrived.'

The first piece of business with Peter Taylor's fingerprints all over it was the signing of Peter Withe from Birmingham City. Withe thrived on crosses, scoring on his debut and taking over as the focal point of the team's attack, but his career had taken him on an eccentric route up until that point, starting at Southport and Barrow and including stints in South Africa and the United States. He was coming up to twenty-five and, according to Clough, on his way to becoming 'one of the game's angry and disillusioned drifters complaining he would have made the grade if only somebody had been bright enough to spot what he could do'.

Taylor also wanted to know some more about the young striker who had barely been seen since having the audacity to ask Clough not to bawl at him when he was playing.

Woodcock had been loaned to Lincoln City and Doncaster Rovers since that crushing conversation in the car park of the City Ground, and for a long while he had reluctantly concluded he was wasting his time waiting for Clough to change his opinion. 'I stood in the car park that day telling myself I had to forget Nottingham Forest, forget Brian Clough, forget the fans, forget everything. I didn't think I would ever get another chance in the first team. My brain had gone – and it had gone to another club. I was convinced I had no future at Forest and that I needed to go and play somewhere else.'

Lincoln had made a £5,000 bid. Brighton were interested as well, but Taylor had made Clough promise not to move out anyone until he had made a personal check. Taylor went to see Woodcock in a reserve game at Kettering. He liked what he saw and he almost punched the air with joy when he heard of Woodcock's yearning to leave his wide role and operate as a striker. Taylor wanted someone fast and nimble to play off Withe, the bigger man, and he was impressed by Woodcock's enthusiasm to accept that responsibility.

Clough was also starting to wonder if he was missing something given that Graham Taylor, then managing Lincoln, was so persistent about trying to sign Woodcock. The next time Woodcock knocked on Clough's door, he imagined it would probably be their last conversation and, summoning up his courage, said he wanted to be given a chance to play as a centre-forward.

Clough asked him what he would do if he was given that chance. 'I'm going to score goals,' Woodcock replied. And, finally, he saw the soft-focus Clough. 'Good answer, young man.'

For a few seconds, Woodcock braced himself for another bone-jarring putdown, but it never came. 'There are all these clubs inquiring about you,' Clough told him, 'I suppose I had better give you a chance to see if I am wrong.'

Woodcock was in the team a couple of weeks later to play Ayr in the Anglo-Scottish Cup and scored a fine goal to warrant keeping his place. In the next game, he set up two of the goals in a 3–0 win over Blackburn and one newspaper called him an 'overnight star'. It had actually taken him thirty months since making his debut to reach that point but, restored to the team, his speed and elegance on the ball immediately improved Forest's attack.

Taylor then set about trying to find an upgrade for Chapman and the player he wanted was Larry Lloyd from Coventry City. The problem was Lloyd would not agree anything more than a month's loan initially because – and he made no bones about it – he generally considered Forest were beneath him.

Lloyd had won a championship medal for Liverpool and already thought he was slumming it at Coventry, with their annual fight against relegation from the First Division. His ego was vast and that made it difficult for him to contemplate dropping down even further to a club among the hoi polloi of the Second Division. 'Liverpool,' Lloyd recalls, 'had a dedicated training ground with all the top equipment. At Forest they used to get changed at the City Ground then jog down by the Trent to a little bit of waste ground at the old Boots site. That was the training ground, through a load of bloody nettles.'

The first game of his loan spell was at Hull and when the team caught the train back to Nottingham the new arrival was the centre of attention, puffing away on a huge cigar as he gave O'Neill, Robertson and Bowyer a rundown of what it was like at Liverpool, explaining in great detail the adrenaline rush of passing beneath the sign for 'This is Anfield', running out under the floodlights, looking into the ocean of faces on the Kop and hearing them sing his name.

Robertson asked him what he made of his first week at

Forest and Lloyd blew out a couple of smoke rings. 'It's a nice little club you've got here, boys,' he informed his new team-mates.

'You like it?' Robertson asked.

Another smoke ring was despatched into the air. 'Yeah, it's not a bad little place this, boys.'

The boys, according to Robertson, were all thinking the same thing: 'Who the hell does this big-headed bastard think he is?'

Lloyd had started his career at Bristol Rovers, the club he used to watch from the terraces, and was signed by Liverpool in 1969 because Bill Shankly wanted someone who could eventually ease out Ron Yeats and form the meanest and most uncompromising central defensive partnership in the league with Tommy Smith. Lloyd played in the FA Cup final two years later and was part of the team in 1973 that won the league and beat Borussia Moenchengladbach in the UEFA Cup final.

He was a big, burly Bristolian, full of testosterone and arrogance and, a bit like Frankenstein, he had the look of someone who had been put together in a scientific experiment – thighs like oil drums, chest built from concrete, neck as wide as a medicine ball. 'Larry,' Shankly said to him on the day they met, 'I have come to the conclusion that you would kick your grandmother for a fiver.' Lloyd said he would do it for half that. Yet he ended up falling out with Shankly and Bob Paisley, football royalty as far as everyone else at Anfield was concerned, and was so full of himself it had put everyone's backs up at Coventry. Lloyd had a reputation for letting off steam on the pitch and esteem off it. He was a 'big-time Charlie' – and that, by the way, was his own description.

Lloyd had three England caps, referred to himself in the third person and introduced himself to the other players with the payoff line: 'I'm here for a month and then I'm out of here.' He was never allowed to forget that one. Or what he said to Clough when he came to the end of his loan and decided he would rather go back to Coventry than hang around in the Second Division. 'I've not seen anything here that's turned me on,' he explained.

Taylor's advice to Lloyd was to look at the way Roy McFarland conducted himself at Derby County, stop thinking he knew it all and learn some discipline. 'He seemed to imagine he was dealing with a pair of non-league managers,' Taylor said. 'Interruptions from players were forbidden when either Brian or myself were speaking, but Lloyd cut in continually. He thought he had the right to say what he liked, when he liked.'

Yet behind that brash exterior there were more likeable traits. Lloyd was good company – witty, opinionated and fond of a good debate – and had a nice line in self-deprecating humour that endeared him to his new team-mates. He was also fiercely competitive and determined to get his football back on an upward trajectory. He knew he had let his career slide and it pained him to think of the trophies he had missed out on at Anfield.

'I had played a lot of games at Liverpool and got into the international team. Then I went to Coventry and in the very first training session I realised I had made a terrible mistake. I was stuck there for two not-very-happy years, but at least

70

they were in the First Division. Then the manager Gordon Milne called me into the office and said: "That fellow Clough at Nottingham Forest wants you to go up there." My first reaction was: "Why would I want to go to Nottingham Forest? What division are they in?" All I knew about Clough was that he was the mouthy git who was always on television. I was twenty-six and I didn't want to drop down a division, but Gordon said to me: "To be honest, Larry, you're not wanted here."'

Lloyd went straight into the team against Hull and quickly became aware it wasn't going to be as easy as he thought. Chapman had been a fixture in defence since becoming Forest's youngest-ever player in 1964, aged seventeen years and five months. He was a loyal one-club man who had been awarded a testimonial match and, to Lloyd, it felt like the older man went out of his way to make him feel unwelcome.

Lloyd had also underestimated Chapman's popularity with the fans. 'I knew there was a problem when the announcer came out to say there was a change to the teams that had been printed in the programme. "For Forest," he said, "replacing number five, Sammy Chapman, is Larry Lloyd." The booing was the loudest I ever remember hearing, probably because it was aimed at me, and when I turned round I realised it wasn't the Hull supporters, it was the red bank of Forest fans at the other end. It was horrible. I still remember my thoughts. Hey, what do you mean "who the fuck is Larry Lloyd?" What's going on? I'm ex-Liverpool, for Christ's sake. Oh, I felt very ordinary and my bruised ego was hurting badly.'

The loan spell went well and when Lloyd returned to

Coventry he won his place back and probably had his best run of form since playing for Liverpool. Yet Lloyd had already burned his bridges at Highfield Road. 'Eventually, Gordon Milne came on again to say Clough still wanted me. I said: "Wait a minute, Gordon, I'm in the team here, playing well." He spelt it out: "I'm sorry, we still want you to go."'

Forest were preparing for league games against Bristol Rovers, Millwall and Plymouth Argyle and Lloyd wasn't exactly ecstatic about the thought of dropping down a level to play for a club where a lot of the supporters seemed to prefer the previous guy. Clough, however, was as persistent as ever to make the deal happen and, with the exception perhaps of Chapman, the other players liked the idea of an ex-Liverpool man signing. Martin O'Neill remembers being 'desperate' for it to happen. 'We knew he was going to improve us and we also felt he could look after us. By that, I don't even mean necessarily on the pitch. A couple of years later, he was fighting with Clough – not fighting, literally, but he was willing to stand up to him. You could sense that about Lloyd.'

The club, at last, were showing some ambition and it had been so long coming it didn't really bother the other players if Lloyd was earning more money than them or that, to quote one of the dressing-room jokes of the time, he gave the impression sometimes he was the kind of bloke who probably shouted his own name during sex. 'I'd have to say that Lloyd was the first major signing,' O'Neill says. 'And I think he'd probably agree.'

The deal had gone through for £60,000, roughly a quarter of what Coventry had paid Liverpool, but it needed Clough to come up with something special – in this case, a bribe – to persuade Lloyd that Forest was the right place to be. 'I was still unsure whether I wanted to sign,' Lloyd says, 'but Clough said: "Wait a minute, how are you doing for kitchen equipment in your house?" I didn't know where the conversation was going but I told him that, as it happened, my wife's washing machine was broken.

'The following day, two blokes turned up outside my house in Coventry wearing overalls and carrying a new washing machine. "Fair play to him," I thought. I let these two guys in and as they carried the washing machine through the hallway into the kitchen there was water dripping out of the pipe at the back. I didn't think too much of it, to be honest. I just presumed they had tested it in the shop and there was still a bit of water left in the back. The next day, I went over to Nottingham for my first day's training and these two women came out pointing their fingers at me. "Hey, are you that Larry Lloyd? You've nicked our washing machine." It turns out they were the laundry women. So that was my signing-on fee: a washing machine.'

Clough called him 'Big Head' – the equivalent, if you like, of John McEnroe complaining someone was a sore loser – and went out of his way not to feed the player's ravenous ego. Lloyd's first game after returning to the club was a 4–2 win at home to Bristol Rovers. 'I think Larry must have been nervous,' McGovern recalls. 'He was geeing himself up in the dressing room beforehand and eventually he went over to Brian and said: "How do you want me to play, boss?" Clough gave him a withering look and said: "I've paid good money for you, Larry, and if you don't know how to play at centre-half

I've made a big mistake." Larry, in fairness, then went out and played as if he had been there years.'

Forest had not won any of their first four league games and Martin O'Neill remembers the team had plenty of imperfections during the opening months of that 1976–77 season. 'We used to infuriate the manager because we were winning games at the City Ground, often scoring heavily, yet going away the following week and losing 1–0 in a lousy game. Clough was apoplectic, and rightly so, that we could be so careless. This was the year, remember, we really had to make inroads and try to get up, but as soon as we were gaining some momentum at home we were losing it just as quickly.'

Those Jekyll and Hyde tendencies were summed up by an erratic run around the time that Lloyd signed. First, a 5–1 thrashing of Carlisle was followed by the game at Hull, a 1–0 defeat with Clough's old nemesis, Billy Bremner, scoring the goal. Sheffield United were defeated 6–1 at the City Ground, but Forest's biggest win for nineteen years was followed by another 1–0 loss, this time at Blackpool, now managed by Allan Brown. When Burnley were beaten 5–2 that made it sixteen goals in three home matches. True to form, a third successive 1–0 away league defeat followed at Oldham Athletic.

That inconsistency looked for a long time like it might sabotage their promotion campaign, and the win against Burnley came at a heavy price bearing in mind Terry Curran left the ground on crutches. The Yorkshireman had started the season with four goals in his five matches and earned the nickname 'the electric Curran' because of his favourite tactic simply to knock the ball past defenders and then run like hell to get there first. He was establishing himself as one of the best wingers outside the top division and had set up one goal by pushing the ball past two defenders and still managing to beat them for pace, even though it meant taking a wide berth round the outside of the pitch, skating down the perimeter track and then coming back into play. Now he was in hospital for a knee operation. Ken Smales remembers Clough being a picture of dejection in his office that night. 'Promotion,' Clough said, 'has just limped out of the door.'

By Christmas, though, Forest had put together a run of form to climb into the top three and reached the Anglo-Scottish Cup final, beating Orient over two legs to give them their first taste of success. Robertson was starting to look like a proper footballer and enough momentum was building for a crowd of 38,284 to pack into the City Ground for an FA Cup fourth-round tie against Southampton. It finished as a 3–3 draw but Forest lost the replay 2–1. The next league game was at Wolves and they lost again by the same score. Then Luton visited the City Ground and it ended with a third successive 2–1 defeat. Suddenly, out of nowhere, the momentum had gone and everything was threatening to unravel.

The next match brought Southampton back to the City Ground on a freezing Wednesday night and Forest were suffering badly, 1–0 down and looking as dishevelled as any time in the Clough era, when the fog started rolling in from the Trent. Fog had often been a problem during Forest's home matches but this was only the third time in fifteen years it had been bad enough to call one off. Forest's luck was in. The game was abandoned two minutes into the second half and Clough, for once, missed a trick not pointing out that he and Taylor now seemed to have Zeus looking out for them. 'The weather kept Nottingham Forest's hopes of promotion alive,' one report began the next day. McGovern reckoned the team 'could have played until midnight without scoring'.

That was the same week Clough was offered the chance to return to Derby and the First Division and gave them the distinct impression he was going to accept the invitation. Derby had sacked Mackay after a poor start to the season and decided that his replacement, Colin Murphy, was not up to it. Taylor, in particular, thought there was unfinished business for him and Clough at the Baseball Ground, where their old club was now languishing in seventeenth position. The terms were agreed, a press conference was arranged and the *Derby Evening Telegraph* billboards were boldly proclaiming: 'He's Coming Home'.

Brian Appleby was said to have arrived at the City Ground on the morning of 21 February and inquired: 'Has he gone yet?' Appleby had given Derby permission to speak to Clough and negotiations appeared to have gone well, only for Clough to change his mind at the last minute, on the advice of wife Barbara. In the space of six days Forest had almost lost their management team, any realistic chance of promotion and in one or two cases perhaps even their sanity. Ken Smales sounded emotionally drained in his next programme notes. If the club had lost 'B and P,' he wrote, 'it would have taken a long period of convalescence to restore my health.'

A sense of normality slowly returned to the City Ground but the team were trailing in eighth position going into March and seven points off the three promotion places (in the era of two points for a win). The fog had been merciful. Forest won the rearranged game against Southampton five weeks later and then went on a run that saw them leapfrog Notts County into third place heading into the run-in. The pressure was too much for County, who finished the season with only one win out of seven matches, but Bolton Wanderers had games in hand and were looming in Forest's wing-mirrors.

Forest slipped again, losing back-to-back games against Chelsea and Cardiff, before beating Oldham at home. The next game was at Bristol Rovers and a 1–1 draw felt like another grievous setback, given that Bolton beat Hereford on the same day to move even closer. 'We really thought we had blown it,' O'Neill says. 'There was dejection in the dressing room afterwards. Clough was trying to keep a brave face on it, but I really think it was an act on his part and, deep down, he thought that was it. That draw meant promotion was no longer in our hands, even if we won all our remaining games.'

The team travelled to Tavistock that night because they were playing Plymouth Argyle two days later, and it summed up their mood that when they checked into their hotel even the genial Robertson lost his temper. David Soul, from *Starsky & Hutch* fame, was in the lobby. 'John saw him immediately and went over to ask for an autograph,' O'Neill says. 'David Soul took the piece of paper but clearly wasn't happy about it. "I must have signed five hundred of these today," he said. Maybe it was because we were all so dejected about the result, but John was very cut up about it. "Well, if that's the way you feel," he said, and tore it up in front of him.'

Woodcock and Withe, a partnership that had quickly flowered, scored the goals in a 2–1 victory and when that was followed up with a nervous 1–0 win in their final game at home to Millwall, courtesy of an own-goal, Forest had taken eighteen points from their final dozen games. Woodcock had started the season as an outcast and finished it with seventeen goals, the club's player-of-the-season trophy and a call-up to the England Under-21s, for whom he scored a hat-trick on his debut. Withe, nicknamed 'Googie' after the actress Googie Withers, had scored nineteen times and led the line with command and authority. Bowyer had weighed in with fourteen of his own and the team had scored twenty-two more times than the previous season. 'It had changed,' Bowyer says, 'from being "not a bad little club" to being a good club.'

Robertson had become so influential that the managers of the Second Division clubs voted him as their player of the year and the Professional Footballers' Association included him in their team. Clark had played every game for the second consecutive season, which was not bad for someone Newcastle had decided was over the hill, and O'Neill finished second to Woodcock in the supporters' vote. O'Neill's relationship with Clough – difficult, begrudging, with points-scoring from both sides – meant he still found praise hard to come by, but he had played with great trickery and tenacity and chipped in with eleven goals from midfield.

As for the rejuvenated Clough, it was difficult to overstate the importance of that summer's day when he invited Stuart Dryden, one of the few committee members he liked and respected, to a charity match at Widmerpool Cricket Club and, still in his whites, casually dropped into conversation that it was time 'to fetch Taylor'.

One letter appeared in the programme midway through the season from a pair of Derby fans complaining that their team were 'sadly lacking in management, personality and aggression' and making another request for Clough and Taylor to go back.

Mostly, they were letters of gratitude on the page marked 'City Ground Postbag'. Norman Gough of Mapperley Park wrote to say 'thank you for putting the pride back into Nottingham Forest.' C Rook of Riddings, Derbyshire, described the Clough–Taylor partnership as 'the best thing that had happened to Nottingham Forest for a long time'. Clough complained sometimes that the average attendance that season was not much over 18,000, but that was a 50 per cent rise from when he took over and another letter showed the keenness of some supporters to be part of the brave new world. It was a request to 'thank Mr Clough for the lift he gave me when hitching from Derby to the City Ground'.

And yet, there was still the distinct possibility that everything could go horribly wrong.

Bolton, incredibly, still had three games to go. They won the first one against Cardiff the following Tuesday and that left them needing three more points to replace Forest in third position and pinch the final promotion spot behind Wolves and Chelsea. A win and a draw – and a sledgehammer would have been taken to Forest's season.

Clough and his players were taking off on an end-of-season jolly to Majorca when Bolton kicked off against Wolves in their penultimate match and the tension as the team boarded that plane at East Midlands airport was almost unbearable. O'Neill's view was that Bolton were 'probably the strongest side in the division'. Wolves had already been confirmed as champions and there was a strong suspicion on the runway that the team from Molineux had been out on the razz all week to celebrate.

The first bulletin came somewhere over northern France. 'This is your captain speaking . . . we have the Nottingham Forest team flying with us today and, for anyone who is interested, you may like to know that Wolves have taken the lead in their game at Bolton.'

Garry Birtles was on his first trip abroad, invited along to make up the numbers because Chapman was terrified of flying, and the rookie striker remembers the plane rocking in mid-air. 'It wasn't turbulence – it was us jumping around on the plane.' There was a sing-song. Drinks were ordered. A toast was raised at 37,000 feet to the goal-scorer Kenny Hibbitt. 'I don't think there was any champagne left on the plane,' McGovern says. 'We were just singing anything we could.'

Yet others remember it slightly differently. The game at Burnden Park was still going on and after the initial announcement the pilot was worryingly silent. 'That was when the nervousness took over,' O'Neill says. 'You might have imagined the pilot would keep us involved, but that was the last we heard from him until we landed.'

Nerves started to fray – even Clough's. At one point Barrett was sent to the cockpit to find out if there was an update. 'I came back and told him Bolton were still losing,' Barrett says. 'He said: "They had better be because you're on the next flight home if we get off this flight and Wolves haven't won."'

Those were the days before mobile phones or the Internet and Clough was reluctant to take it as gospel. Another message came back that the Wolves goalkeeper Gary Pierce had been injured during the second half and a striker, Bobby Gould, had pulled on the gloves to take over. That cranked up the tension another few notches as the players – some of them already half-cut – disembarked at Palma airport.

What they didn't know at the time was that fans were already making their way to Nottingham's Old Market Square to celebrate. Or that there were two coaches of Forest supporters who had made the trip to Molineux to cheer on Wolves and had joined in the pitch invasion at the final whistle, with one stealing the corner flag as a souvenir.

Through passport control, a semi-circle formed around a pay phone as Clough asked the long-distance operator to put him through to a Nottingham number.

He was ringing Stuart Dryden but it was the vice-chairman's wife, Mary, who answered and it was a crackling, almost impossible line.

Clough could just about make out one sentence before the phone went dead – but those six words turned the blood in his veins into red wine.

'I suppose congratulations are in order.'

Chapter Four
Fourteen Chip Cobs

'Clough, I've had enough. Stop it.' *Muhammad Ali*

After training, it was a greasy spoon called McKay's, just along the road from the ground, where the players usually congregated. For beers, they would head to the King John, a hundred yards down the hill from Nottingham railway station, or maybe the Pepper Mill or Uriah Heeps if it was shaping up to be a proper night out. Yet the most popular meeting place was always McKay's. It was there where the players put the world to rights, tucking into the kind of unpretentious grub that never seemed such a big deal in the days before football opened its doors to nutritionists and sports scientists and the strange new world of pasta, green-leaf salads and mineral water. 'Fourteen chip cobs,' became such a regular order that the owner, Bill, had to get in extra supplies of bread and potatoes.

In the summer of 1977, there was a lot of conversation in that little cafe about what needed to be done to ensure Forest did not drop back into the Second Division. To put it bluntly, the players were apprehensive about what might happen now they were in the top league. Forest had sneaked up in third position with fifty-two points from forty-two games, the fifth lowest total of any promoted club in history. There might have been the occasional disagreement in McKay's about whether it was a cob, a roll, a bun, a bap or, for a Mancunian such as Colin Barrett, a barm. But there was an acceptance over their steaming mugs of tea that the next step of the adventure would be a difficult one, and that there was a risk some of the players might be cut free.

Martin O'Neill had the occasional lapse into insecurity even during that week of celebrations by the hotel pool in Cala Millor, drinking beer out of plastic cups and listening to his Jethro Tull tape or the cassette John McGovern had brought with him of Fleetwood Mac's latest album, 'Rumours'. 'There was euphoria,' O'Neill remembers. 'It was congratulations all round. But then, of course, you spend the next few months worrying whether we are actually capable of playing in the higher league and whether we would even get the chance. Will it be too big for us? Will the step be enormous? We knew Brian Clough and Peter Taylor wouldn't hang around and they would be bringing in some new players.'

Taylor had told the *Evening Post* the team should be aiming high, and possibly even trying to qualify for Europe, but the players could probably be forgiven for thinking that was stretching the boundaries of credibility. Forest had never been higher than third and lost over a quarter of their games the previous season, beaten by Wolves (twice), Hull, Blackpool, Oldham, Charlton, Luton, Sheffield United, Chelsea and Cardiff, as well as what the club's match-day programme called 'the annual smash-and-grab raid by Notts County'. They had not beaten either of the two teams that had gone up ahead of them, and when it came to the betting-shop chalkboards they were nearer the bottom than the top. 'We had got up by the skin of our teeth,' Larry Lloyd says. 'You didn't have to be a brain surgeon to realise that team would not have survived and that Clough had to make some signings.'

Three arrived before October, including a goalkeeper, Peter Shilton, who gave the impression sometimes that if someone threw a handful of rice at his net he would keep out every single grain. The other two were Scots. One had more baggage than an airport carousel and the other was five feet four inches of pride, adrenaline and competitive courage. 'A hooligan from Birmingham City called Kenny Burns and a little midfield nasty-man called Archie Gemmill', to use Lloyd's description. 'Three world-class players; that was the point I started thinking maybe this guy Clough wanted to do something in this division.'

Burns arrived first and, to put Lloyd's words into context, even the club that was selling him told Clough he must be mad thinking he could tame the Glaswegian. Burns was notorious. He had committed one tackle in an Aston Villa– Birmingham derby that thirty years later made it into a feature in *The Times* about the fifty most X-rated challenges of all time. He spent his nights at the dog track and he was not even on speaking terms with some of his team-mates at St Andrew's. 'Don't buy him,' Birmingham's chairman, David Wiseman, warned Clough. 'He's trouble.'

Clough had trusted Taylor implicitly with the transfer of Lloyd but his information was that Burns drove around in a battered Vauxhall Viva with no MOT or insurance ('Not true,' Burns always insisted). A picture developed of an untamed, hard-drinking pub-brawler. Clough didn't want someone bringing bad headlines to the club and was so opposed to the idea it caused friction between him and Taylor. 'Forget it,'

Clough said, when Taylor came up with the idea. 'I don't want troublemakers, I don't want shit-houses and I don't want an ugly bastard like Kenny Burns littering my club.'

But Taylor wouldn't let it go. He had heard Burns was a stone overweight and losing money hand over fist to the bookmakers, but he still thought it was worth investigating and went incognito to the Perry Barr dog track in Birmingham to find out whether the gossip was true. 'He didn't recognise me in my disguise of flat cap and dark glasses,' Taylor later reported. 'Nor did he realise that the punter so often at his shoulder as he placed a bet was Forest's chief scout Maurice Edwards.'

Taylor's report back to Clough was that it was moderate stuff – 'tens and twenties, nothing higher' – and nothing they couldn't handle. Birmingham accepted a £150,000 offer and Clough told Burns to have a shave, buy himself a decent coat and meet him the next day at a garden centre in Long Eaton, on the road from Nottingham to Derby.

When Burns turned up, he discovered they were naming some flowers after Clough at an exhibition of sweet peas. Maybe Clough was trying to work out if there was a softer side to his new signing, or perhaps he was just letting him know that life at Forest would not be like his previous clubs. 'I didn't have a clue,' Burns says. 'I thought we were going to look at some peas – as in, garden peas. I mean, peas are peas, aren't they? Green things. What kind of peas are sweet peas? I know what green peas are. I know mushy peas. In Scotland, flowers are just things whose heads you kick off when you've had a few pints on a Saturday night.'

The horticultural lesson over, there was another surprise

waiting for the man Clough insisted on calling 'Kenneth'. Burns had scored twenty goals in thirty-eight games the previous season as a centre-forward, including four in one game against Derby and what is known as the perfect hat-trick in another match against Leicester – one right-footed, one left-footed and one off his head. Yet Clough, going by Taylor's recommendation, had something different planned. 'Perhaps it sounded insane to switch a goal-taker into defence, but there was good reason for our madness,' Taylor would later explain. 'I suspected Burns didn't relish life up front because the running didn't suit his lazy nature. What's more, we desperately needed a sweeper alongside Larry Lloyd and I visualised Kenny turning into a Scottish Bobby Moore. He was as skilful as Moore and certainly more ruthless.'

Nobody, however, had bothered to tell the man himself. 'Peter Withe and Tony Woodcock thought I was being signed to take their place,' Burns says. 'Clough signed me on the Sunday. Then pre-season training started on the Monday and I didn't see him again for another ten days. It was Jimmy Gordon who let me know. "Right," he said, "bibs on – Middleton, Anderson, Barrett, Lloyd, Burns, McGovern, O'Neill, Bowyer, Withe, Woodcock, Robertson." And that was it. That was the first I knew about the new partnership with big Larry.'

Shilton came next in mid-September after what seemed to take an eternity haggling over the fee with Stoke City, a club record for Forest at £270,000, and a wrangle over his own financial arrangements, which perhaps explains why Clough was waiting with his squash racket to trip up the goalkeeper's agents. A lot of other managers might have been happy to have an England Under-21 international in goal, but John Middleton had allowed a soft shot to beat him in a pre-season game and Taylor had never fully trusted him anyway. Shilton was a clear upgrade, but not everyone put up the bunting. Middleton had come through Forest's ranks and a lot of supporters didn't like seeing one of their own being barged out of the way.

Gemmill had played for Clough at Derby and signing him the second time was certainly a lot more straightforward than it had been in 1970. Gemmill was playing for Preston North End back then and had offers from other clubs, including one from the newly crowned champions Everton. His wife, Betty, didn't particularly like what she saw of Clough from his television appearances (her exact words being 'I can't stand that man'). But the rest was vintage Clough, turning up at their front door and refusing to be put off when he couldn't talk them round that evening. Most managers would have called it a night and gone home. Clough announced he would sleep in the spare room, woke up with his charm on full beam and clinched the deal over a breakfast of eggs and bacon. The deal done, he then proceeded to get stuck into the washing up, still wearing his vest while talking Betty through some of the places to visit in the Derbyshire Peak District.

This time, he did not have to work anything like so hard. Gemmill had just turned thirty and had history with Derby's new manager, Tommy Docherty, going back to a 1–0 defeat for Scotland against England at Hampden Park in 1972. Docherty was managing Scotland at the time. He blamed Gemmill for the goal and when Clough pulled the midfielder out of Scotland's tour to South America at the end of the season, Docherty never picked him again. Gemmill had assumed, five years on, they could wipe the slate clean but Docherty had no intention of starting again. 'He asked me to meet him at the Midland Hotel,' Gemmill says. 'I went to his room and he said: "You're finished here – you're too old, you've lost your pace, you're no good for the team I want." And that was that.'

Clough was on the case already and offered £20,000 for Gemmill with Middleton included in the same package. 'The boss didn't have to sell Nottingham Forest to me,' Gemmill says. 'It was him being there that sold it to me. He told me Peter Taylor had said I was the final piece of the jigsaw. "You'll be winning another title and a cup," he said, and there was one thing I knew about the boss – ninety-nine per cent of the time he told you something was going to happen, it did happen.'

Clough must have been emboldened by what he had seen in his first month back in the First Division, but that was still some claim when Forest had been dismissed as potential relegation candidates, or mid-table at best, in all the newspapers' pre-season predictions. Liverpool had won the championship in three of the previous five seasons and finished second in the other two. Manchester City had a vibrant and thrilling side. Ipswich, managed by Bobby Robson, had finished third in two of the three previous years. Manchester United had Steve Coppell, Martin Buchan and Gordon Hill. These were the clubs that attracted all the column inches when it came to identifying who would fight it out for the championship.

Forest, in stark contrast, had scraped an unconvincing promotion and brought in only one player in the close season. The writers thought they lacked speed and finesse and would be overwhelmed in midfield where, as one scribe later put it, the popular belief was that 'the names of Bowyer, McGovern and O'Neill were hardly likely to strike fear into the hearts of Case, McDermott, Kennedy and Dalglish.'

Forest were the nouveaux arrivés and in their first match, away at Everton, it was quiet on the bus going into Goodison Park. A letter had appeared in the *Nottingham Evening Post* that day predicting 'that Forest will come straight down, while Notts County clinch promotion'. The sign-off, 'Faithful Magpie', gave a clue as to the author's loyalties, but the players on that bus were anticipating a long, hard slog. John Robertson was sitting beside O'Neill. 'I was nervous as hell,' he remembers. 'I think we all were.'

Taylor sensed it too and came into his own before kick-off with a ten-minute routine of jokes and anecdotes that worked wonders to change the mood. All the same, it was an intimidating place to start, with the Everton fans welcoming them on to the pitch with chants of 'Lambs to the slaughter'. Woodcock remembers the noise when Everton ran out being 'so loud you felt you almost had to duck down'. Forest played the first twenty minutes, according to O'Neill, 'in our own penalty box'. The pace was ferocious and Woodcock found out the hard way that seasoned First Division players didn't want a young buck trying to show them up.

Mick Lyons, the Everton captain, was once described as a

'horse of a man'. He was raised on the same estate in Croxteth where Wayne Rooney was later brought up and he once scored a goal against Leeds that involved throwing himself at a diving header even though Norman Hunter, one of the era's category-A hatchet-men, was swinging his boot at the ball merely inches away. 'I thought he had broken my leg,' Woodcock says of one introductory challenge. 'I was lying on the ground in absolute agony. That was Mick's way of saying: welcome to the big boys.'

Everton had reached the League Cup final the previous season as well as the FA Cup semi-finals. They were another team with title aspirations and the pressure on Forest's goal was almost unremitting during the early exchanges. 'I honestly thought this was really too much,' O'Neill says. 'We couldn't get a breather.' But the new defence held out. Burns had moved in seamlessly alongside Lloyd and, twenty minutes in, Forest broke out to win a corner. Robertson swung it over. The ball thudded off Withe's forehead. Forest's number nine had scored at the ground where he had once stood outside selling programmes – and the team had lift-off.

Dave Jones, Everton's right-back, described what followed as the best performance from an away side he could remember at Goodison. Lyons had written in the programme he had a strange feeling Forest might be 'the surprise team of the season', but the performance was a sensation. Duncan McKenzie, who had joined Everton the previous season, said he was amazed at how slick and efficient his old team were. Robertson, who had cleaned McKenzie's boots when he was an apprentice, doubled the lead with a shot into the top corner before Jim Pearson pulled one back just before half-time. O'Neill added Forest's third in the second half and there could have been more. Bowyer was indefatigable in midfield. Lloyd puffed out his chest and sucked in the air of the top division, where he had always thought he belonged. Burns passed his first real test with distinction. Anderson showed he was not fazed and Clark wore the unflappable look of a man who had seen it all before. Clark had played over 400 games for Newcastle and commanded the respect of his team-mates. They called him the 'old gouger'.

McGovern thought he had done pretty well too, only to find out afterwards that Clough disagreed. 'He started giving me the rollicking of my life in the dressing room,' McGovern recalls. 'I'd gone forward too much for his liking and I'd had the temerity to think I might score and tried a couple of shots from just outside the penalty area. He was telling me I should have given it to somebody else – "Give it to a good player because a good player has a chance of scoring and you don't" – when someone started knocking on the door.

'That dressing room was usually sacrosanct. Clough wouldn't even let in the chairman, but when he swung open the door his face changed. "Come in," he said, "delighted to see you." We couldn't see who it was at first, but he said it like it must be the Pope or the Prime Minister. "Bill, I'm just giving them a rollicking, telling them how poor they were, but I think you should do it." And it was Bill Shankly, the former Liverpool manager. Clough sat down with the rest of us and suddenly it was Shankly, this legend of the game, giving the team-talk for the next fifteen minutes, with his hands in his pockets, in the classic gunslinger pose.'

That quarter of an hour gave the Forest players an insight

into why Kevin Keegan once said of Shankly that 'he made you feel any mountain could be climbed.' Keep your feet on the ground, was the crux of it, because there was still a hell of a way to go. But he also said there was no way Forest should undersell themselves if they could play that well and Clough was manager. 'You can win it,' Shankly told them. 'Don't just be in the First Division, go and win it. Keep playing like that and you can win the championship.'

The media's view was that a combination of Shankly, Clough, Jock Stein, Mario Zagallo and Rinus Michels might not be able to sustain that level of performance throughout the rest of the season. Promoted teams often get off to a flier because of the momentum of the previous season, and the win was largely put down to a combination of adrenaline and beginners' luck. 'Brian Clough is quite a subdued fellow these days,' read the report in the *Guardian*. 'The Nottingham Forest manager did not get carried away by his team's demonstration of their abilities on their return to the First Division after five years, and neither should anyone else. One cannot go overboard yet. They have the element of surprise at the moment. However, the skills of players such as Tony Woodcock and John Robertson are quickly to be recognised by more competent defenders than those on display at Goodison Park. When that happens, Forest should be prepared for hard times.'

Except the following week the players in that shiny new kit – Garibaldi-red shirts, white shorts, three Adidas stripes on the sleeves – beat Bristol City courtesy of another goal from Withe. 'Forest,' one report began, 'may not have the players to reach the peaks of the First Division, but their attractive and intelligent football will give a great deal of pleasure.'

That was followed up with a resounding 3–0 win over Derby, in the first game pitting Clough and Taylor against their old club, with the television commentator Hugh Johns eulogising about 'some of the most electrifying football I've seen for a long time'. In three games, Withe had scored four times. Forest were the only team with a 100 per cent record and they were even more rampant in their next match, beating West Ham 5–0 in the League Cup.

Something had changed and, though it isn't easy pinpointing exactly when the nerves and apprehension made way for a sudden burst of self-belief, the win at Everton clearly had a lot to do with it. Robertson remembers a moment at Goodison thinking: 'Hey, we're not actually too bad, here.' Woodcock was playing with so much distinction Clough would happily admit he had misjudged him. Withe was the early front-runner in the scoring charts. What McGovern lacked in pace he made up for by seeing everything so quickly. The team was new, impressionable and desperate to test themselves against the best. The league table in August can always be a deception but Forest were top and to see Clough around this time, even just his walk to the dugout, was to see a man who seemed to believe a natural order had been restored.

Other managers would just get in the dugout without any fuss whatsoever. Clough made it an art form. He ambled: straight-backed, insouciant, mesmerising. Sometimes, if he was wearing a tie, he might tighten the knot. He would look over the perimeter wall, even at away matches, as if to check the crowd knew he was there. But they were already looking. Clough was not just telegenic, he had the ability to draw everyone's attention and hold it. He was also back on top, which was just the way he liked it.

All of which made the 3–0 defeat at Arsenal in Forest's next match feel like a crashing disappointment. 'It was,' according to John Lawson in the *Evening Post*, 'like returning from a holiday and waking up to the realities of everyday life.' Forest suddenly looked what they were: a team that had reached the First Division through the back door. Everyone had been waiting for the fall and now it was pointed out that Carlisle, promoted as the Second Division's third-placed team three years earlier, had also been top of the table three games into the 1974–75 season – and ended up relegated in bottom place. Clough's Derby County had a similarly impressive start in their first season after promotion only to drop away around the New Year. Most journalists saw history repeating itself and there was a told-you-so element to some of the write-ups. 'Perhaps,' one report concluded, 'deep down the provincials were over-awed by the marble halls of north London.'

The 'provincials' had certainly irritated Clough, leading to an almighty showdown the following Monday, and his mood was hardly improved when he saw the television pictures of Burns reverting to old habits while he lined up at a defensive wall. 'There was a bit of something going on there,' the television commentator Brian Moore told ITV's viewers, as Richie Powling started backing into the wall. That something was Burns introducing his opponent to an old friend, the Glaswegian kiss, and a slyly administered headbutt.

Burns had already stepped out of line when he tried to

keep up with Lloyd during an afternoon drinking session on the pre-season trip to Germany and was so pie-eyed he ended up passing out and spewing up in front of Clough, Taylor and their respective wives. He apologised profusely but his 'stitch that' moment at Highbury was his second indiscretion already and the season was barely a month old. Burns claimed his headbutt had actually been a sneeze – which made you wonder what might happen if he ever developed hayfever – but Clough fined him, condemned him in the newspapers and warned him, only five games into the season, that he would be back at the dog track, unemployed, if there was any more indiscipline.

Those were the days before the Football Association set up panels to take retrospective action on video evidence. Clough kept Burns in his team and their response to the hiccup at Highbury, winning their next three games, was a fine riposte to everyone who assumed their start to the season had been a fluke. Forest climbed back to the top of the league after beating Ipswich 4–0 at the start of October, Withe becoming the club's first player since 1907 to score four goals in a single match, and when they beat second-placed Manchester City it was starting to feel like a trick of the mind that on the corresponding weekend the previous season they had just lost at Blackpool. 'Where is this all going to end?' one report asked. Nobody, however, seemed willing to entertain the notion this 'team of basically ordinary souls', as *The Times* put it, were at the top to stay and Bob Wilson, the former Arsenal goalkeeper who had become one of the BBC's main football pundits, predicted it was only a matter of time before everything unravelled.

No team had won the championship in their first year after promotion since Alf Ramsey's Ipswich in 1962 and, before then, there had been only Tottenham in 1951 that had done it since the war. The difference was both those sides had gone up as Second Division champions. No side had ever done it from Forest's position and, with a game coming up at QPR, Wilson had worked out they had not won any of their last five trips to the capital. Could Forest, he asked, really go all the way through the season playing the way they had done during the opening couple of months? And his conclusion was that, no, it was implausible, and it wouldn't be long 'before the bubble burst'.

If there was one thing Clough did not like, it was anyone else running down his players and, ignoring the fact that he used to take aim indiscriminately during his own television appearances, there was no way he was going to let Wilson get away with being so dismissive. 'He has expressed an opinion that has put him up there to be shot at – and I'm doing the shooting,' Clough said. 'If I make wrong decisions, I could find myself out of work. But will someone at the BBC get rid of Bob Wilson for not getting things right?'

On the face of it, Wilson's wasn't the most outlandish statement in the world when the Forest players were surprising even themselves. Otherwise, why had none of those players even bothered asking at the start of the season if there was a bonus for winning the league? They simply hadn't thought it necessary. 'We were just happy to be in the First Division and on the pitch with these teams,' Burns says. 'Then we got on the pitch with them and found out we were better than them.'

Robertson played so majestically during those opening months that Taylor used to ring him sometimes first thing in the morning to make sure he hadn't lapsed into old ways. 'Straight away he would be checking up on me,' Robertson says. 'It would be a crackly line sometimes. "Is that bacon I can hear sizzling in the background?" he would say. "Have you had that frying pan out again?"'

Robertson still smoked like a trooper. He held the cigarette, Mafioso-style, in the palm of his hand so it wasn't always obvious and he had a habit of hiding behind a rubber plant in the entrance to the Jubilee Club, a drinks lounge that had just opened behind the Main Stand, taking in the last few puffs before shuffling on to the team coach. Some players would bound up the steps in the surefooted way of a natural athlete. Robertson, Clough used to say, heaved himself up one at a time. He was the only player to use the handrail to get himself through the door and those battered suede shoes were still a point of contention. Clough didn't even need to say anything sometimes. He would simply look Robertson in the eye, slowly transfer his gaze to the shoes and then back to the player's face. Robertson would shift uncomfortably and attempt a nervous smile. Neither would utter a word, but Robertson was left in no doubt what Clough made of his dress sense.

Gemmill's relationship with Clough was even more complex. He had been with him through the glories at Derby, when Clough's fire really started to burn, but their personalities could rub against one another like sandpaper. Gemmill has never stopped referring to Clough as 'the boss', but it is not always easy differentiating between the various stages where he loved him, loathed him and sometimes a bit of both. 'I hate the bastard sometimes, but I would give him my last half-crown,' he said once.

Gemmill received the ultimate compliment in his first game, a 1–1 draw against Norwich City, when Clough picked him ahead of McGovern and also handed him the captaincy. Clough then dropped him for the next three matches, saying the little Scotsman had picked up 'too many bad habits' at Derby. 'The real Archie Gemmill must have been put in chains in recent years,' Clough complained. 'He's forgotten all his good habits, playing the ball back to defenders all the time. He wouldn't have been allowed to play like that when I was at Derby and he won't play that way here.'

The other players, meanwhile, tell a story about Gemmill going to see Clough after being left out.

'I'm not happy,' Gemmill, the smallest man in the squad, announced.

Clough's reply was delivered with comedic timing that Tommy Cooper would have been proud of.

'Which one are you then?'

Forest's players certainly had to develop a tough skin, and expect anything, when Clough and Taylor were around.

Another time, it was O'Neill's turn to cop it in front of all the other players and Taylor was jabbing a finger to help win the argument. 'I'll tell you why you're in the team and we're winning the game,' Taylor raged, pointing around the dressing room. 'You're in the team because of good players like him (pointing at Robertson), him (Burns), him (Lloyd), not so much him (Barrett), him (Gemmill) and him (Shilton).'

That 'not so much' was even worse for Barrett – a player

Clough rated as one of his best ever pieces of business – than it was for the man Taylor had actually been arguing with. Yet it was one of Taylor's idiosyncrasies that, Robertson aside, he always preferred the players he considered to be his own signings.

When Clough grew bored of training at Forest, and sometimes that was after five minutes, he had a habit of sending everyone on a run through the adjoining field of brambles and nettles three feet high. Sometimes they would have to go on piggyback. At others they would run, single file, with their hands in front of their faces, knocking the brambles and thorns aside so they inevitably swung back on to the next person. Tracksuit bottoms weren't allowed so the players' legs would take most of the punishment, red-raw with scratches and nettle stings. And when they came back out, Clough would inevitably shout: 'Right, back you go again.'

On Fridays, when the team trained at the City Ground, he would send them scattering into the stands for an impromptu game of hide and seek. 'Maybe one lap of jogging round the pitch,' Tony Woodcock remembers, 'then he'd shout: "Last man out of sight" and there would be grown men scrambling up to the directors' box, hiding behind the seats and looking at each other thinking: "What are we doing here?"' The loser – the last man out of sight – had to go first through the nettles the next time.

Forest's 2–0 win at QPR was described by Taylor as their best performance since the opening day of the season, featuring an exquisitely taken free-kick from Burns for the second goal, and Bowyer remembers Clough bringing up the offending line again and again. 'He used to say to us: "Is this the week?" Everybody in the media was talking about the Forest bubble, and when it would burst, and he made sure we were aware of it. It was all he needed to say really, because there was already an element of us against the media. It hadn't taken us long to realise our little provincial club wasn't going to get the credit our style of football and our results deserved.'

The journalists riding on Clough's coat-tails didn't think a team that had just made it out of the Second Division could have any staying power and, as such, shouldn't be treated too seriously. Football writers are reluctant sometimes to confess they might have got something wrong. But McGovern thinks there was more to it. 'The media loved Clough. He was outspoken, he said outrageous things, and they loved all that, but you can't win everyone over. If we played in London or Liverpool and the journalists asked inane questions, Clough would round on them. He'd give them a volley and there were some who didn't like him because of it. "He's a bighead," they would say. Then we started getting "lucky Forest" and "Their bubble will burst." They were waiting for him, and us, to trip up.'

Not all the praise was begrudging though. Forest were acclaimed in one newspaper for playing 'beautifully simple football' during the autumn of 1977. Clough was hailed for his ability to create teams with an 'almost excessive belief in themselves' and there was praise for the players too. Frank Clough once wrote in the *Sun* that if Clough's Derby won the league he would eat his own match report (and he kept his promise). Now he said Robertson 'would walk into the England team if he weren't a Scot' and noted Woodcock's 'ability to turn any defender grey'. Geoffrey Green in *The Times* summed up Forest's principles in his own erudite way: 'The secret of Forest's success is teamwork. Each man plays for his fellows; they have peace, spirit and vision of a wide field.'

There was certainly a sense of togetherness about the league leaders and, as the rest of the world waited for them to run out of steam, they were also showing the qualities that were essential for any team who wanted to be thought of as genuine contenders. Against Manchester City, they were losing after twenty minutes but still managed to win courtesy of Woodcock's equaliser and another goal for Withe four minutes from the end. Manchester United also took the lead when they visited the City Ground in November and, again, Forest showed their durability, with second-half goals from Burns and Gemmill turning the game upside down. Gemmill's header was a peach and Forest were so good that day Clough said the performance should have been set to music.

Shilton was a perfectionist, striving always for a flawless performance and treating every goal against him like a personal affront. Burns had settled down after that unfortunate 'sneezing' incident at Arsenal and it was obvious already that Tommy Docherty might have dropped an almighty rick thinking Gemmill was past it. When they were managing Derby, Clough and Taylor regarded Alan Hinton as one of their best acquisitions, at £29,000 from Forest, and never forgot hearing on the night of the signing that one of the Forest committee members had been crowing about how

'We've done them two good and proper.' The roles had been reversed with Gemmill. News quickly spread that Docherty had been boasting that he had 'sold Cloughie a pup'.

By November, Derby were eighteenth after winning three out of their first fifteen games. Wolves and Chelsea, the clubs promoted with Forest, were both in the bottom half of the table while the team at the top had a three-point lead over Everton in second and were six clear of Liverpool in fifth. The leaders were showing no signs of relenting and the newspapers were also waking up to the fact there was a player on Forest's left who seemed to be on first-name terms with the ball. 'Is Nottingham Forest's runaway leadership of the First Division all to do with Brian Clough's talent for striding across the otherwise troubled waters of English soccer?' James Lawton wrote in the *Express*. 'Or is it because the majority of their rivals have yet to show the gumption required to identify the source of Forest's strength – and the basic know-how to deal with it?

'Forest scored seventeen goals against two last month and even a casual observer could note that their pale-faced, dark-haired twenty-four-year-old Scottish winger John Robertson was the man at the heart of it all. Whether he is dawdling in a deep position down the left wing, driving either side of his shadow or delivering balls of deep penetration early or late, he is clearly the man who matters.'

That was becoming apparent to everyone, but it had taken a change of heart from Clough and Taylor in pre-season before the crucial decision to make Robertson the focal point of the team. The initial idea was for Forest to channel most of their attacks through Curran on the right wing. Robertson was going to be what O'Neill called 'the support player' on the other side. As for O'Neill, he hardly had a look-in during the pre-season fixtures and was wondering where it left him. 'Peter Taylor had this idea, more perhaps than Brian Clough himself, to play with two out-and-out wide players and take teams by storm.' But the balance wasn't quite right. Curran was a flier with little thought for defensive duties. Robertson, as Clough tirelessly reminded everyone, was not a natural runner, especially in a semi-defensive role. O'Neill, on the other hand, was a prodigious worker who could track Robertson's runs and help the midfield keep its shape. Barrett called him the 'lungs of the team'.

The change was implemented after a pre-season game against Notts County five days before the start of the new campaign. O'Neill then became the support act and Robertson took over the lead role. Curran was so put out about losing his place he stormed into Taylor's office with a transfer request and threw it on the desk. 'He'd got his envelopes mixed up,' Robertson says. 'Peter opened it and said: "Do you want me to pay this or something?" It was Terry's gas bill.' Curran, the self-styled 'poor man's George Best', didn't play a single minute for Forest in the First Division and went on loan to Bury before joining Derby.

Robertson was more of a poor man's George Wendt (Norm from the television show *Cheers*) in his lost years, but now he was flourishing as the most effective British winger since Best himself – and possibly the most unorthodox one too. He didn't have Curran's ability to knock the ball ten yards ahead and beat an opponent for pace. He didn't specialise in fancy tricks and, though he could dribble, it wasn't a blur of step-overs, nutmegs and dazzling footwork. He was one of the slowest players in the league and Gemmill was only half-joking when he described Robertson's usual preparation as consisting of 'bacon rolls, pints of lager, pints of Guinness and a warm-up of a fag and a wee nip of whisky'. Robertson was nothing like the usual wide man and that, perhaps, is one of the reasons why opposition defences found it so difficult knowing what to do about him.

One certainty though: Robertson was establishing himself as the star of the team. His crossing under pressure was peerless and, though he wasn't fast over ten or twenty yards, his brain was so quick he had the first two yards on anybody. 'He would go past people who were quick and leave them for dead,' Gemmill says. 'Eight times out of ten he would go past the full-back, or drop his shoulder and play the ball inside. No pace whatsoever, couldn't tackle a fish supper, but left foot, right foot, genius. He was phenomenal, for somebody so fat.'

Robertson was that rarity, genuinely two-footed, as a legacy of all those hours of practice when he was a youngster, knocking the ball back and forth against a brick wall, developing the touch and composure that made it seem like the ball was never going to run away from his foot. When he first moved to the left, he had a tendency to play his pass too quickly without weighing up all his options. Clough encouraged him to delay and use his ability to see if there was something better on, manoeuvre the space and then deliver the ball. At other times, Robertson liked to spray long passes from one side of the pitch to the other, getting a kick from showing off his accuracy over distance and knowing it was the kind of thing the crowd would applaud. Clough quickly knocked that out of him. 'Decoration,' he called it.

Bill Shankly would later say that Robertson passed the ball along the ground with the accuracy of a snooker player potting the black. Burns says Robertson 'didn't just kick the ball, he stroked the ball'. The instructions were simple: get it to Robbo.

'I remember when I first came and we used to train behind the old East Stand,' O'Hare says. 'There was a bit of patchy land there, no grass, and that was the first time I saw in really tight situations just how good he was. He could go past people like they weren't there. He could almost beat people without touching the ball. He just dropped his shoulder and he was gone.'

More than anything, Clough let Robertson know he had it in him to be a great footballer and made his player feel the same. 'That's why it riles me when people say Clough ruled by fear,' Robertson says. 'How can any footballer go on the field and weave magic if they are scared stiff? I'll tell you what I wanted. I wanted that sign he did, the little circle, to show you he was happy with something you had done. Because when I got that sign, I wanted that ball back and I wanted to show him again and again.'

Robertson saw a lot of that sign in those months when Forest started upsetting the status quo, clambering to the top of the table and then squatting there, defiantly. The game against West Ham was just one example. Robertson set up four of the five goals that night and gave his marker, Frank Lampard senior, such a chasing he can remember Billy Bonds coming over late in the match with the intention of trying to kick him into the stand. 'Robertson is the best winger around,' Lampard said afterwards. 'He goes either side, which isn't really fair.'

The amazing thing is that Robertson had not won a single Scotland cap by the time the rest of the First Division started trying to fathom out how someone with that almost nonchalant half-walk, half-run could be so effective. Perhaps thinking it was just a flash in the pan, few sides thought it was necessary to put more than one defender on him. When they cottoned on, there was a queue of opponents waiting for Robertson, but that didn't bother him either. Robertson was happy to take the easy option and lay the ball off, knowing that by drawing two or more players he was giving his team an advantage anyway. He clung to the touchline – 'Chalk on your feet,' Clough would shout, 'I want chalk on your feet' – and stretched the game, pulling opponents out of place and creating space for his team-mates to exploit. All he needed was half a yard and that's when the ball would be whipped in, either with vicious swing to the near post or with greater lift to the far side.

Lloyd regards him as the most talented winger he has ever seen. 'He couldn't run. He wasn't quick. But you couldn't believe some of the things he used to do when the ball was at his feet. If someone put it down the line for him to chase, he wouldn't even chase it. He just wanted it to his feet. All the time: "To my feet, to my feet." He'd get it to his feet, shimmy, he'd drop his shoulder to the right, the full-back would go to the right, 30,000 people would go to the right. He'd put his fat arse to the right – and then, hey presto, he was off, down the left.

'I've seen other wingers who had more pace but would end up running it out of play, and I've seen wingers who would try to cross it and the ball would end up in the Trent.

Robbo pinpointed his crosses. He rarely wasted one. And he was our outlet. I used to like the occasional sortie upfield and when I suddenly reached a position that was totally alien to me, I didn't know what to do. My first thought was always the same: "Where's Robbo? Oh, there he is, thank God, and remember: to his feet. Now, you do the rest, Robbo." He was slower even than me, but the little fat bastard was a magician.'

The dynamic between Clough and Robertson was changing too. Clough carried on badgering Robertson about his appearance but his once despairing tone, complaining it was driving him barmy, now had the unmistakable tint of affection. Clough would sit in the dressing room sometimes with his arm draped around Robertson's shoulder. 'Give him a ball and a yard of grass, and he is an artist,' Clough would say. He would even turn a blind eye sometimes to the fact more smoke came out of Robertson than nearby Kegworth Power Station. 'I often think Robbo could have been Clough's secret son,' Lloyd says. 'We'd come in at half-time and if things weren't going well, Clough would be telling us what to change. You'd look around and realise Robbo wasn't there. Then you'd notice a plume of smoke coming from the toilets and you knew the little man was sitting in there having a crafty fag. Clough would just tell us: "Leave him, he'll pick it up when we get back on the pitch." Nobody else could have got away with that.'

On the other side of the pitch, O'Neill could find it difficult sometimes in a team that had made the player furthest away from him the first point of reference. 'You would think the fulcrum of the team would normally be someone in central midfield or one of the centre-backs,' O'Neill says. 'No, the fulcrum of our side was outside left. It went there every time.

'John would get the ball on the left and my job was to try to get to the back post for any crosses coming in. If John checked back, rather than going down the line, that meant I had to check back. I'd be doing all these runs back and forwards – doggies, we called them – and I'd be every bit as tired as they were the other side. I just hadn't touched the ball. So I would be thinking: "Do you think, just once, someone might turn this way?" We could literally go thirteen or fourteen minutes without the ball coming to the right but, if nothing else, it meant I was in a good position to judge all these players. And John was brilliant. Over twenty yards he wouldn't have beaten anybody; he wouldn't have beaten my father. Over two or three yards, he was sensational.'

O'Neill had been there during the years when Robertson was hovering on the brink of professional failure and, pre-Clough, lined up for a move to Partick Thistle by a manager who could not get his name right. The key, O'Neill believes, was having someone who could see what Robertson was good at, rather than what he couldn't do. 'Allan Brown couldn't see John's talent at all. We used to go out on Saturday nights and John's head would be in total turmoil. He really had to have someone to believe in him all the time. We all do, but John in particular. Clough used to give him that little sign and it made him feel ten feet tall. And John was mesmeric when his confidence was up.'

All of which can make it feel like a trick of the mind sometimes that if Brown had got his way, Robertson would have been back in Scotland at the club Billy Connolly grew up calling 'Partick Thistle Nil'. Partick dropped into the second tier of Scottish football in the season Brown tried to arrange that deal and Ronnie Glavin, the other half of the proposed exchange, moved to Celtic instead, where he ended up in court accused of setting fire to his own sports shop and allegedly trying to swindle £20,000 from his insurance company.

He was acquitted and eventually moved to Barnsley, helping them win promotion from the Third Division. Yet it is fair to say Forest got the better end of the deal. By that stage, Robertson was on his way to becoming the most unassuming and unlikely superstar of the era.

'I remember meeting him,' Jimmy Case, the Liverpool player, once said. 'I was quite surprised to see him with a fag in his mouth.'

Chapter Five
A Lesson In Football

'Takes some believing, eh?' *John McGovern*

As winter started to arrive in 1977, a football club with a century of almost non-achievement behind them were still at the top of the First Division. A campaign was building for Clough to be made England manager and Nottingham was in the national news after the manager of the Virgin record store in King Street was arrested for displaying the sleeve of 'Never Mind the Bollocks, Here's the Sex Pistols' in its window. Other stores in Camden and Notting Hill were threatened with prosecution but the test case was held in Nottingham, under the 1899 Indecent Advertisement Act, only to collapse when the defence lawyers argued 'bollocks' was a legitimate Old English term with various meanings. Apparently, Sid Vicious and the other Sex Pistols might have been referring to a priest or an orchid. And if you believe that you would probably believe any, well, bollocks.

Clough had been leading his own clean-up campaign and posed next to a billboard at the side of the pitch before one match with a message for spectators to mind their language. Clough had already tackled Forest's reputation for having some of the most violent supporters in the country, the infamous 'Mad Squad', in his first programme notes back in 1975: 'My message to troublemakers is simply get lost!' Now he arranged a placard with the message: 'Gentlemen, no swearing please! Brian.' For the next few games the Trent End responded with cleaned-up versions of their usual songs – 'What the flipping heck was that?' and 'The referee's a naughty' – and Clough was unconcerned presumably by the whiff of hypocrisy after his side had knocked Aston Villa out of the League Cup and he let the occupants of the pressbox know exactly what he thought of their profession. 'I want nothing more to do with the fucking press,' he said. 'I've finished with the fuckers. They are a shower and they stink in my opinion.' Clough then walked out before returning a few minutes later to make his point again. 'In case you did not hear correctly, I'll repeat it.' And he did, word for word.

His grievance was their coverage of the previous game, a goalless draw against West Bromwich Albion, but it was also a culmination of the way Forest kept being portrayed as what Robertson used to call a 'rag, tag and bob-tail team'. Clough thought the journalists should have paid more attention to the fact he and Taylor had already won the league with a team he had managed in the Second Division and recalled the words of Derby's former chairman, Sydney Bradley, when he proclaimed that 'Brian and Peter built an ocean liner out of a shipwreck.' The difference was that Derby side went up as champions in 1969, seven points clear of Crystal Palace in second, and it took them another three years to win the title. Forest were threatening to do it in a single season: a team described in one newspaper as 'a mixture of fresh and well-worn faces who ought to be slogging it out at the bottom of the table'.

The banner at one game read 'Clough's Bionic Bubble Will

Never Burst' but there had been a slight wobble and Forest had not scored in three of the previous four league games. After starting the season at the top of his form, Peter Withe had gone half a dozen matches without a goal and, to Clough's intense displeasure, one of those blanks was a 1–0 defeat at Leeds in the manager's first game back at Elland Road. Nobody believed Clough when he said it was 'just another game', even if a lot of the people he regarded as enemies were no longer there. Ray Hankin scored the decisive goal and Clough's impressions of Leeds and their relationship with fair play was not greatly enhanced. Peter Shilton had been concussed, losing a couple of teeth, just before the goal went in.

The defeat was slightly misleading – Peter Taylor described the performance as even better than the one at Everton – and when Forest drew 0–0 at West Ham one conversation on the train journey home demonstrated how attitudes had changed. 'Hello, Mr Clough,' the train guard said. 'What went wrong today then?'

Nonetheless, there was still a steady queue of football people and journalists willing to parrot Bob Wilson's view that it was only a matter of time before Forest, like the pace-setter in a long-distance race, obediently stepped aside for the stronger competitors to power through. Mick Mills, the Ipswich and England player, was among them and the constant scepticism was wearing thin judging by the programme column Ken Smales penned against Manchester United in November and a two-page rant, almost Clough-esque, about the 'birds of prey' that had been pecking at them.

Football programmes tend to be the blandest of reads but

Smales, like Clough, had some of the traits that Harry Enfield picked up for his 1990s comedy character, the Yorkshireman – 'I say what I like and I bloody well like what I say' – and it was easy to see why he and Clough had become allies. 'The vultures are patiently circling overhead waiting for exhaustion to overtake us and halt our progress in the inhospitable desert of the upper reaches of the First Division,' Smales began. 'They are waiting to swoop down and pick our bones dry, waiting to boast to the world that "I told you the Forest bubble would burst." But these scavengers will have to stay aloft a bit longer before this happens and they would be advised to search for an alternative source of food. Our caravan is still pressing on and can go a bit further yet.'

Wilson, according to Smales, was lucky to be holding down his job after the way he had 'made a fool of himself with his hasty judgments'. Smales, a former Yorkshire and Nottinghamshire cricketer who had been part of the club's administrative staff since 1961, made the point that 'the 4–0 humiliation' for Ipswich had made Mills look 'a trifle silly'. And finally there was a message for anyone else who needed their wings clipping. 'Many others of the species Sarcoramphus papa have jumped on the bandwagon: "Wait till the heavy grounds come, wait till they sustain a few injuries . . . wait till . . . wait . . . wait." But they won't be able to wait forever. I have news for them. It is no bubble they are hovering around. It is a barrage balloon and we know what they are for. So they had better watch where they are flying.'

Fighting talk, and it was certainly fair to assume that Mills wished he had said nothing ahead of Ipswich's date at the City Ground. The man who went on to captain England in the 1982 World Cup had made the mistake of thinking John Robertson was an orthodox left-winger. 'He tried to show Robbo inside,' Colin Barrett says. 'Ipswich clearly all thought he was left-footed and, in fairness, I used to think the same until I saw him taking a penalty. Of course, he was right-footed too. He could flat-foot defenders, pass them down the outside or come inside. And he skinned Mills every time.'

Don Revie had given up his job as England manager during the summer to take a more lavishly paid role in charge of the United Arab Emirates, writing in his resignation letter that he had come to find the pressures 'intolerable' and following it up with a newspaper interview in which he said 'nearly everyone in the country seems to want me out.'

The FA responded by charging Revie with bringing the game into disrepute, accusing him of a 'flagrant breach of contract', before a series of articles appeared in the *Daily Mirror* alleging he had been involved with four or five different cases of bribery and attempted match-fixing. One of them suggested he had offered Bob Stokoe, then player-manager of Bury, a £500 bribe in 1962 to 'take it easy' in a relegation match with Leeds. Revie was alleged to have used a middle-man to ask the Wolves players to do the same when Leeds were going for the championship in 1972. Forest were another of the clubs named with Jim Barron, the club's former goal-keeper, saying they had rejected a request to 'go easy' before another crucial match for Leeds in 1971.

Clough, naturally, could barely disguise his *schadenfreude*, describing himself as 'wearing a black armband for football' and writing a ghosted newspaper article in which he predicted his old adversary would find Abu Dhabi 'the most luxurious prison in the world'. The article, 'Revie – By Clough' was printed in the *Sunday Mirror* and even by Clough's standards it was a brutal slaying. 'Don Revie could have ordered champagne and caviar at breakfast this morning,' it began. 'One telephone call in his £50-a-night Intercontinental Hotel would have been enough. The taste, I suspect, would have been like the porridge at Wormwood Scrubs or water from a dirty stream.' Revie, he said, had 'degraded' the sport. 'I'm a professional man and he has sold me short by quitting England as he did. He has sold football short. What's worse, he has sold himself short.'

No doubt Clough enjoyed sticking in the boot, but it was that outspoken streak and the rough edges to his personality that probably explain why he was not invited to take over from Revie as England manager, despite being the only manager on the FA's shortlist – the others being Ron Greenwood, Jack Charlton, Lawrie McMenemy and Dave Sexton – who had won a league championship. He was the obvious candidate and it gnawed away at him for years that the FA gave the job to Greenwood when every newspaper poll of the time made it clear Clough was the people's choice; outside, that is, of Forest's own fan-base. When the speculation was at its height, Forest's supporters paraded a billboard of their own: 'Brian, no leaving please! The Gentlemen.'

The issue had been hanging over Forest for months and can be added to the already extensive list of what-ifs that had intermittently threatened a derailment. What if Clough had been lured away by Derby's offer the previous February? Or what if the weather had not saved them on that foggy night against Southampton? What would have happened to Forest's title push if the FA's chairman Sir Harold Thompson had not been, in the words of Clough's great friend Geoffrey Boycott, so 'gutless'? The damage caused by losing Clough might have been irreparable. 'I think Sir Harold and his colleagues were wrong,' Ken Smales later said, 'and how delighted I am.'

The relief was immense because Clough was at the height of his powers, still young at forty-two and bloodying so many people's noses with Forest that most people outside the FA had concluded he was the right man for the job. His team were defying all reasonable expectations and there wasn't a trace of discernible self-doubt whenever Clough was asked about their ability to stay there, just a mild form of sadness that so many others could not see it too.

That point was reinforced in Forest's first game after Greenwood's appointment, twelve days after Clough had sat in front of the FA's selection panel and – classic Clough – started the biggest interview of his professional life by informing the FA secretary Ted Croker that the new England kit was 'hideous'.

In one respect, Forest's game at Manchester United in mid-December was not the most important fixture of the season, bearing in mind Dave Sexton's team were fourteenth and had no chance of catching the cluster of teams challenging for the title. They had lost at the City Ground the previous month and there had already been the first mutinous cries of 'Sexton out' at Old Trafford, despite the fact he was not even halfway through his first season in the job. But they were the FA Cup holders and had already beaten Liverpool earlier in the season. Old Trafford had a special aura and a tradition of excellence that meant Forest knew if they were going to turn the volume down on their critics, it was the perfect place to do it.

They wore their away strip that day – all-yellow with blue trim – and the highlights package can be found by typing 'A Lesson in Football' into YouTube. United had never lost a league match 4–0 at home in the post-war years and, by the time it was all done, Forest were applauded off the pitch and the home players wore the body language of zombies, in search of smelling salts or possibly something stronger. 'The best display,' according to Barry Davies, covering the game for *Match of the Day*, 'that I have had the privilege of seeing this season.'

That was the day, more than any other that season, the world found out that the rag-tags were actually the real deal. Every season, there is always one game when everything clicks for the team that is going to win the title. That was it for Forest and the location they chose – the ground that, in 1957, a twenty-year-old Bobby Charlton described as the 'Theatre of Dreams' – was perfect to make their point.

For Tony Woodcock in particular, it was a special day. He had been brought up in Eastwood, DH Lawrence country on the cusp of Nottinghamshire and Derbyshire, but as a kid the first team that meant anything to him had Matt Busby as their manager. He grew up 'worshipping Denis Law', covering his bedroom walls with pictures of the Busby Babes and trying to imagine what it might be like to stand in, or play in front of, those baying crowds.

Woodcock's one previous appearance at Old Trafford was in the reserves. 'I can remember running back out after the match and going on my own to stand in the Stretford End, because I had never been there before and I just wanted to have a proper look at this stadium, which I had dreamt about all those years. So to play there when it was full was a really big moment for me. Ian Bowyer came over to me before the game. He said: "If you want to do it anywhere, this is the place to do it." So we did. We went out and we did it.'

Perhaps it was Woodcock's old allegiances that explained why he celebrated the first goal by turning towards the Stretford End to pump his fists. His shot had come back off the post and went in off Brian Greenhoff for an own-goal and that was effectively the last United saw of the game. It was a blur of yellow: quick, incisive, pass-them-to-death foot-ball. Woodcock scored one with his right foot and one with his left. Robertson stroked in the other but there were numerous other chances and at the final whistle, as the players made their way off, Barry Davies left it for a few seconds. The best commentators always know when silence works and when to let the pictures tell their own story. Then came his verdict, beautifully delivered. 'Manchester United,' he observed, 'buried in their own backyard.'

John McGovern did the post-match interviews that day and can remember waiting in the bowels of the stadium as United's manager faced a very different set of questions. 'I actually felt sorry for Dave Sexton that day. Imagine being the manager of such a massive club when you have lost 4–0 at home and it could have been ten. He had to explain it to the cameras and I felt for him, because that was as good as it ever got in terms of every single player on one side playing to their maximum. If you had tried to pick a man-of-the-match that day, you would have struggled. We were flying, and we ran them to death.'

Sexton did not even attempt to make excuses. 'Forest showed us up,' he said. 'They don't play with eleven men. They seem to have sixteen or seventeen. When they are attacking they have seven coming at you, and when they are defending there are about nine of them.' It could, he admitted, have been 'double the score' and it was certainly true that United's suffering might have been even worse. One report mentioned that Viv Anderson – a right-back, lest it be forgotten – might have scored a hat-trick. 'For years,' Clough said, 'this place has been held up by all as the home of skill, but today my team showed them what skill is all about.'

On the bus journey back to Nottingham, Clough could be heard singing one of his favourite Sinatra songs.

> You've either got or you haven't got style
> If you got it, you stand out a mile.

His team had plenty of style and it was an affirmative performance for anyone still wondering whether Forest's position at the top of the league was phoney.

'Those who have doubts should be prepared to shed them now,' Tom German wrote in *The Times*. 'Nottingham Forest are equipped to win the championship and assuredly will if the exciting style which demolished and demoralised Manchester United sets their standard for the second half of the season.'

Paul Fitzpatrick was equally effusive in the *Guardian*. 'A question many people were pondering afterwards was whether Forest were so good because United were so poor,' he wrote. 'United were wretched, as bad as one can recall, but to seek in any way to diminish Forest's performance would be unforgivable. Observers with long memories of Old Trafford football would say they were the best side seen on the ground for many a long year. They will not be surprised if Forest win the championship, rather if they don't.'

More importantly, something changed with the players that day. Bill Shankly had told them they should have a stab at winning the league. Clough had promised Archie Gemmill it was going to happen, though not necessarily that season, and Martin O'Neill can recall going for a few drinks with his family after the opening-day win at Everton and being taken aback by his brother's verdict. 'I remember him saying he thought we could win the league. "Don't be silly," I replied. "Do you know what it was like in the first twenty minutes today? Are you completely off your rocker?"'

Forest had been top since 4 October but there had still been that nagging sense that it was too good to be true. 'Whether we really believed we could win the league at that stage, I very much doubt it,' Robertson says. But they did on the way back from Old Trafford, once they had demolished several rounds of celebratory drinks in Manchester's Playboy Club, and so did the journalists who had previously dismissed them as caretaker leaders. How could anyone not when they had been at the summit for ten weeks and just demolished the most famous team in the land? 'We showed all those clever clogs in the media that we were good enough,' Clough said. 'I enjoyed that.'

Clough immediately took everyone away for a few days of sunshine in Benidorm where they found an English pub, the aptly named Robin Hood, and John O'Hare used a snorkel to pretend he was playing the bagpipes as the players, half-cut, sang along to the new Wings song, 'Mull of Kintyre'. But it wasn't the booze that had O'Hare telling his team-mates there was nothing left to fear in the First Division. 'I don't think they could believe how good they were,' he says. 'Maybe, being an older head with Frank Clark, I could see it better. "You can win this league," I told them. "Look at the way you are playing, you're destroying teams – you're not just winning, you're hammering everyone." It had all happened so quickly they didn't realise how good they actually were.'

O'Hare had first-hand knowledge of what elements were required from his title-winning days at Derby, and O'Neill remembers the conversation. 'The younger lads such as myself, John Robertson, Viv and Tony Woodcock would hang on to a lot of what John O'Hare said, because we knew he had done it before. He never boasted about it, but we had great regard for him. That was the first time I'd heard John say: "You can win this league." He didn't say "we", he said "you". He hadn't played that often and he was distancing himself from it.

"You're ripping teams apart," he said. I thought: "If he thinks it, we might actually have a chance here.'"

O'Neill had felt concerned before the game at Old Trafford that there was still time for everything to unravel, but his mentality changed after that game. 'To hammer them like that, absolutely hammer them – we won 4–0 but it could have been twice as much – what a feeling that was to know we could do that at the place known as the Theatre of Dreams, the club of George Best, Bobby Charlton, Denis Law and all those great players. If ever there was a result to give us a surge of confidence, that was it.'

The next game was against Liverpool on Boxing Day and another test of nerve that would let the football world know more about Forest's chances. 'Before the match Clough said he had something to tell us,' O'Neill says. 'He said he had been speaking to Bob Paisley and Bob had told the Liverpool players that if they didn't match us for energy, he knew they would be beaten. It might have been just the way he said it, deliberately to give us a lift, but I remember those words resonating and thinking: "My God, are Liverpool really concerned about us now?"'

Gemmill scored first but Steve Heighway equalised before half-time and the referee gave Phil Thompson the benefit of the doubt after Woodcock went down late on in the penalty area. 'We had dropped points at home, which we weren't used to, but that result at least meant they hadn't gained anything on us,' O'Neill says. 'From that point onwards, having beaten Manchester United and not lost to Liverpool, we knew we could do it.'

The momentum was building. A crowd of 47,218 was

shoehorned into the City Ground that day and the Trent End was so packed it had to be closed at a quarter to two. At the next home game, a 1–1 draw against second-placed Everton, there were 44,030 packed inside. 'It's a bit like the old days this, isn't it?' Smales said, but not the old days the players could remember. Forest, Robertson could not help thinking, had come a long way since the Christmas period three years earlier. 'We played Blackpool,' he recalls, 'and got about eight thousand.' To be precise, 8,480.

The season had reached its midway point and, in between facing the Merseyside clubs, there was a 2–0 win at Newcastle that again could have been more emphatic. 'I was in the bath afterwards and David Needham said to me: "What do you think?"' McGovern says. 'We had gone five points clear and I said: "Nobody will catch us now, we'll win it now." Even at Christmas I was convinced we had all the elements to take on anybody, home or away.'

McGovern was captaining a Forest side that was in the process of winning four successive away matches in the top division for the first time since 1894. 'When I was at Derby, our away record wasn't actually that brilliant. This Forest side were a lot better than the team where I had won the championship already. We were a better side, so why wouldn't I feel confident?'

Needham had signed from QPR and made his debut at Old Trafford, 'panicking like hell,' after Larry Lloyd had broken a bone in his foot during a 2–1 win over Coventry the previous weekend. Needham was twenty-eight and had been at QPR only half a season. He had spent the previous twelve years at Notts County, where he had been a regular thorn in Forest's side, and it did cross his mind that, politically, it might be an unpopular switch when Clough invited him to Trattoria Antonio, the Italian restaurant on the cusp of Trent Bridge, to arrange the transfer. Needham had played 429 league games for County and now he was joining the enemy from across the river. 'I was going to upset everybody at Notts County,' Needham says. 'And I wasn't sure how the Forest players would accept me either.'

As it turned out, there was only player who was put out and that was the one with his foot in plaster. On Needham's first day at the club, he went around everyone to shake hands and introduce himself.

'Are you all right?' he asked Lloyd.

Lloyd was never well disposed to anyone he suspected might challenge him for his place and the injured centre-half did not bother with superficial niceties.

'I'm not that fucking well, mate, otherwise you wouldn't be here.'

Lloyd might not have been happy, but Needham's acquisition was a clever piece of business because Forest were approaching the point of the season when the most serious danger was fatigue. They were slogging it out on three fronts and had used only fifteen players up until that point. They were also having to do it on pitches that often needed only a few drops of rain to turn into mudbaths. It was a grind and those were the moments when the players appreciated why Clough did not go in for the same training regimes that other managers of that time swore by.

'Clough knew that if you had a few days off you would go back into work with a bounce in your step,' Kenny Burns recalls. 'He'd come in on Monday, smoking a cigar, and say: "Right, I don't want to see anyone until Thursday." I would push my luck: "Friday is actually better for me boss." He'd say: "Thursday, you fat lazy bugger. Take your wives and girlfriends out and get some bonus points because if they're happy, you're happy and I'm happy. And if I find out anyone has been training or out running, I'll fine them."'

To some, the regime at Forest must have seemed terribly lax. Football teams in the 1970s were generally flogged to the sound of the managers' whips. It was the era of hard running, punishing cross-country slogs and the general attitude that the first rule of success was to train them harder than the other lot. One more circuit of the pitch, a hundred press-ups for whoever came last, and all that.

Frank Clark had been brought up the old-fashioned way at Newcastle and it was a culture shock for him at Forest. 'I was thirty-one, I wanted to carry on playing as long as I possibly could and I'd read a newspaper article where someone asked Muhammad Ali: "Do you train less, now you are getting older?" Typical Muhammad Ali, he said: "No, I train more." So I thought if that was good enough for him, it was good enough for me.

'I wasn't comfortable with all the days off Clough kept giving us, so I started running on the roads around where I lived. Nothing too strenuous or too far, just something to keep ticking over. But someone wrote to the local paper about seeing me. It was a nice letter. But Clough got hold of me and he went absolutely berserk. "When I give you a day off, you have a day off. And if I find out you've been training on your day off again, I'll fine you." I tried to argue with him but lost the argument obviously, and over the next two seasons I played one hundred and eight consecutive games. At the end of the second season he called me in again. "Well, who was right then?" I looked at him and thought: "What's he talking about here, like?" But that's what he was talking about from two years before. He'd never forgotten about it.'

Clough's view is that a team that was expected to play sixty-odd games a season only needed to tick over between matches. Sammy Chung, the Wolves manager, once boasted to Clough that he worked his team so hard he could make Forest's fittest player sick within three minutes. Clough replied that when two points were awarded for being sick, he would give Chung a job.

His own methods were very different, but there was always a competitive edge in training. McGovern reckons the runs through nettles were punishments if the team had under-performed and a reminder that Clough didn't expect it to happen again. There were five-a-side games, he says, that were 'played like cup finals'. Nobody shirked a tackle. 'There was always that competitive edge,' Gemmill adds. 'It was never mundane. Someone would say we were playing ten minutes each way. An hour later, we would still be playing for the winning goal.'

Mostly, though, it was nothing more onerous than light jogging, a few basic drills and an exercise or game – sometimes it wasn't clear which of the two – when the players would have to scurry through each other's legs and then be carried, piggyback, to the other end of the field. Forest wouldn't send their players lapping the ground while carrying sandbags or on midwinter cross-country marathons. 'The proof of the pudding is on match days when no one can question our physical endeavour and staying power,' Taylor used to say. 'Our system works; that is its justification.'

Sometimes the players would turn up for training and wouldn't even have to get changed. Clough would simply announce they were going for a walk instead. They would find a nice spot by the Trent and spend the next thirty minutes tossing bread to the ducks. 'Amazing good can come from walking and talking beside the river,' was Taylor's take.

Burns was always amazed how pre-season training at Forest compared with what he heard from other clubs. But he also says that over the course of the season they were as fit as any other team in the league, and the 2–0 win against Arsenal in January was a prime example. Needham, a regular threat at set-pieces, opened the scoring and Gemmill sealed it with a goal he started on the edge of his own penalty box and finished inside the six-yard area. In between, Withe was the only other player to touch the ball. Gemmill had pinched it off an opponent's toe, played it out to Withe on the left and then set off on an eighty-yard dash, driving forward over the rutted pitch, picking up speed and running like his life depended on it. His legs seemed to be doing a mile a minute and, finally, he was in the goalmouth to turn in the return pass. It was one of the longest one-twos there can ever have been.

By the end of the month, a media stampede had started in the other direction and the newspapers were asking whether

English football was about to witness an unprecedented treble. Forest had navigated a route to the League Cup semi-finals and reached the FA Cup's fifth round at the expense of a Manchester City side that had climbed above Everton into second position in the league. Liverpool were not making up any ground back in fourth and the result at Old Trafford was put into perspective by United thrashing Everton 6–2 in their next match. Three days later, Everton lost 3–1 at Leeds and Forest's position was strengthened again. Their lead was now six points and Clough, like his players, was on top form. 'We played away at Bristol City in one of my first games,' Needham says. 'As I came out of the shower area, I could hear Cloughie talking to someone. "That Needham's a good player, isn't he?" he was saying. To this day, I don't know if he knew I was there or not. If he did, it was great management because it made me feel good. Hearing that really helped get me through.'

Clough always knew the value of his own compliments. Woodcock can remember floating out of the ground after Clough announced to everyone the striker had proved him wrong and was 'an absolute credit to the game'. Then there was the line to Barrett, deputising for the injured Clark, after Forest had beaten Leeds over two legs to reach the League Cup final. 'Just how long can you keep up this superb form?' Clough wanted to know, bending down in front of him in the dressing room.

Forest had done the hard part in the first leg, winning 3–1 at Elland Road, with O'Hare scoring against his former club. That was followed by a 4–2 victory in the return game, and for the other ex-Leeds player on Forest's books it was a sweet moment. 'I played from the age of sixteen to thirty-four and the one game where I nearly produced perfection, out of six hundred and seventy-odd, was against Leeds,' McGovern says. 'It was the game we lost 1–0 earlier in the season. For me, that was the closest I got to perfection. I never hit a bad ball and the manager noticed it as well. "You didn't misplace one pass today," he said. There was a reason for it. I still had a grudge against Leeds because of the way they stitched me up and got rid of the manager who signed me.'

McGovern's loyalty to Clough was unstinting, and though he always said it was purely a business arrangement and a normal player-manager relationship – 'He would give me a rollicking the same as anyone else' – there was plainly more to it. In 1960, McGovern's father was killed in a road accident while in Ghana to work on the Volta Dam. McGovern was eleven and not looking for another father-figure, but Clough did become his mentor and an almost paternal influence on his life. 'He was the only male person I could get advice from,' he says. 'Though I didn't ask for advice, it was just kind of thrown at me.'

On the first day they met, McGovern was still at school and had been on trial at Hartlepools when the players were told to line up to meet the team's manager. McGovern was fifteen and tells the story with his well-practised Clough impersonation. 'I was stood at the end of the line and, being a Mick Jagger fan, the only one with shoulder-length hair. I could see Clough shaking hands with the others before he came to me. Then it was my turn. His first words to me were: "Stand up straight, put your shoulders back and get your hair cut. You look like a girl."'

McGovern took the advice and became the classic short-back-and-sides prototype that Clough wanted: neat, polite and obedient. Clough persuaded the headmaster from McGovern's rugby-only school to let the teenager play football rather than go to university and, within four years, McGovern had become the youngest ever player to appear in all four divisions.

Wherever Clough went, McGovern tended to follow like a homing pigeon. The only time the link was broken was at Brighton but, even then, the bond was so strong that Clough still rang McGovern to ask whether he wanted to leave a title-winning Derby side for life on the south coast. 'I said: "But you're in Division Three" and the phone went dead,' McGovern recalls. 'Then he called back and said he'd make me skipper. I said: "But you'll still be in Division Three."'

The *Guardian* once described McGovern's role at Forest as 'Clough's consigliere, the on-field manager who calmly dealt with trouble and kept his nerve when others were flagging.' He was a play-breaker and a playmaker, but it wasn't a fashionable job in those days. McGovern worked out the *Nottingham Evening Post* had somehow failed to mention him in twelve successive match reports and, though it was nothing like as vicious as at Leeds, there were times when Forest's boo-boys targeted him as their default setting.

McGovern was not far short of Robertson as the slowest player at the club and had an unorthodox running style as a legacy of being born missing one of his back muscles, meaning he had an unusually rounded left shoulder. More than once, Clough had to defend his captain from the crowd's dissatisfaction. But it wasn't just the fans questioning McGovern's style. McGovern once read he had the gait of a 'horse running through treacle'. Gemmill, who became a close friend, told him he looked as though he permanently had a broken arm. Clough used to say a director at one club asked why he had signed a 'sparrow-footed, innocuous, frail weakling'. At Hartlepools, one of Clough's journalist friends told him he could see nothing special in the young McGovern. 'That's why I am a manager and you are a journalist,' Clough replied.

Clough and Taylor knew everything about McGovern down to his fingerprints and appreciated the work that others did not see. He was dedicated, trustworthy and, though he knew his own limitations, he played with complete self-belief and was blessed with that priceless asset, the football brain. 'The computer,' McGovern called it. He saw things early and there was a nice balance in midfield, where Gemmill had the licence to break forward and the pace to get in beyond the front players. 'John did all the donkey work,' Gemmill says. 'I could more or less please myself. I could run forward eight, ten, twelve times in a match. It might break down and in the next minute John would be in the perfect spot. He would feed the ball to me and we'd start again.'

Gemmill has shared a football pitch with Graeme Souness, Billy Bremner and countless others but rates McGovern as 'by far the best midfielder I played with' and it does feel remarkable that the captain of the team leading that title charge in spring 1978 never won a single Scotland cap.

That was the footnote to the 4–0 win at Old Trafford and it is a story – a true story – that probably encapsulates the history of the Scotland national team and why an anonymous member of their squad was famously once quoted as saying the manager Ally MacLeod thought 'tactics were a new kind of peppermint.'

MacLeod was in the crowd in Manchester that day and excitedly announced some time afterwards that Forest were so good he would have to include all of Clough's Scottish players in his squad for the World Cup the next summer. Robertson had established himself as the outstanding wide player in the First Division. Burns had re-invented himself as a centre-half of great distinction. Gemmill was playing as though he was absolutely desperate to ram Tommy Docherty's words back down his throat and McGovern was the leader of the best team in England at the time. It all made perfect sense. How could any of them possibly not be there?

McGovern made a mental note not to book a holiday in the wrong part of summer and to brush up on the words to 'Flower of Scotland'. It had been five years since he made his second and final appearance for Scotland's Under-23s. He knew his relatives in Montrose – where he had lived until the age of seven – would be proud, and if he was following the press reports he would also have been aware of MacLeod's *Braveheart* speeches, when the manager talked about Scotland going to the World Cup with the intention of winning it.

Meanwhile, a quick-thinking photographer, sensing a pay day, set up a picture of McGovern with Burns, Gemmill and Robertson by the side of the City Ground pitch. Clough went in the middle, with the four players wearing kilts that been hired from a local fancy-dress shop. The five of them danced a Highland Fling and the photograph – 'The Clan McClough' – was ready to be wired to the newspapers as soon as every-thing was confirmed.

When Scotland's squad was announced, Burns, Gemmill and Robertson were all in. But McGovern wasn't. The photographer rang MacLeod to find out what was going on.

'Where's McGovern?' he asked.

There was an awkward silence.

'McGovern's Scottish?' MacLeod replied.

Chapter Six
Champions

'It is magic how they are doing it, but how long can the Forest miracle last?' *Danny Blanchflower*

Twenty years after giving up playing, John O'Hare was doing some scouting work for Leicester City and was asked to cover a game at Liverpool. His route was planned to Anfield and he had left plenty of time for the drive north from his house in Derby. What he didn't know was where to park. 'I pulled up at the big car park at Stanley Park. I wound down my window and said: "Excuse me, John O'Hare, Leicester City."' Football clubs usually leave passes on the door for officials from other clubs. But the man at the gate had clocked who it was and it wasn't the fondest of welcomes. O'Hare: 'His exact words were: "Fuck off, we don't like you here."'

The enmity between Forest and Liverpool was only in its infancy in the spring of 1978 but there is no doubt the giants of Merseyside didn't like it that another team in red was looking down on everyone from the top of the table and turning the league into such a formality that the Manchester City manager Tony Book had suggested it 'might take an earthquake to crack them'.

All the same, there was none of the simmering resentment that marked out Liverpool's relationship with Manchester United and, at that stage, nothing really to suggest 'We hate

Nottingham Forest' would become a standard part of the Kop's songbook, still regularly heard four decades on. Bill Shankly was a guest of Clough's for one game in Nottingham and when the two sides were preparing to face each other in the League Cup final, there was a little touch that perhaps sums up how much simpler and more attractive football could be in the old days. Only one of the clubs could play in red. The other would have to wear their away strip and it was settled, in private, by Bob Paisley arranging to drop into the City Ground to have a drink with Clough and toss a coin. The person entrusted to flip it in the air was an eleven-year-old who always had plenty of stories to share in the playground. Nigel Clough was a first-year pupil at Woodlands Comprehensive in Allestree, Derby. Paisley called heads, Nigel threw tails, and dad ruffled son's hair to say well done. 'I can't even win the bloody toss against you lot,' Paisley grumbled on the way out.

By that stage, there had been an admission from Bob Wilson that Forest's bubble was made out of something more substantial than soap and water. Gordon McQueen had just become the most expensive footballer in history, moving from Leeds to Manchester United for £495,000. Ian Botham had struck his first Test century. Liverpool's players were embarking on the 'Year of the Scouse Perm'. Dr David Banner had burst out of his shirt for the first time as the Incredible Hulk and Ken Dodd, by all accounts, had badly misjudged his audience when he marked the opening of the newly renovated Nottingham Theatre Royal with a series of references to the size of a certain manager's mouth.

That manager, incidentally, had just decided it was time for his team to make a pop record, not only enthusiastically joining in the vocals himself but also roping in Peter Taylor and even trainer Jimmy Gordon, who was sixty-two and an Engelbert Humperdinck fan. 'We've Got The Whole World In Our Hands' was an adaptation of Laurie London's number one hit from 1958. Paper Lace, a Nottingham band who won *Opportunity Knocks* (imagine *X Factor* with more moustaches and bigger hair) and scored two top-ten hits in 1974, came up with the new version and a slot was lined up for the players on *Jim'll Fix It*. Clough now shared a record label with Frank Zappa, James Taylor, Van Halen and the rest of the Warner Bros empire. The song lasted six weeks in the charts and peaked at number twenty-four without ever threatening to dislodge Kate Bush and 'Wuthering Heights' from the top spot. It did, however, make an unexpected entry into the top ten in Sweden and, best of all, reached number one in Holland.

All a bit of fun, but it was easy to imagine Forest's rivals thinking Clough's crew had some nerve proclaiming to be 'the best team in the land' before they had won a single thing. Until that point, the players had made absolutely certain not to do anything that could lead to accusations of being big-time and overly presumptuous. Now they were waiting to find out if there was a slot on *Top of the Pops* and bobbing up and down to a song predicting a clean sweep of the season's silverware. A video was shot on the pitch with the team singing in front of an empty Trent End and the players were handed the sheet lyrics on the bus so they could learn the words. The lines included 'we're gonna win, we're gonna win everything' and a tribute to 'Peter the keeper with nothing to do.' The final verse was a belter – 'Peter Taylor and Ian and Johnnie O'Hare / Jimmy the trainer, he's taking good care / No one can stop us, they wouldn't dare' – and finished with Clough, as ever, having the final word. 'Yarwood,' came that familiar voice, 'follow that!'

A song like that would have been difficult to live down if Forest had imploded before the end of the season and one interviewer, suspecting exactly that, asked John McGovern straight: 'Is there a feeling, even now, that everything could blow up in your faces?' But there was no sign of it, other than losing at West Brom in an FA Cup quarter-final, and the League Cup final should have washed away any last trace of doubt.

It was certainly some calling card that Forest left with Liverpool, bearing in mind Clough had to prepare for the Wembley showdown with his usual squad of sixteen missing key players. Archie Gemmill and David Needham were cup-tied because they had already played in the competition for their previous clubs. McGovern went into the match with a groin injury and Colin Barrett was out with a stress fracture of the ankle. Most worrying of all, Peter Shilton was also ineligible and, with John Middleton now at Derby, that meant entrusting a rookie goalkeeper, Chris Woods, against the club Shankly once called a 'bastion of invincibility'. Woods was eighteen, the son of a Lincolnshire farmer and an occasional Friday-morning partner for Clough on the squash courts. He had never been in a squad for a league match but had become Forest's only eligible goalkeeper for the League Cup and, unusually, he preferred to play with his bare hands rather than wearing gloves.

Liverpool's team was packed with experience and achievement. Their goalkeeper, Ray Clemence, was Shilton's rival for the England team. Their back four of Phil Neal, Phil Thompson, Tommy Smith and Emlyn Hughes all had England caps. Ian Callaghan, a former footballer of the year, had been around so long he had already been awarded an MBE, and Kenny Dalglish had cost £440,000, then a British record transfer, when he signed from Celtic at the start of the season to take over the number seven shirt from Kevin Keegan. 'Is he better in midfield or up front?' the Celtic manager, Jock Stein, once asked of Dalglish. 'Och, just let him on the park.' John Smith, Liverpool's chairman, described him as the 'signing of the century' and Clough was another admirer. 'When he scored he had a better smile than Clark Gable,' he once said. 'Beautiful teeth, arms wide, that's how he celebrated.'

Forest had an abysmal record in the League Cup. They had never even got past the fourth round before that season, and on the last occasion they made it that far it ended in a home defeat against an Oxford side that was seventeenth in the Second Division. The only other time was back in the season 1960–61, when the league president Joe Richards set up the competition, liking the idea so much he had his own name engraved on the side of the trophy. Forest didn't bother entering for four seasons and, incredibly, in the eighteen years since the competition was launched they had not beaten a single side that was higher than them in the league. Forest's guests for the final included eight of the side that had won the FA Cup in 1959, but the presence of those ageing men,

139

some now well into their fifties, was a reminder of how long it had been since they were last at Wembley, when a ticket cost three shillings and sixpence and the team included Roy Dwight, Elton John's uncle.

Liverpool, on the other hand, regarded Wembley almost like a second home. Forest's run to the final had been a blitz of goals, scoring sixteen times in their four games against West Ham, Notts County, Aston Villa and Bury before, most satisfyingly for Clough, the aggregate 7–3 against Leeds. Now, though, the team Clough called 'Wembley virgins' were facing what one newspaper described as a 'meeting with Armageddon'. Liverpool had won the European Cup the previous season and had just beaten Benfica, home and away, to reach another semi-final. It had been an unusual season for them in the league, including three successive defeats in November to spark whispers of a crisis at Anfield, but Liverpool in those days never froze on the big occasion. If you were watching in black and white, the joke used to go, Liverpool were the team with the ball.

That was certainly true on that Wembley day of 18 March 1978, when Forest had to withstand some relentless pressure once the managers had led the two lines of players out of the tunnel. Clough, scoring the first minor victory, had held up proceedings by stopping to turn to the end housing the Forest supporters, with their home-made banners for 'Robbo will make Phil Kneel' and 'Woodcock's Sharper than Jimmy Hill's Chin'. As the Forest manager told his players to wave, Bob Paisley didn't notice and walked on a few steps. When he realised, he and his team obediently had to wait for Clough to catch up. 'Well, that's never happened before,' Brian Moore exclaimed in the commentary box.

Woods, the youngest goalkeeper to appear in a Wembley final, played heroically – 'If it hadn't been for him,' Robertson says, 'we'd have been beaten seven-nil' – and walked off the pitch at the end with his arms aloft and the Forest supporters singing his name. Liverpool were still entitled, however, to feel they had had enough of the ball to win with something to spare, and they had other grievances about the referee, Pat Partridge, who had disallowed a goal from Terry McDermott and turned down what Paisley called a 'blatant penalty' after a challenge from Burns on Dalglish. 'We were shelled for ninety minutes,' Clough admitted.

There were no penalty shoot-outs in those days and the 0–0 draw meant a replay at Old Trafford four days later when, once again, Woods played beyond his years. This time, however, Forest passed the ball with greater elegance. They also seemed to gain encouragement from the first tell-tale signs that Liverpool's players were frustrated by their inability to turn their superiority at Wembley into the hard currency of goals.

Seven minutes into the second half, Liverpool had a corner and Clark knocked the ball clear. Withe nodded it down to Woodcock and O'Hare, playing instead of the injured McGovern, had already set off on his run from the edge of his own penalty area, picking up speed through the centre-circle. Woodcock's pass was beautifully weighted and suddenly O'Hare was streaking clear on the counter-attack and bearing down on the Liverpool goal. 'People say I must have got a taxi to get there,' O'Hare says. 'But I got there.' Then, just as he was bringing back his foot to shoot, something happened that changed the relationship between the two clubs forever.

Phil Thompson knew he was not going to reach the ball and the Liverpool centre-half confessed afterwards that he had deliberately gone for the man instead, referring to 'a professional foul', a term that had never been used before but has stuck ever since. The speed of the move had caught him out and in those days there was no rule about a player being sent off for taking someone down as the last man. 'It was my only chance,' Thompson said. 'I had to kick him outside the box. I know it sounds bad but any professional would have done it.'

Partridge was a long way behind play and struggling to catch up. The referee pointed to the penalty spot, thinking it was inside the area, and all hell broke loose.

O'Hare's estimation was that he was 'probably a foot outside'. Burns reckons his team-mate 'might have got his fingertips into the box'. As for Thompson, he cannot talk about it without his face contorting with anger. 'Two yards outside,' he says. 'But the referee must have been about twenty-five yards away.'

Robertson tucked the penalty past Clemence and there were little puffs of toxic smoke coming from the ears of Liverpool's players when Partridge disallowed another goal from McDermott five minutes later, this time for an apparent handball. Television replays showed he had controlled the ball on his chest. Partridge then brought out his yellow card and booked Callaghan for the first time in his 849 games as a Liverpool player.

The final whistle went and as Burns collected the trophy the Liverpool players were still remonstrating with the referee and boiling with a perceived sense of injustice. One or two seemed on the point of spontaneous combustion. On the bus journey back to Nottingham, Clough's men declared that justice had been done, congratulated O'Hare for what Lloyd called a 'great dive' and made jokes about the prominent feature that would later saddle Thompson with his Pinocchio nickname. They knew by that stage that Partridge had made the wrong call, but they would have backed O'Hare to score anyway and Clough did point out there were quite a few teams over the years with complaints of their own about penalties in Liverpool's favour. Forest had won their first major trophy of the new era and the mood was euphoric. 'Bollocks to them!' someone shouted from the back of the bus, to loud cheers.

Clough was a big fan of the bollocks-to-them philosophy and so was Taylor, judging by his television interview with Gerald Sinstadt after the match. Taylor turned up with an arm around Robertson's shoulder and, showing the acting skills that Robert De Niro would have been proud of, looked absolutely nonplussed when it was put to him the game was mired in controversy.

Taylor: 'Obvious penalty. No one's doubting it, surely?'

Sinstadt: 'What was John O'Hare's feeling about it?'

Robertson (unconvincing): 'Oh, he says it was certainly inside . . . certainly . . .'

Taylor (interrupting): 'Your cameras will catch it, surely?'

Sinstadt: 'Yes, and I think they show it outside.'

Taylor (smirking): 'It also shows we've got the cup, that's the main thing.'

Liverpool were seething. Tommy Smith said Partridge 'should be shot, as simple as that'. Thompson was later fined

£300 by the FA with bringing the game into disrepute and it was just a pity there were no cameras recording the moment when he got back to the dressing room that night. Thompson took out his rage on a model trophy – made from cardboard, an old washing-up bottle and silver foil – that one of his relatives had given him as a bit of fun. 'I booted it to pieces. Its head fell off. Then its legs. I was so angry.'

Smith did congratulate Clough but the dynamic between the two clubs was never the same again, and when O'Hare talks about the way 'they have long memories up there' he is not just referring to the friendly gateman at Stanley Park.

A few years after that trip to Anfield, O'Hare was on another scouting trip for Leicester, this time at Sheffield United, when he saw someone ahead of him who looked familiar. The hair was different. The perm had gone and there were a few more lines on the face. But he recognised the scowl. 'I was walking down the stairs and it was Phil Thompson, six or seven steps in front of me. He spotted me and turned round. "You cheating bastard," he shouted. That must have been almost twenty-five years on and he still had a grudge.'

O'Hare had learned from Clough there was an art to getting in the last word.

'Fuck off, big nose,' he shouted back.

For Forest, it had been a defining moment. Liverpool had given everything but had not managed to find a way past a teenage goalkeeper once in two matches, the first including a thirty-minute period of extra-time. Forest had absorbed everything, refused to buckle and come out on top despite missing five players who might have fancied their chances of being in the team. Liverpool had been restricted mostly to shots from twenty yards or more, and that brings us to the key point about Forest's defence and, in particular, the double act holding it together.

Lloyd and Burns were certainly hard men and, yes, there were times when they blurred the lines between what was fair and what was not, operating with a loose interpretation of the rules of the day. Over the years they had played up to that reputation and if they had been any different they could not have flourished the same way in an era when it was obligatory for every successful team to have at least one guy acting as the team's minder. Yet they could play beautifully in their own right. It wasn't all about intimidation and brute force. They were aficionados in the art of defending – and sometimes that was overlooked when their reputation always came back to their fondness for the rough stuff.

Clough once described Lloyd as the 'Great Wall': a barn door of a defender, six foot two, tough as nails and gobby as hell. Burns was a couple of inches smaller and had a nose that had been broken more times than he could probably remember. His front teeth had been lost years ago – a legacy of previous aerial battles – and he had a reputation in the game for having a fuse like Tommy DeVito, Joe Pesci's character in *Goodfellas*. Treat with caution. Don't, whatever you do, call him funny.

Clark recalls Burns having a 'terrible reputation' at Birmingham and wondering whether Forest had signed a 'bit of a thug'. Burns had been thrown out of Glasgow Rangers, the club he supported as a boy, after being sent off three times in four matches. The headbutt on Richie Powling added to his crime-sheet and, before then, there was the pre-season incident in Germany when he was carried to his bed, completely sozzled after a hard afternoon's drinking. The whole thing sounds like an episode from *Auf Wiedersehen Pet* – 'The waitress put his chicken and chips down and he collapsed into it,' Clark remembers – and ended with Lloyd and Bowyer pulling him out of the hospitality tent and dragging him to his room to sleep it off.

When Peter Taylor offered to show Burns the areas of Nottingham where he might want to move, it only dawned on the player afterwards that they had been house-hunting on the opposite side of the city to where Taylor lived himself. Taylor had a running joke with Burns that the number of broken gas meters went down when Burns was out of the country. And then there was the story about committee member Brian Appleby collaring Clough when the England job was available. 'Don't leave me with Burns,' he reputedly said, 'or I'll slash my wrists.'

Yet Burns had been low maintenance since that headbutt at Arsenal. Bowyer, who had a nice line in humour, had broken the ice on the Glaswegian's first day at the club – 'Don't hit me, Kenny,' cowering into a corner of the dressing room – and the players were pleasantly surprised to find out the new signing wasn't the lunatic hell-raiser they had all heard about.

Taylor reckoned Burns was 'a lamb underneath' and, on away games, Anderson and Woodcock used to ambush their new team-mate, two on one, to have a bit of fun at his expense, jumping out of cupboards and wardrobes and modelling their style on the way Chinese manservant Cato Fong used to surprise Inspector Clouseau in the *Pink Panther* films. 'We all knew about this big tough Scot with a reputation for being the hard-man,' Woodcock says. 'It turned out he was a really nice guy, but Viv and I would always have a go at him. We'd get him on the floor and hold him down. I'd get one arm, Viv would have the other arm. Kenny would be lying there, looking at us, bright red, shouting, swearing. "One on one," he'd be growling. But there were two of us. Slap! "Quiet you! You big tough old man, got a reputation, have you?" Slap! Slap! Bosh! Boosh! "Go on, give him one, Viv." Slap! "And here's one from me, you big toughie." Slap!'

The difficult part was releasing Burns and getting away before he could get to his feet and come after them. 'It was like letting go of a raging bull so we had to time it to perfection. One, two – okay, give him one more before we go . . . boosh! – and three! Then out of there. Fast.'

Burns knew he was on to a good thing at Forest and one story probably sums up the way his attitude changed after the Powling flare-up. The following month, Burns committed one of the centre-half's cardinal sins by playing a careless pass across the edge of his own penalty area during a game against Manchester City. Dennis Tueart almost scored from the mistake and Clough told Burns he was being fined £50 for his carelessness. 'From his reputation, you might have expected Kenny to blow up,' Clark says. Burns was, after all, still a relative novice in the position. But there were no complaints. Burns accepted the fine, told Clough he would be more careful in the future and made sure he never did it again.

Don Dorman was the Birmingham City scout who had brought Burns south of the border. 'The first time I met Kenny after he had gone to Forest, I couldn't believe it was the same person. In the old days he was like a lad who had just come out of Borstal. But I'd never witnessed such a change in someone as when he came to my office a month or so after he'd gone to Forest and asked: "Can I come in, Mr Dorman?" I was absolutely shocked. And he conducted himself so well.'

Clough, in turn, developed a soft spot for Burns that even extended to inviting himself to his player's wedding, turning up with Barbara and a second guest – Pete, his gardener. Clough had been playing squash on the morning of the service and was still wearing his sports kit with his racket under his arm. 'Oh, he did make an effort,' Burns says, deadpan. 'He'd put new white laces in his trainers.'

Burns didn't even object to being called 'Kenneth', a name that hardly suited his hard-man image, just like Dave Mackay had to get used to being 'David' when Clough was managing Derby and in later years Des Walker was 'Desmond' and Teddy Sheringham 'Edward'.

'There were only two people who used to call me Kenneth – one was Clough and one was my mum. It started in one of the pre-season games in Germany. Tackles were flying in and they had an international centre-half who broke Peter Withe's nose. I always had that wee bit of devilment in me and when I saw this guy running down the touchline, I went over and hit him with a tackle that put him right through the fence. And that was the first time I got the call: "Kenneth!"

I turned round and Clough had his thumb and his finger together in that little circle he used to make.'

That sign meant 'perfect' and became a source of irritation to the other half of Clough's central defensive partnership. 'He would do it all the time to Burnsy,' Lloyd says. 'I'd get nothing and it used to drive me mad. I'd be thinking: "I know I'm having a good game, why doesn't he ever say well done? Just give me that sign, will you?" But he never did.' It was his man-management. He knew how to press the buttons of each individual in the team. He knew that I craved praise and that I would strive to get a pat on the back and that all I wanted was a "Well done, big fella." And he knew I would play out of my skin to get it if he kept me waiting.'

Lloyd came off with blood pouring from his head after one game against Leeds and bristling with satisfaction about how he had played. 'There was me with my nose across my face and a stitch in my head after keeping Joe Jordan, a real handful, quiet for most of the game, and Cloughie didn't say a word. So I said to myself: "Fuck him, I'll show him again next week." And he was probably thinking: "I know Larry will do it again next week if I ignore him." It was a very clever way of managing the team.'

Burns and Lloyd hunted in twos. They would do anything to stop the opposition as long as they could get away with it, but they also had to be clever in the days when players accrued disciplinary points under a totting-up process. Twenty meant an automatic suspension and Lloyd remembers a typical conversation.

'How many points are you on, Ken?'

'Fourteen – how about you?'

'Only ten – I'll take him out first.'

In Lloyd's first season, he wasn't so good with his calculations, and Clough decided enough was enough when his player went over the disciplinary threshold only two months after signing for the club.

Lloyd had been engaged in a running feud with Peter Osgood, an old enemy from his time at Liverpool, in the fog-abandoned game against Southampton and eventually dropped the nut on him ('Come on, you bastard, over here – whoosh!') once he thought the visibility was so poor that nobody would see. The referee missed it but Clough, naturally, saw everything and dropped him from the team. 'Lloyd has to be taught a lesson, even if it damages our chances of promotion,' Clough said. 'Whether I'm manager of England, Forest or Nottingham Pork Butchers, I'm determined to preserve my standards of team behaviour and discipline.' Clough liked his central defenders to be able to mix it with the opposition and maybe even frighten them a little, but he had to draw a line and Forest, for all their faults, did have a reputation for fair play. When Sammy Chapman was sent off against Leeds in 1971, it ended a run of thirty-two years without one of their players being ordered to the dressing rooms early. Clough even invited one referee, Clive Thomas, into his office after Burns had been booked for a late challenge. 'Well done,' he said. 'You keep doing that.'

Clough knew what he was getting with Lloyd and Burns though. He never actively told them to base their game around intimidation, but there were times when he was willing to turn a blind eye to their tricks. 'I'd be getting warmed up,' Burns says, 'and I would hear that voice again. "Kenneth! Kenneth!"

Clough would shout: "Number ten, no shin-pads." So I would give the number ten a kick down the shins. Then once I'd kicked him, I'd make sure to pick him up and say sorry to the referee. Except at the same time as I'm saying sorry to the referee, I've got hold of the player I've just kicked and I'm telling him: "I'm going to smack you again in a minute" . . . "Oh, I'm sorry, ref, sorry" . . . then back to the player and "I'm going to come right through you," just to put that little bit of doubt in his mind. I got away with a lot of things under Clough. We understood each other, put it that way.'

Lloyd's relationship with Clough, on the other hand, was more a marriage of necessity. Clough told him straight one day – 'I don't like you' – and wanted to know what Lloyd thought of him. Lloyd thought about it for a few seconds and then said, all things considered, he respected Clough as a manager but often hated him as a man. If he was ever in a bar, he said, and Clough walked in to have a drink, he would leave his own pint and walk out. 'Good lad,' Clough said.

Lloyd was known at Coventry as 'Albert' after Albert Tatlock, the old grump on *Coronation Street*. He was not an easy character to manage and ultimately he had the dubious honour of being fined more times than any other Forest player. If Clough ever fined someone, the letter came in a white envelope with the red Forest crest on the front. They were known as 'red trees' and Lloyd had enough to fill a suitcase.

'He was troubled by a back injury but it was less of a problem than his big mouth,' Taylor once said, recounting how he had been warned off signing Lloyd. 'My friends in football said: "You're crackers, this fellow is the big I-am, he's full of himself and no one can tell him anything." I said: "But on the other hand, he is big, he can head the ball, he is an international, he is tough and, besides, I like arrogant players. If he gets too cocky, Brian and I will sort him out." But I have to confess that Lloyd needed more than an average sorting-out. He was murder for the first few months.'

There was, however, usually a certain charm attached to most of Lloyd's indiscretions. The time, for example, when Forest played Toronto Blizzard on a pre-season visit to Canada and the teams were told to walk out in tandem for the national anthems. 'My problem was that the bigger the game the better I was,' Lloyd says. 'The smaller the game, I couldn't care less. And for this one, I couldn't give two fucks.'

It was a boiling hot day and Lloyd had his socks rolled down. The maple-leaf flag was about to be hoisted when the referee marched over – and Lloyd finishes the story by putting on a Canadian accent.

'Hey man, pull your socks up.'

'Pull my socks up?'

'Socks up for the national anthem, please.'

'You taking the piss?'

'Listen man, show some respect for the flag. Socks up!'

'Get the fuck out of here.'

A few moments later, Lloyd heard a commotion by the sideline. Clough was on his feet, holding up the board to substitute him before the game had even kicked off.

Lloyd clearly didn't have the mind for friendly fixtures, because that wasn't the only time an exhibition match caused friction between him and Clough. Another time, Forest played Tampa Bay Rowdies at the City Ground and when the ball came his way for the first time he was in a daft mood again. 'I went to back-heel it to Frank Clark and fell over. Up went the board – number five – and I was substituted four minutes into the game. I walked back to Clough and shouted: "You're a fucking loony, you are." He yelled back: "So are you."'

Clough chopped him down again before the replayed final against Liverpool at Old Trafford. When McGovern was injured during the game at Wembley, Lloyd had taken it upon himself to take over the captain's duties. Before the replay, the players were in the dressing room and Lloyd was gearing up for the same role. Clough threw the ball at Burns. 'Hey, Kenneth,' he said. 'Take them out.'

Clough's choice of cigar, in common with Winston Churchill, was the Romeo y Julietas. 'Clough used to come into the dressing room at a quarter to three,' Burns recalls. 'He'd tell whoever was substitute to fetch him a whisky. Then he'd sit there with his whisky and a cigar. He'd have a drag, look at me . . . then blow the smoke all over big Larry. Larry would be coughing: "Jesus, boss, that's awful." Clough would turn back to me: "I just do that to annoy the big bugger." Oh, how he loved to wind him up.' But they were good for one another, even if they were not always willing to admit it.

David Needham had played impeccably while Lloyd was injured and been part of a team that had won eight games out of eleven and drawn the other three. He had also chipped in with three goals and was showing why they thought of him as an idol on the other side of the Trent.

Needham was nicknamed 'Pigfarmer' by the other Forest players because of his love of the countryside, often turning up for training in a pair of wellies. He had a nice way about

him, calling Clough 'sir' when they first met, and he had
played so imperiously alongside Burns that a debate was
brewing about whether Lloyd would win back his place when
he was fit again.

Eventually, Lloyd's foot healed. He had spent the previous
two months feeling unnerved by Needham's form, thinking
'that bastard is doing too well for my liking', and he was fret-
ting about his place when he started training again. Forest
had the second leg of their semi-final against Leeds coming
up and Clough called a team meeting the day before. The
starting eleven was read out. Lloyd was in and Needham was
out. The explanation, Lloyd says, was the greatest compliment
he ever received from Clough.

'David, you're probably wondering why I have left you out,
and you're entitled to,' Clough said. 'David, you've done ever
so well since I bought you. You know you've done brilliantly
and I can't fault you. David, you're a lovely boy. If my daughter
were looking to bring home a man to marry, you'd be that
man. You're that nice I'd have you as a son-in-law.'

That was when he pointed in Lloyd's direction. 'I hate that
fucking bastard over there. Absolutely hate him. And that,
David, is why you're not in the team. You're not a bastard
like Larry Lloyd. And son, I want a bastard in my defence.'

Forest actually had two bastards but the other players have
always felt the reputation of Burns and Lloyd was, as Clark
says, 'way overblown'. A lot of that might be their own doing
when Lloyd, for instance, has a book on which the front cover
boasts: 'When I played for Liverpool and Forest there was no
messing – we took 'em out!' Yet Clark might have a point,
judging by the number of letters that arrived at the club from

supporters of other teams praising Clough for the team's style of play and good manners on the pitch. A typical one came from the headmaster of a Rotherham junior school after a game at Leeds. 'I feel I must write to you to say thank you for restoring my faith in football,' it began. 'I had become disenchanted by the gamesmanship on the field. I went to Leeds to watch the match. What a pleasure it was to see your players retiring ten yards when there was a free-kick and their self-discipline under provocation.'

What Lloyd and Burns did provide was the studs-and-thuds ruthlessness that was vital for any successful defence of that era. Viv Anderson was now an England Under-21 international, described by O'Neill as 'one of the best full-backs there has ever been'. Clark had a brilliant knack of knowing how to stay on his feet and face down his opponent rather than diving in – or, as Burns puts it, understanding that 'God didn't put studs in your arse.' Needham and Barrett would have been automatic first-team picks at most clubs and, behind them, there was the goalkeeper Clough credited for making the crucial difference.

Peter Shilton's presence, according to Clough, automatically meant another ten points in the bag every season, and he never grew tired of bringing that up within earshot of the Forest committee members who had tackled him about spending so much on a goalkeeper. 'The opposition might get through our midfield,' he would say. 'Very occasionally, they might get beyond Larry Lloyd and Kenny Burns. But when they'd done all that, once they thought they were in the clear, they'd look up and see a bloody gorilla standing there with shoulders like Mr Universe and they'd wonder where the goal had gone.'

Shilton certainly had a formidable frame, even if he was not the tallest of goalkeepers. At Stoke, they played a trick on him one day because of the way that after training he would shower then pick up his sports bag and head straight off, without hanging around to gossip with the other other lads. When Shilton was getting washed the other players filled his bag with metal weights from the club's gymnasium. Shilton came out, dried himself down and changed into his clothes. Then he picked up his bag and walked out of the door – without even noticing.

Clough had wanted to sign him at least twice before and Taylor was a regular at Leicester's youth games when Shilton started getting accolades at the club where Gordon Banks made his reputation. Shilton was not just an outstanding prospect when he was younger, he also gave the impression he was born for his trade. As a schoolboy, he was so obsessed with making it his life he would hang by his arms from the banisters of his parent's grocery store to try to stretch those powerful limbs a few more millimetres. Taylor, a former goalkeeper himself, spotted the raw potential on those reconnaissance missions he liked so much – his collar turned up, hat pulled low. 'He used to say to me: "You didn't know I was there, did you?"' Shilton says. 'He was there every game apparently, so I knew he liked me.'

The first time Clough tried to sign him, Shilton was twenty-one and already a fixture in Leicester's side as well as setting out on his international career. Clough was managing Derby, about to embark on their championship season, and had a safe pair of hands already in the form of Colin Boulton. Yet he was still willing to equal the British transfer record and make Shilton the most expensive goalkeeper in history.

Shilton remembers it being one of the few times Clough did not get his way: 'Clough went to the chairman at Leicester, Len Shipman, and said: "I want to sign Peter Shilton, how much do you want?" Shipman told him £200,000 and to put it in writing so he could present it to the board. He actually took it to the bank and said: "Look, I've got a letter confirming Peter Shilton is worth £200,000," and used it as a way to increase Leicester's overdraft facility. He then went back to Clough and said he didn't have to sell me because he had solved the club's money problems another way. I reckon that that was probably the last time Clough was turned over in a transfer deal.'

Shilton tells another story about how he became disillusioned after moving to Stoke and felt he needed to talk to someone in the game whose opinion he respected. 'We had sold all our best players. The roof had blown off the stand and they weren't insured. I wasn't getting picked for the England team and I was very down. I liked Clough. He was at Forest at the time, so I got a number for him and phoned him up. He told me to come over for a bite to eat. Tapping up, they would call it now, but I wanted to meet him and I needed some good advice. We had lunch and it was a real lift for me that he was speaking to me about football, on the same wavelength.

'He seemed to know exactly how I felt, and when Stoke

were relegated I had a reasonable idea he might want to sign me. It was all over at Stoke. The best players had left and I watched Forest on TV. They were doing well in the league. I could see the potential and I knew about the likes of Viv Anderson, Tony Woodcock and John Robertson. I could see they could play.'

Shilton's form was undoubtedly a major factor in why Forest had gradually turned the title race into a procession. Clough was so convinced everything was going according to plan – and it is difficult to imagine anyone else ever getting away with this – he went to Majorca on holiday rather than watching his team's game at Norwich in February. Forest blew a three-goal lead to draw 3–3 but, even then, it felt like a one-off rather than a sign of capitulation. 'They are dead certain to win it,' John Bond, the Norwich manager, said. 'They will win it by a mile. Archie Gemmill will run them there on his own.'

All of which eventually brought the champions-in-waiting to Highfield Road, Coventry, on a bright April day and a game preceded by Clough insisting every player in his team knocked back an alcoholic drink. Forest had beaten QPR the previous Tuesday, courtesy of Robertson's eighth penalty of the season, to leave themselves on the brink of settling everything. A goalless draw at Maine Road earlier in the month had effectively taken Manchester City out of the equation, while Everton's chances were virtually extinguished when they lost against Liverpool on the same day Woodcock's late goal gave Forest a 1–0 win against Aston Villa. All Forest now required was a draw at Coventry for everything to be mathematically certain with four games still to play. 'It had got to the stage where, if we didn't win it at Coventry, we were going to win it the next week,' Martin O'Neill says, 'and if we didn't win it the next week, we were going to win it the week after. It had got to the stage where it was inevitable.'

The game is remembered now for Shilton, as Colin Barrett puts it, having 'one of those days when you could aim a thousand shots at him and still wouldn't beat him'. One in particular – a header from the bearded Mick Ferguson, to be more accurate – was remarkable.

'That's the save that people remember me by,' Shilton says. 'I don't know how I got to it. It was just a reaction, all that hard training, going for everything. I still replay it in my mind. Ian Wallace had got to the byline and chipped the ball across the goal. I was at the near post and had to go back across the goal as Ferguson came in and bulleted his header from about four or five yards out. I managed to turn it over the bar and it was made even more dramatic because of the way Ferguson sank to his knees and put his head in his hands. I put my hand on his shoulder to commiserate and people, to this day, still come up to me to say they were there that afternoon.'

Larry Lloyd was suspended and watched from the stands as the game finished goalless and the victorious players celebrated in front of a sea of red on the away terrace. When he was playing for Coventry, Lloyd was in the canteen one day when the chairman Jimmy Hill walked in with a guest from Saudi Arabia and introduced Lloyd as 'the player Liverpool sold us with a bad back'. The new title-winner remembered that moment when he bumped into Hill in the reception area. 'Oh Jim,' he said, shaking hands warmly. 'Delighted to see you. I owe you a big vote of thanks. You sold me to Nottingham Forest with a bad back and now I'd like to show you my medals.'

In the dressing room, however, there was no crowing. 'You see all these pictures in the modern game of after-match hysteria, champagne being tossed everywhere and people yelling and screaming,' Shilton says. 'We just sat down and had half a glass of champagne each, as though it was another day's work. But that was typical of our attitude and profes-sionalism. We didn't get too excited. It sunk in when we went on the pitch before the next match against Birmingham to collect the trophy. We wore green tracksuits and didn't exactly look very fashionable, but I didn't care what I was wearing because we were going to lift that trophy.'

Forest had let in five goals in their previous two games before Shilton signed. They conceded one in the next five matches and only twenty-four over the whole season. But it was not just his agility and reflexes that improved the team. Shilton was so vocal and demonstrative, always on top of his defenders, cajoling them, handing out rollickings or whatever was needed, the players around him could never let their concentration slip. He gave them no choice.

No team had ever won the league having conceded fewer goals. Forest had let in only eight in their twenty-one home games and Burns's metamorphosis from dog-track drop-out to defensive doyen was duly completed when he was named player of the year by the Football Writers' Association. Burns collected his prize at a black-tie dinner at the Cafe Royal and was even allowed to miss the end-of-season game at Liverpool to accept his prize. Liverpool had moved up to second place by then but, again, they could not get past Forest's defence, drawing 0–0 as Burns headed to London to join some of the greats of his profession. 'Can you believe it?' Ian Bowyer said. 'A rogue like Kenny Burns alongside gentlemen of the game such as Stanley Matthews and Tom Finney.'

Liverpool reached fifty-seven points in the end, the same number that had won the league in 1977. Their problem was Forest finished with seven more and, in doing so, became the first team to complete the double of the First Division title and League Cup. Wolves, the Second Division champions a year earlier, finished fifteenth. Chelsea, who went up as runners-up, were sixteenth. Forest had the highest points total since Arsenal's sixty-five in 1970–71. They took twelve more points than they had managed in the Second Division and thirty-nine more than their last stab at the top flight, in 1971–72, when Forest were slithering towards relegation and their only form of national exposure tended to be Richard Williams presenting *The Old Grey Whistle Test* wearing his home-made 'Forest 2 Chelsea 1' badge.

Burns also won the Midland Sports Writers' prize and the supporters' player of the year award, with O'Neill second and Woodcock third. Gemmill's lung-splitting break out of defence against Arsenal earned him the BBC's goal-of-the-season award – not bad for someone who had been told the previous September he had lost his pace – and Robertson won the ATV counterpart for his goal against Manchester City in the FA Cup.

Shilton won the Professional Footballers' Association player of the year vote, with Gemmill runner-up and Robertson among the six contenders. Woodcock was young player of the year and Ken Smales, returning to his favourite subject, did wonder among all the acceptance speeches and clinking of wine glasses whether Forest might get a 'Bob Wilson Bubble-Bursting Plaque'. Some of the players nominated who they thought had been the outstanding individual. Burns chose Woodcock. Lloyd, Withe, Anderson and Bowyer went for Burns, while Barrett, McGovern and O'Neill picked Robertson – O'Neill explaining it was because 'he owes me twelve quid and might pay me back now.'

The strange thing was that Everton and Manchester City, third and fourth respectively, both scored more than Forest's sixty-nine goals. Forest's top scorers, Withe and Robertson, had twelve each, but even that put together was still half a dozen short of Bob Latchford's thirty goals for Everton. What Forest had done well was spreading the load. Woodcock had eleven, O'Neill eight and McGovern, Burns, Bowyer and Needham had chipped in with four.

Throughout the entire season, Forest had used sixteen players, and at one period over the New Year they had fielded the same side in nine successive league games. What would have happened if injuries had bitten harder is another matter, but that consistency was vital when it came to developing the rhythmical passing style that made them so easy on the eye.

Forest – playing the ball on the floor, with width and penetration and soft-touch football – even survived an attempt from the supernatural to derail them.

It's a great story. In the spring of 1978, Hereford United were enduring such a poor run of results in the Third Division that their manager Tony Ford brought in a psychic and hypnotist called 'Romark' – real name, Ronald Markham – to help them beat relegation. Markham's first game was against Chesterfield and to general amazement his prediction – 'Hereford will win 2–1 and Peter Spiring will score the winning goal' – turned out to be absolutely spot on. Unfortunately his next prediction, that Hereford would win at Cambridge, was followed by a 2–0 defeat and Romark, desperate to show he was the real deal, then offered a 'free sample' of his work by casting a spell on Forest, announcing they would finish the season empty-handed.

It was two weeks later that O'Hare went running through Liverpool's defence in the League Cup final and Forest won their first major trophy for two decades. Hereford went down to the Fourth Division and the mysterious Romark, boasting he could 'outclass anything Uri Geller can do', was later sent to prison for dishonesty. He also attempted to prove his powers by driving a yellow Renault blindfolded – or rather, with two coins, a slice of dough and a thick band over his eyes – through the streets of Ilford, only for his journey to end twenty yards later when he crashed into the back of a police van. 'That van was parked in a place that logic told me it wouldn't be,' he claimed, before being banged up for stealing £68,000-worth of jewellery and antiques from his elderly mother.

The more people tried to burst Forest's balloon, the more they inflated it. It had been floating at the top of the table for seven months and their longevity was a triumph for Clough's policy of not overworking his team and the light training sessions on the practice pitch Taylor described as 'a squelchy stretch beside the Trent without shelter or fences'. Ten players were involved in thirty or more league games.

Frank Clark says it shows Clough was 'simply ahead of his time', understanding the benefits of rest and not overworking his players. Those piggyback runs through the nettles and games of hide-and-seek never did catch on elsewhere, though.

Clough, of course, was named manager of the year to go with the four manager of the month awards that had already gone his way, a record for one season. He and Taylor took the players back to Cala Millor to celebrate properly once the season was over and they picked a run-down old restaurant-pub called the Shack to do their drinking, play cards, plan the future and get merry. Clark took his guitar and Barrett led the sing-song of country and western classics.

On the day of coronation, Clough had stayed in the away dressing room at Coventry swigging champagne from a paper cup while the newspaper correspondents waited in the corridors for his verdict. Clough had done some legend-building as the only other manager apart from Herbert Chapman, with Huddersfield Town and Arsenal half a century earlier, to win the championship with two teams. Yet he kept it simple that day. 'We've done it how I would assume everyone likes to do their job,' Clough said. 'Nicely, honourably and well.' There was no gloating and on the way back he told Taylor he would celebrate by removing his car from the drive and having a night in with Barbara and the kids. The next morning, he woke early and was back on the A52 over to Nottinghamshire to help sell the Sunday papers at the shop his brother, Gerry, owned in Bramcote. There was still work to be done.

Chapter Seven
They've Burst Your Pretty Balloon

'They had a plan in that each player knew what was expected of them and each did his job with excellent efficiency.' *Sir Alf Ramsey*

Brian Clough had overseen the most unexpected and impudent league title in history. His team had kicked off the dust of the Second Division to become champions of England and, in the process, Clough had rebuilt his reputation in a way that barely seemed plausible after the ordeals at Leeds and Brighton. A smallish club from a smallish city – unfashionable, unheralded Nottingham Forest – had qualified for the European Cup and Clough had done it in a way that left everyone scratching their heads, even his own colleagues. Stuart Dryden, Forest's newly appointed chairman, was so fascinated by Clough's eccentricities he had started referring to him as the 'Quare Fellow'.

Even when the players were awarded the championship trophy, Clough made sure it wasn't just another bog-standard presentation, inviting half a dozen police officers on to the pitch to line up in the traditional team photograph. The youngest constable was instructed to hold the trophy. One of his colleagues was given the League Cup and another was put in charge of Kenny Burns's player of the year trophy. They were flanked by their commanders and by the time they were all in line, wearing their custodian helmets, they had inadvertently blocked out just about every player in the back row. The moment was captured with John O'Hare looking completely nonplussed, hands on hips, and at least four of his team-mates obliterated from the picture.

Clough had made the ordinary extraordinary. Players who were regarded elsewhere as run-of-the-mill pros had suddenly become First Division champions. A shift in power was taking place, with Liverpool as its principal victim, and nobody could have expected that Clough would embark on Forest's title defence by moving out one of the players whose contribution had been essential in getting them to that position in the first place.

Peter Withe lasted one week of the 1978–79 campaign before he was sold to relegated Newcastle. Nobody had been identified to take his place and the economic engineering of selling a player for five times what the club had paid for him felt like a strange kind of victory when it left a considerable hole in the team. Forest did not win any of their first five matches. They did not even score in four of them and Alex Montgomery, one of Fleet Street's big-hitters, summed up what most people were thinking, including some of Clough's own players, during that period when the goals dried up and the newly crowned champions suddenly looked lightweight in attack. Clough, he wrote, had 'dropped an almighty clanger'.

Questioning Clough had become a hazardous occupation given the number of sportswriters who had misjudged his team over the previous year, but it was certainly one of his more unexpected transactions. Withe had been the focal point of Forest's attack for the previous two years. His partnership with Tony Woodcock had been fundamental to the team's success and the move was peculiar all round, bearing in mind it meant a player of twenty-seven, at the peak of his powers, leaving the champions to drop back into the second tier. Forest had cut their leading scorer loose just as they were embarking on their first-ever season in Europe's premier club competition. Withe, meanwhile, had Cambridge, Wrexham and Orient to come in his opening month. The whole thing felt bizarre and unsatisfactory, especially when the young reserve taking his place, Steve Elliott, was raw and untried.

Yet Clough, to use Peter Taylor's description, was 'always riding' Withe. He did it with everyone but Withe in particular. When Withe went through his first barren spell, Clough publicly threatened to put him in the reserves and complained 'if he drops back any further he will be impeding Peter Shilton.' When Withe scored four against Ipswich and requested the ball as a souvenir, Clough asked the players to sign it and presented it himself. The sting came later when Clough – as difficult to read sometimes as hieroglyphs – announced to the press that Withe would 'get no ball until he learns how to play with one'.

In another game Withe took a bang to his foot and could hardly walk as he left the pitch at half-time. Forest's medical staff wanted to take him for an X-ray. 'Peter had to be carried off on Jimmy Gordon's back,' Woodcock recalls. 'As we went into the changing rooms they were delicately taking off his boot when Clough came in. "What are you doing?" he said. "Get back out there!" Peter couldn't even walk let alone run. He just stood on the centre-spot for forty-five minutes, hobbling around to keep himself warm.'

Withe's flow of goals had dried up towards the end of the

season, scoring only once in his last twelve appearances, and Clough was so irritated by his performance in an end-of-season game at Ipswich he substituted him at half-time and brought on Frank Clark to take over in attack, telling the veteran left-back he could do no worse than the guy he was replacing. Clark had never played centre-forward in his life and, as his team-mates frequently reminded him, he was approaching the age when most people's idea of sport was trying to find their spectacles in the morning. He actually scored – his only league goal in a career spanning more than 500 appearances – and Clough did a jig of delight on the touchline. But that was not the point. 'We got a corner and I was embarrassed because I didn't even know where to stand,' Clark says. 'When Clough said he wanted me to go up front, Larry Lloyd actually burst out laughing.' Nobody, however, could have been more embarrassed than Withe – and that, almost certainly, was Clough's intention.

Clark's foray into the world of goal-scoring was a one-off and when Clough went back to the Withe–Woodcock partnership Forest thrashed Ipswich 5–0 to win the Charity Shield. It was a record score and Ipswich's manager, Bobby Robson, left himself open to a classic piece of Clough wit when he came to the winners' dressing room, congratulated Forest on the win but mentioned that he didn't think the margin of victory was a true reflection of the game. 'You're quite right, Bobby,' Clough agreed, 'if we hadn't been playing at half-pace it would have been ten.'

Withe played in Forest's opening league game, a 1–1 draw against a Tottenham side featuring their two new Argentinian signings, Ossie Ardiles and Ricky Villa, but was sold the following Monday and that was followed by a sapping run of four 0–0 draws. Even when the goals finally arrived in the replay of a League Cup tie against Oldham, resulting in a 4–2 victory, Clough sounded flat. 'I'm more depressed than ever,' he said. Two of the goals, he pointed out, came from corners. Another was a penalty. 'We just didn't function at all.'

Elliott, a regular scorer for the reserves, was promoted to the first-team a month before his twentieth birthday, but when the teenager made his debut against Coventry he had a good chance to win the game only to turn his shot against the post. He didn't score in any of his next four appearances either. Woodcock seemed to be missing Withe and when the draw was made for the first round of the European Cup, bringing the considerable downer of a two-legged tie against Liverpool, it took a while before the old 'bollocks-to-them' mindset resurfaced.

Liverpool had what Clough called a 'fourteen-year headstart' on Forest bearing in mind their long association with the competition, going back to 1964 and those famous black and white television pictures of a swaying, heaving Kop going through their repertoire of Beatles songs. Kenny Dalglish's ice-cool finish against Bruges was enough to win the last final and, in the process, soothe the disappointment of releasing their grip, finger by finger, on the First Division. Now they were aiming to emulate the Ajax side that pioneered Total Football and the great Bayern Munich side of Beckenbauer, Müller et al by winning the European Cup for a third successive year.

Forest, on the other hand, were dipping their toes into the competition for the first time and couldn't score a goal to save their lives. It was the last draw they had wanted – 'horrible' is the word Woodcock applies – and though it wasn't something anybody admitted at the time, at least one player can remember thinking the worst. 'Liverpool were the bee's knees,' John Robertson says. 'I thought: "Oh Jesus, we're not even going to get a proper trip into Europe here." I was a bit sick, to be honest. If I'm telling the truth, I did think: "Maybe we aren't going to do this."'

There wasn't a great deal of support in the media either judging by the column Reg Drury penned in the *News of the World* saying the country should want Liverpool to reach the next round because Forest 'didn't have the know-how' to do well in the European Cup. 'That's why Liverpool must beat them if the trophy is to stay in England,' Drury explained. 'Forest are European novices and do not inspire the same awe as Liverpool.'

Ken Smales cut out that article and added it to his little black book of other press clippings but, in fairness to Drury, Montgomery and everyone else who questioned Forest's staying power, there were people in Clough's ranks secretly thinking the same. Forest had begun the new season like a marathon runner with a pebble lodged in his shoe. The momentum appeared to have been lost, or at least inter-rupted, and football was littered with stories of teams having one exceptional season and then fading away.

Liverpool, meanwhile, had set off like greyhounds and seemed to be in a hurry to re-establish their position at the top of English football. They had just thrashed Tottenham

7–0 at Anfield, including a goal from Terry McDermott that was so spellbinding in its build-up that Bob Paisley described it as 'probably the finest ever seen on this ground'. They had knocked in four at Manchester City and three at Birmingham and they still had a lingering grievance, lest it be forgotten, from that rancorous night at Old Trafford six months earlier when they remained convinced they would have won the League Cup but for Pat Partridge's refereeing.

So it was fair to say that in September 1978 the team from Anfield were after revenge and most people in the country thought they would probably get it. 'We had usurped them the previous year and now they wanted their own back,' Martin O'Neill says. 'I think every single pundit and journalist out there thought we were going to get our comeuppance.' The tendency to lean towards Liverpool was not just confined to the media. A poll of the other twenty First Division managers asked them to predict who would get through. 'Clough,' O'Neill recalls, 'made sure we all knew there was only one who thought we had a chance.'

In truth, it was more than one. Alan Dicks at Bristol City, John Neal of Middlesbrough and Chelsea's Ken Shellito all backed Forest. It was the other seventeen who went the other way. Ron Atkinson at West Brom, Gordon Lee at Everton and Bobby Robson all tipped Liverpool, as did Terry Neill at Arsenal, Ron Saunders at Aston Villa, Dave Sexton at Manchester United and Gordon Milne of Coventry. Jock Stein, in his short stint at Leeds, went for the holders and it was the same for Keith Burkinshaw at Spurs, Tony Book at Manchester City, John Bond at Norwich and Bolton's Ian Greaves. The draw had fallen favourably for Liverpool: away leg first, home leg second, exactly as they liked it. Also ticking the same box were Tommy Docherty at Derby, Sammy Chung from Wolves, Steve Burtenshaw of QPR, Lawrie McMenemy at Southampton and Birmingham's Jim Smith.

Clough sensed his players' foreboding and did his best to shake it out of everyone, but it wasn't easy. There were also people at Forest who suspected something fishy about the draw. O'Neill says there was 'a lot of talk about fixing . . . two English teams, and wanting one of us out quickly, who knows?' Smales said he would rather the team had been drawn against an unpronounceable outpost in Albania rather than have to play Liverpool. 'It didn't appear to be fiddled,' he assured everyone in his programme notes.

Yet he did call it a 'catastrophe' and the players did not feel any better. 'I had played in Europe,' Lloyd says. 'Most of the other lads hadn't and were looking forward to a nice trip somewhere, easing themselves into the European Cup. I remember Clough telling us: "If we're going to win it, we are going to have to beat Liverpool at some stage, so we might as well get it out of the way in the first round." But the whole of Europe thought Liverpool would beat us. We were novices and Liverpool, well, they were the kings of Europe.'

John McGovern also remembers the way Clough tried to lift everyone's mood. 'He got us all together and he said: "Listen, do you know what they'll be saying in Liverpool's dressing room?" Clough's view was that the Liverpool players would have been saying: "Not them again." He was so confident. "Trust me," he said, "their heads will have gone down when they found out they were playing you."'

Clough also had an appearance lined up on *ATV Today*.

The trophy was the centre-point of the set and the presenter Gary Newbon asked Clough whether Liverpool's trouncing of Spurs had frightened him.

'Not that much,' Clough replied, making it sound as if it was the daftest question he had ever heard. 'We should have stuck seven past Spurs in the first match of the season.'

'Do Liverpool have any weaknesses?' he was asked.

'Their weakness is they couldn't score a goal against us last season,' Clough said, and that was when his voice hardened. 'That's not a bad one for a start. So don't ram seven goals down my throat, or anybody else's.'

Clough took the trophy, adorned in Liverpool's ribbons, in both hands and gave it a hearty pat. 'The first thing is it feels very, very heavy. But if we can get it at the end of this season, it will feel like a feather. And I would like our name on it.'

'Keep holding it,' Newbon said. 'It suits you.'

Clough might also have pointed out his side were closing in on the record Leeds had set in 1968–69 of thirty-four games unbeaten in the top division. Yet Forest's opening month to the new season had been described in one broadsheet as a 'depressing start' and anyone flicking through the early league tables might have noted there were only five clubs in the entire four divisions who had scored only once in their first four games. One was Oxford at the bottom of the Third Division. Crewe, Torquay and Darlington were all in the lower reaches of Division Four and the fifth team were the First Division champions. 'Forest Withe-ring' had become a familiar headline and, deep down, the players were wondering whether selling their leading marksman might blow up in Clough's face. 'Withe had been brilliant for us,'

O'Neill says matter-of-factly. 'He had scored a lot of goals for us but, gosh almighty, even in the period when he wasn't scoring he was still the best centre-forward in England.'

All of which brings us to the young, rake-thin striker whose career until that point had incorporated one nondescript appearance in the Second Division, a couple of bland seasons in the reserves and a background in amateur football that, with all due respect to Long Eaton United, was hardly likely to frighten the 50,000 partisan Merseysiders who would be waiting for Forest at Anfield.

Garry Birtles had been working as a carpet-fitter in Nottingham when a rumour reached Clough a few months into Forest's promotion season that Manchester United were tailing a young striker at Long Eaton who was apparently showing a bit of potential. Clough had never heard of Birtles, but the idea he might lose a player from his own patch was a potential embarrassment. Clough left Taylor in charge of Forest's next league game and went to see what all the fuss was about. 'We were playing Enderby Town in an FA Cup qualifying tie,' Birtles says. 'Forest had a game that day at Oldham, but I think Clough's attitude must have been "No Nottingham lad is going anywhere until I've seen him." I was never certain he was going to turn up, but the mere suggestion had my stomach churning.' Forest lost 1–0 at Oldham while a hundred miles south it wasn't going so well for Birtles either. Ten minutes into the game, his shin pad was split in half by the opposition centre-half and he was taken off on a stretcher.

Birtles was left with an ugly gash to his shin but, limping heavily, insisted on going back on. 'All I could think was that some hairy-arsed centre-back had just screwed up my fifteen minutes of fame in front of Brian Clough. We lost and I didn't score, so I wasn't in the best of moods after the game. I felt I had blown it again.'

Clough, nonetheless, was impressed by the striker's bravery and offered him a month-long trial despite not seeing a great deal else to encourage him. 'His quote afterwards,' Birtles recalls, 'was that the half-time Bovril was better than Birtles.'

Forest certainly had misgivings. Birtles had spent his Sunday mornings doubling up for Long Eaton Rovers in the Nottingham alehouse leagues and the jump in class was huge. He didn't seem strong enough to cope against First Division centre-halves. He had already been rejected by Aston Villa where he operated as a left-winger and, perhaps understandably for a part-timer, he did not appear to have great stamina. Taylor watched him in a reserve game at Coventry and for the first hour he saw nothing to excite him. The triallist fumbled his control and tripped over the ball. He had sharp elbows and skinny knees. He looked like he needed a good meal and when Forest made a few more inquiries it turned out the link with Manchester United was a red herring and it was actually Peterborough United who wanted him.

Taylor was preparing to leave when something happened that made him sit bolt upright in his seat. Birtles had a little trick where he would feign to go to his right, then drag the ball back with the sole of his left boot and change direction in an instant. It was his only moment of the game, but it was enough to convince Taylor that Birtles was worth a punt.

Forest paid Long Eaton £2,000 and Birtles was handed a professional contract, albeit one at the lower end of the scale. 'I was paid the same amount I was earning as a carpet-fitter,' he says. 'The difference was I wasn't stuck on a building site on freezing-cold days, fitting carpets, sticking glue around toilets and putting coving on walls. For £60 a week, I was delighted.'

A few years earlier, Birtles had signed the petition for Clough to be installed as Forest manager and, at the age of ten, he was in the Trent End to see Johnny Carey's side win 4–1 against Manchester United. Yet it was a long slog for him in the reserves, or the 'stiffs' as they were commonly known in the profession, and there were times when it felt like the window of opportunity had been slammed shut and the blinds pulled down.

Birtles made his debut at the age of twenty, in a 2–0 win against Hull in March 1977, but Clough made him play as a central midfielder rather than his usual striking role. The experiment wasn't a great success. 'All I could think was: "Why is he playing me here?"' Birtles says. 'I hated it.' What should have been a momentous occasion finished with Clough wondering if a player who had started at the bottom should have stayed there. 'If I do that again,' he told Birtles, 'the chairman has told me I will get the sack.'

For the next two seasons, Birtles became a fixture in the reserves and summoned only by Clough when he needed a squash partner, the unwritten rule being that if the manager called 'let' there was absolutely no doubt the point had to be replayed. Birtles did not qualify for a championship medal – appearing in two pre-season friendlies in Germany and a

'Now, listen here, young lady . . .' Brian Clough preparing
for one of his TV appearances with his old friend Brian Moore.

Clough with his flock, starting the annual Shrovetide
football match in Ashbourne, 1975.

Left: The word is out – Brian Clough ha arrived at the City Ground.

Below: Clough used to call John Robertson 'the Picasso of our game'. He wasn't always so happy about the player's fondness for a drink and a fag.

Opposite: If ever there was a photo that encapsulated Clough's affection for Peter Taylor, this was it. 'If I was th shop window,' Clough would say, 'he was the goods in the back.'

Below: Garibaldi-red shirts, white shorts, three Adidas stripes – the Forest team line up for their official photograph.

A team photograph with a difference – Clough and his players (and a few special guests) show off their trophies after being presented with the First Division championship.

Above:
Clough helping out in his brother's newsagent's the morning after winning the First Division title.

Above: Clough, perhaps the only manager in history who would verbally spar with Muhammad Ali – and win.

Right: Trevor Francis was English football's first £1 million player – then made his debut in an A-game watched by 40 people.

Right: Garry Birtles, a real-life Roy of the Rovers, went from playing Sunday league football in Nottingham to taking on Liverpool in the European Cup.

Below: Kenny Burns (front) and Larry Lloyd, arguably the best central defensive partnership in Europe.

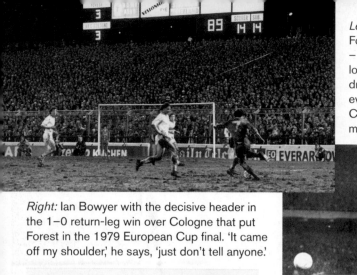

Left: Nottingham Forest 3 Cologne 3 – perhaps the loudest, most dramatic match ever played at the City Ground, on a mudbath of a pitch.

Right: Ian Bowyer with the decisive header in the 1–0 return-leg win over Cologne that put Forest in the 1979 European Cup final. 'It came off my shoulder,' he says, 'just don't tell anyone.'

Left: The Dynamic Duo. 'It was like a renaissance in him,' Martin O'Neill remembers of Clough bringing in Peter Taylor to work by his side.

Trevor Francis landed on the Olympics shot-putter circle after heading in the winner against Malmo. 'I didn't feel a thing,' he says. 'It was the greatest moment of my career.'

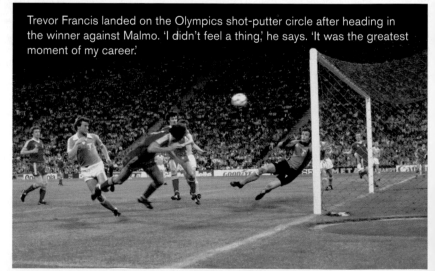

Left: 'I was thinking of my dad.' Franz Beckenbauer is the only man who has lifted the European Cup more times than John McGovern.

Right: The victorious team return to Nottingham. Ian Bowyer was so fond of this blazer and tie combo that it still hangs in his wardrobe now.

Below: Bringing the European Cup back to Nottingham, the first time. An estimated 250,000 people turned out that day to welcome them home.

Right: Tony Woodcock almost left Forest for Lincoln City. Here he is taking on AEK Athens in the European Cup.

Below: 'I hit it and then I thought, whoa, that's got a chance.' John Robertson lets fly with the winning goal against Hamburg in the 1980 European Cup final.

Above: Peter Shilton – as the song went, 'the keeper with nothing to do' – trained on a roundabout ahead of the 1980 European Cup final.

Left: Anyone for a drink? This photo appeared on the front cover of the European Super Cup final programme against Barcelona (another trophy for the collection).

testimonial for Alan Goad at Hartlepools didn't count – and had started to wonder whether he was ever going to get his chance when he was not even included on a pre-season tour to Yugoslavia and Steve Elliott, two years his junior, was promoted ahead of him. Mansfield, towards the bottom of the Third Division, offered to take him off Forest's hands, on £110 a week, but Birtles had become so disaffected he was starting to think about packing in the game for good, until a conversation with Frank Clark persuaded him to stick with it.

Clark had been getting some extra fitness with the reserves because he was returning from an injury, and on the way back from a game against Sheffield Wednesday he sat beside Birtles on the bus. 'His chin was on the floor,' Clark says. 'I just tried to offer him a bit of support, because I could see he was very down. He said he felt like his career wasn't going anywhere, that Clough clearly didn't rate him very much and he was going to pack up and go back to being a carpet-layer. He had a year left on his contract and I said: "If it's only a year, sit tight. You never know what's round the corner in football." But he was really low and I didn't know if he would listen.'

It was good advice because four days before the first leg against Liverpool there was a home game for Forest against Arsenal and Clough had seen enough to realise Elliott was not going to be the answer. Birtles played in a 2–1 win. He did enough to keep his place and it was the next game at the City Ground, the night the *Evening Post* billed as the 'Match of the Century', that Birtles set up a story that wouldn't have looked out of place in a comic strip. *Roy of the Rovers*

177

magazine certainly thought so: Birtles would soon be appearing on its front cover.

Birtles was, to quote Graeme Souness, 'an unknown carpet-layer' and Liverpool's players let him know exactly what they thought about a lad from non-league sharing the same pitch as them. 'No one had heard of me at Liverpool,' he says. 'There was quite a bit of piss-taking coming in my direction from more than the odd member of their squad.' But who could be surprised? Three years earlier, Birtles had been playing his farewell match for Long Eaton Rovers against a team called Clumber Kitchens and Bathrooms on the Sunday league pitches at Nottingham's Victoria Embankment, rummaging through a black bin-bag containing the kit in a changing room he remembers reeking of 'stale bitter fumes'.

Birtles, a true local hero, came of age against Liverpool that night, and not just because he scored a goal that had the journalists in the pressbox desperately flicking through their *Rothmans* yearbooks to find out who the hell he was. He stood up to everything. His favourite little drag-back was the perfect riposte to Thompson's mickey-taking, completely bamboozling the Liverpool defender, and when the tackles started flying in the new kid on the block held his own. And that was important because Liverpool, as well as being a brilliant side, always sought to have a physical edge over their opponents.

Emlyn Hughes once said he would walk into the toughest dockside pub in the world if he was with his Anfield team-mates and not feel worried in the slightest. 'You knew,' he said, 'that if things got tough, nobody would bottle it and scoot off.' There was also no doubt that the first two people through that pub's doors would have been Souness and Jimmy Case: sleeves rolled up, ready for whatever or whoever. Souness was a wonderful footballer but a terrifying one too. 'The nastiest, most ruthless man in football,' Frank Worthington, then at Bolton Wanderers, called him. 'Don Revie's bunch of assassins were bad enough, but there was a streak in Souness that put him top of the list.' Terry Yorath, one of the Leeds players, put it another way: 'I wouldn't go so far as to say he's a complete nutcase, but he comes very close.'

As for Case, he had his own credentials to be regarded as what Woodcock called 'the hardest – or whatever you want to call it – player in the country'. Woodcock found him sinister to the point of being 'frightening' and remembers one game when Case came looking for him. 'I knew he was coming to do me and I jumped – a scissors jump. I got so high I thought he had no chance of catching me, but he still caught me.'

Woodcock can also testify for Souness's flailing studs and has a scar on his shin as a permanent legacy from the first leg of the European tie. Yet the player Souness really went for that night was McGovern. 'Souness kicked him up in the air,' Burns remembers. 'He kicked him and he kicked him. And then he kicked him some more. Souness was a great player, but he was a dirty bugger with it.' Coming from Burns, that is some observation.

Thompson can remember a photograph that summed up the friction between the two teams. 'The picture showed Graeme holding Ian Bowyer by the throat. He had him by the Adam's apple and he was pushing him away. What a photograph. People talk about the old mêlées between

179

Manchester United and Arsenal in the heat of the battle. They had nothing on this.'

He was mistaken, actually. The player in Souness's grip was actually McGovern. Bowyer did not arrive on the scene until a few minutes later when he crunched Souness with a tackle of his own. Yet the most striking part of that photograph was that the victim of all the manhandling did not look like he had any interest in fighting back. 'That was Graeme's retaliation for a tackle I'd made on the halfway line five minutes earlier,' McGovern recalls. 'He grabbed my face and Phil Neal had my arms pinned to my side so I couldn't do much about it. But I never got involved in personal vendettas in case it affected my concentration. Graeme wanted to run midfield. I wanted to run midfield. We both knew that if we dominated midfield it gave our team a chance of winning, and occasionally that meant we ran into one another – and he was a much more physical player than me. Graeme kicked people for fun. He did the kicking. I just carried on doing my job for the betterment of my team.'

McGovern's performance that night reminded Burns of 'one of these little squeezy-toys – no matter how many times he was knocked down, he'd come back up again.' McGovern never ducked a single tackle. His work-rate was prodigious and he wore a seen-it-all-before expression that let Liverpool know they were not getting to him. He stared straight through Souness and then he got into position. And if there was a fifty-fifty, he went in to win it. 'That,' Burns says, 'is why he was our captain.'

Before the draw, Paisley had predicted that Forest posed the biggest threat to Liverpool's hopes of winning the trophy for the third time in a row. That at least showed Liverpool's management took Forest seriously. Souness later admitted, though, that no one took too much notice of Paisley's remarks and that he and his team-mates hadn't expected any real trouble. 'We had had a magnificent start to the season and we were knocking in goals all over the place. As far as we were concerned, it was just a question of how many we were going to score against a team with no experience of the nice-ties of European football.'

Liverpool's self-belief went hand in hand with their trophies and it was only temporarily disrupted when Birtles – 'an unknown,' Ray Clemence later described him, 'whose only apparent claim to fame was that he could play squash' – introduced himself properly. Woodcock set him up, Birtles stroked the ball into the net and, finally, all that hanging around in the reserves felt like it had been worthwhile. 'I still remember the way the ground erupted, drowning out the senses,' he says. 'It was the sort of chance you would see gobbled up on the Embankment every Sunday morning by players still hungover from the night before. It was routine, but it was everything to me.'

After that, Forest played with enough skill and verve to have added more goals before half-time. The crowd was loud and raucous and Forest played with the confidence and rhythm that might have been expected of a team that had gone seven-teen months since losing on their own ground. But Liverpool were strong and experienced and in the second half they started getting a hold of the game. Boney M were in the charts with 'Brown Girl in the Ring' and in the away end the Liverpool fans had adapted the words. 'One goal's not enough,' they sang, unashamedly cocky.

Liverpool's players could hear it too and there was an aggression on the pitch that took Birtles by surprise. 'At 1–0, Phil Thompson ran past me and said: "One won't be enough." He almost spat out the words.'

Other Liverpool players joined in as the game entered its closing stages. 'Emlyn Hughes was going round us all telling us we still had to go to Anfield and that one wouldn't be enough,' Burns says. 'He had that little squeaky voice: "One's not enough! One's not enough!"'

But Souness was still driving his men forward in search of an equaliser and the new scoreboard behind Clemence's goal had just flashed up eighty-seven minutes when Liverpool won a corner. Forest were tiring. 'It was a case of holding out,' Barrett remembers. 'Keep it at 1–0, grind it out.'

Martin O'Neill was not in the team that day and, sitting beside Clough and Taylor in the dugout, he could feel their stress levels rising. 'We were winning but it was tough,' he says. 'Liverpool were having a lot of possession. Time was running out and, trust me, 1–0 at that stage would have done Clough and Taylor. One-nil would at least give us a chance. Two-nil would have been sensational but, at that stage, it wasn't even on the agenda.'

The corner was cleared and there were the first plaintive whistles from the crowd for the referee to signal full-time. Barrett followed the ball out as Case went to play it down the line to Souness and start another attack. The pass was misplaced and Barrett stuck out his leg to block it. Phil Neal was first to the loose ball and tried to pick out Souness again, but Barrett had closed him down too and blocked it for a second time. Now Barrett had the ball by the halfway line and suddenly Forest's left-back, preferred ahead of Clark, was in a position where the usual order – 'Pass it to that little fat bastard,' he remembers it – was out of the question. Robertson was still back in his own half along with most of the team. Barrett had a look around him, realised his usual pass wasn't on and started going forward on his own.

On the other side of the pitch, O'Neill was starting to wonder which of Clough and Taylor was going to burst a blood vessel first. 'As Colin went forward, they were absolutely murdering him. They couldn't believe what they were seeing. The two of them in unison were up on their feet: "Where's he going? Where's he going? What is that lunatic doing? Get back, you lunatic!"'

Birtles had peeled off to the left, with Robertson in absentia, so Barrett knocked it wide, thought about running back to his own defence but decided to carry on going forward instead. Birtles swerved past Case and Liverpool, in their search for an equaliser, had not left enough men at the back. Thompson slid in to tackle Birtles, but it was a poor challenge. Thompson could not get a clean contact on the ball and Birtles was now at the byline. Woodcock was in the middle and Barrett was entering the penalty area. Birtles chipped the ball over. 'Even in that split second,' Woodcock says, 'one thought flashed through my mind: "What the hell is our left-back doing all the way up here?" But it was a gorgeous header he cushioned into Barrett's path, weighted to perfection. And, suddenly, in the eighty-eighth minute of a European Cup tie against Liverpool – mighty, historic Liverpool – everything seemed to go into slow motion and a £29,000 giveaway from Manchester City's reserves was drawing back his right boot.

'My God,' Burns says, 'it was the sweetest volley you will ever see.'

The ball was still rising as it soared past Clemence.

'And that,' Burns adds, 'was the point I ran past Emlyn Hughes and asked him (puts on a high-pitched voice): "Two goals enough?"'

'Fuck off! Fuck off!'

Birtles couldn't resist it either when Thompson went past him at the final whistle.

'One not enough, Phil? Will two do us, then?'

Birtles regretted that later. 'I was a young whippersnapper and there was no way I should have been doing that to a seasoned England international. His face was like thunder. I must have been mad, especially with Souness in their team.'

But the song now reverberating round the City Ground was another Boney M adaptation: 'Two goals is enough, tra la la la la.'

Even McGovern, Forest's Mr Sensible, asked Hughes whether two might do it. 'I think, to a man, we all did,' he says.

Liverpool had made the mistake of playing it like a First Division match, going for the equaliser when they would have better off shutting up shop and accepting that 1–0 was not such a bad result to take back to their place. 'If the game had been abroad we'd have settled for that,' Paisley said afterwards. 'We left ourselves exposed and the result of that over-adventure was a second Forest goal. We let Forest disturb us and what makes it worse is that we knew that's what they would try to do.'

Souness blamed himself, pointing out he was 'tearing off

down the right flank' and hopelessly out of position when Barrett started galloping forward. That night, Souness said, was his 'growing-up game in Europe' but the same could also be said of the side that now had a £2,000 striker running their forward line. Psychologically, Forest had cracked it. Clough likened the impact of Birtles to that of 'a dying man crawling through the desert and finding a green shoot and a spring of water; we were that desperate for goals when he came along.' Any sense of inferiority was gone and Barrett's goal changed everything, even if the shouts of 'Wait until we get you back at Anfield' emanating from Liverpool's dressing room, where walls were being kicked and doors slammed, made it clear Forest were going to take an almighty battering when the two sides renewed hostilities.

Anfield had a reputation in the 1970s as the most intimidating place in football, especially on European nights when the acoustics were turned up. Yet Clough took the view that some teams were so in awe of the place they had waved the white flag of surrender before a ball had even been kicked. His own policy was not to show any reverence whatsoever; hence the fun he had nibbling away at Alan Hansen's heels that time. Paisley used to tell a story about Clough turning up unannounced one day 'standing there in an old tracksuit with a bottle of whisky' and saying he wanted to have a drink and talk football. Paisley's office, Clough later said, was so nondescript and spartan it reminded him of a 'foreman's hut on a Wimpey site'. The truth was Clough had immense respect for Liverpool, but that didn't mean he always had to show it. 'I remember playing here when Liverpool could have fitted their trophies into a biscuit tin,' he used to say.

Clough set up the return leg once the team arrived in Liverpool by ordering several bottles of Chablis for his players over lunch and telling them to pour themselves a glass. The booze was to 'help them sleep' in the afternoon and, as they were staying at a city-centre hotel, it was inevitable it would get back to their opponents. David Johnson said later the Liverpool players found it unnerving. Here was a team Clough had described as 'babes in the wood' in European terms, waiting to play the biggest match of their lives, and he had them 'on the bevvies' a few hours before kick-off. He was either unfathomably confident – or off his head.

Certainly, no other manager in the history of football would have dreamt of preparing for a European game that way, or possibly any serious game, and the Liverpool players might have been even more bewildered when Forest's bus turned into Anfield Road with Bill Shankly perched on the front seat. Clough had insisted on picking up Liverpool's former manager on the way. 'We didn't ask why,' Birtles says. The two of them were chatting away as if it was the most normal thing in the world when, on a night like that, it really wasn't. Imagine, perhaps, today's Chelsea team playing a Champions League tie at Manchester United and José Mourinho ordering their bus to take a diversion to collect Sir Alex Ferguson on the way. Then try to picture Mourinho walking down the bus handing out cans of beer, as Clough did with his players before Anfield's floodlights came into view.

By that stage, there was barely half an hour until kickoff. Clough had deliberately left it late so the players didn't have too much time to sit around in the dressing room, over-think everything and remember how many other teams had found those four walls closing in on them.

Clough did, however, take his players for a pre-match walk on the pitch, still in their blue blazers and grey flannels, and insisted they go right in front of Liverpool's more febrile fans. 'He wanted us to walk in front of the Kop,' Birtles says. 'Anfield was the most hostile place I'd ever been but Clough insisted on it. He sent us out there to make it clear we respected them and we knew all about their fabled powers, but it was effectively us saying you can sing "You'll Never Walk Alone" until you are hoarse, but it won't make any difference.

'Liverpool's fans despised us. The sight of us strolling around laughing and joking just riled them all the more. They were booing us, throwing oranges and everything they could get their hands on. A tennis ball came on the pitch. Quick as a flash, John Robertson flicked it up, volleyed it – and stuck it in the top corner of the net. All of a sudden, the mood changed and the Kop started to applaud. How to take the pressure off, in one easy lesson. But that was Robbo, wasn't it?'

Back in the dressing room, Clough's team-talk was typically succinct.

'Gentlemen,' he said, without a hint of concern in his voice. 'There is a sign out there that says "This is Anfield." Now, shall we show them we are not bothered?'

Clough had taken umbrage beforehand when a television interviewer asked him whether Forest would simply try to contain their opponents. 'We don't try to contain anyone,' he shot back, 'apart from you.' But that night was the first time, with Liverpool's crowd screaming 'Attack, attack, attack', that Forest abandoned the Clough credo of width and adventure to operate with a tight, compact system and try to stymie the opposition.

Clough didn't usually bend for anyone and prided himself on how little, if ever, he mentioned the opposition. Yet he did make an exception for the bigger games. Gemmill was ordered to tuck in ahead of Anderson because Alan Kennedy loved pushing forward from defence to join in Liverpool's attacks on the left. Woodcock and Birtles were told to drop back to the halfway line. Clough knew that Liverpool – bearing a grudge, under the floodlights, in front of their own fans – would still fancy themselves to overturn a two-goal deficit.

Frank Clark describes it being 'like the Alamo'. He was back in the team because Barrett had suffered a bad knee injury and Forest's left-back epitomised the toughness that was essential if they were to stand any chance. Clark needed nine stitches in his shin at half-time and the identity of the man who left that calling card didn't remove the strong suspicion it was a deliberate act. Jimmy Case's studs-up challenge meant Clark missed the next two games, but he came back out for the second half, bandaged up, refusing to let anyone see how much pain he was suffering.

On the opposite side, Viv Anderson played elegantly enough for David Miller to inform readers of the *Daily Express* that Forest had a player who 'can develop into an attacking full-back comparable to the memorable Djalmar Santos of Brazil's 1962 World Cup-winning team'. Anderson was no longer the raw, coltish defender who was guilty sometimes of making careless passes and losing his concentration. Clough had turned him into a reliable and often exceptional full-back, known as 'Spider' or 'Extension' because of his long legs and high-kneed running style. 'The timing of his tackling and interceptions is as clean and sharp as any defender in the First Division,' Miller added. 'It reminded one of Bobby Moore at times.' For any defender, there could be no higher compliment.

Peter Shilton commanded his box that night like a man who wanted to show the world he took goalkeeping to its highest level, while Kenny Burns and Larry Lloyd provided more evidence to back up their credentials to be known as the best central defensive partnership in the business. Kenny Dalglish tried to rattle Burns with an early challenge. Burns turned towards him. His face hardened. He fixed his gaze and pointed a finger. No words, no physical contact or retribution – just a pointed finger, held there long enough to let his opponent know that was his only warning. 'I think Dalglish finished up on the Kop,' Clough said later. 'We didn't see him again.'

The home side were desperate for an early goal to shift the psychological balance back in their favour and swarmed all over Forest from the start. 'Liverpool used to try to rush teams out of the game,' McGovern says. 'If they won the kickoff they would aim it just to stay in play by your corner flag. Then they would advance like a wave to close you down and keep you trapped in your own half.'

John Robertson realised early on there wasn't going to be much opportunity to show off his creative sparks. Instead, he tucked inside as Forest repelled wave after wave of Liverpool attacks. The pressure was close to intolerable, but McGovern shielded Burns and Lloyd while Gemmill doubled up with Anderson, snapping into tackles. 'Archie could be nasty when he wanted to,' Woodcock says, 'You need people in a team like that.' Ian Bowyer, with his granite jaw and marathon runner's lungs, was the same. The occasion demanded personality and nerve and Forest had both during the long passages of play when Liverpool threatened to overwhelm them.

The modern term would be 'parking the bus'. Forest didn't just park the bus, they locked the handbrake and threw the keys down the nearest drain, but when they did break out Woodcock showed for everything and nobody could have known that Birtles was not long out of the thud and blunder of non-league. Birtles was willing to run himself into the ground. 'He'd gone from the obscurity of non-league, with nobody knowing who he was, to headline fame almost overnight,' McGovern says. 'Garry was our own Roy of the Rovers. It didn't bother him whether he was playing in front of forty or fifty thousand people at Liverpool or three or four hundred at Long Eaton; another classic Clough signing.'

It was a defensive masterclass and by the time it was done, John Motson was breathlessly telling BBC's viewers that, for Liverpool, it was 'the end of an era'. The European champions had found no way past an immovable barrier. They were out of a competition they had come to believe they owned and Phil Thompson had collapsed to his knees, so distraught that a couple of young fans ran on to peel him off the pitch. It was the fifth time in a row Forest had stopped Liverpool scoring. 'The Kop is silent,' Motson exclaimed, and Lloyd's arms were up in celebration. Lloyd had loved being a Liverpool player, but that was forgotten now. 'I see players today going back to their old clubs and not celebrating out of respect,' Lloyd says. 'What a load of nonsense. I was playing for

Nottingham Forest, they paid my wages, I'll celebrate as much as I want – and I gave it plenty.'

Lloyd's performance had helped to 'shut up one or two Liverpool players' and this was one of those nights that demonstrated why the old bruiser – a player even Burns admitted being intimidated by sometimes – had much more to his artillery than just overwhelming power.

Lloyd had worked out that a central defender should not get too close behind Dalglish because it played to the forward's strengths. Dalglish had a great knack of using his close control to back in, wait for the challenge then spin in an instant and roll off the defender. Lloyd deliberately started a yard away, figuring that it would be better to hold his opponent up rather than allowing a player with Dalglish's sophistication to turn and get in behind.

The strategy worked so well Lloyd used to have a running joke with his team-mates where he would peer into his shirt pocket on nights out and pretend Dalglish was still in there. 'Come on, Kenny,' he would say, 'you can come out now.' Team-mates would ask if Pocket Kenny wanted a drink or some crisps. The two men bumped into one another several years later, after Lloyd had stopped playing, and Dalglish paid him the ultimate compliment. 'Thank fuck you are out of the First Division,' he said.

Above everything else, there was a brotherly spirit about Forest that night and a togetherness that had been fostered on the journey from the Second Division. 'No one,' as Clark says, 'could possibly believe this mob would beat Liverpool over two legs.'

Before that night, Clark had not played a single minute all

season, and Liverpool clearly suspected the oldest player in Forest's team might be rusty and vulnerable, five months after he last started a first-team game. As they piled forward on that side of the pitch, Robertson of all people could be seen chasing back to help out his team-mate. 'You had to have a certain mindset when you went to Liverpool,' Robertson says. 'You had to dig in. Even me, who couldn't tackle my granny.'

Bowyer's attitude also summed up the competitive courage that helped Forest withstand the onslaught. 'It was personal for me,' he says. 'I was brought up on the Wirral and when we used to go across the river to Liverpool it was like entering a different world. We played against Liverpool schoolboys when I was fourteen. I was one of the smallest in the team, playing lads a year older than me and I always remember one of our lads threw the ball to me and, as I went to head it, one of the Liverpool players headed the back of my head. His nose had blood pouring out of it. He said to me through all this blood: "You do that again and I'll effing burst you." I had never heard that expression before, but it prepared me for the nights at Anfield when it was going to be aggressive. And, yeah, I loved it. I used to love the battles against Liverpool.'

Shankly was asked once whether Anfield could make opposition players freeze. 'Only bad ones,' he replied. Forest, refusing point-blank to surrender their position, had proven it. Souness talked afterwards about the way Forest 'kept us dangling on a piece a string.' It was, Hughes said, a 'nightmare', and the BBC used Nat King Cole's 'The Party's Over' as the backdrop to the pictures of Liverpool's players traipsing disconsolately off the pitch.

The party's over
It's time to call it a day
They've burst your pretty balloon
And taken the moon away.

Liverpool had played one hundred times in Europe before meeting Forest, winning fifty-seven, drawing nineteen and losing twenty-four. Forest, in stark contrast, had no experience of European competitions other than a couple of undistinguished seasons in the Inter-Cities Fairs Cup, and on the last occasion, in 1967, their lack of know-how at that level brought an element of farce to their exit.

Forest had beaten Eintracht Frankfurt over two legs to reach the second leg and were drawn against FC Zurich. They won 2–1 in the home leg but lost the return game 1–0 in Switzerland. Nobody had explained the away goals rule properly and at the final whistle the Forest players remained on the pitch, unaware they had been knocked out and waiting for a period of extra-time that never came.

Before that, the only other occasion was in 1961 when the first-round opposition was provided by Valencia. Forest lost 7–1 on aggregate – 2–0 in the Mestalla and 5–1 at the City Ground. How times had changed.

Peter Taylor described the performance at Anfield as the most committed and exceptional display Forest had put together in his time at the club and said he had been 'absolutely staggered' by the poll that showed only three First Division managers had backed them to do it. The other seventeen, he said, needed to wise up and realise Forest were every bit as good as Liverpool, and probably better. 'It concerned me that men in our profession had not done their homework,' he added.

A 2–0 aggregate win was a satisfying way to make the point and now Forest could look forward to some bona fide European excursions, maybe even the trip to Albania that Smales had mentioned, and see if Bob Paisley's prediction was right. Paisley kept a diary of every Liverpool game and had filled his latest entry with a long passage about the frustrations of dominating a team for so long without being able to find a way past them. Forest, he concluded, had a team spirit he had never seen in any of Liverpool's opponents. 'As soon as I closed my diary,' he said, 'I picked up the telephone and rang a bookie to place a bet on Forest for the European Cup.'

Forest's players had already cashed in, because Clough had devised a bonus system whereby beating Liverpool over two legs was worth 'a Birtles' – i.e. £2,000 per man. Clough had valued the first-round tie so highly the bonuses were more lucrative at that stage than any other round to the final.

They had met Liverpool six times now since scraping promotion and not lost to them once. 'It's not a jinx,' Clough volunteered. 'It's talent.'

A lot of teams would have celebrated by cracking open a few bottles of wine. Forest, of course, had done that before the game and Woodcock remembers it being a lot less lively in the dressing room. 'Clough kept it brief. His first words were: "I don't want any of you going into the players' bar, we don't want anyone gloating so let's get showered, get on the bus and get back to Nottingham. You've done the job, you've got rid of the European champions." And that was it. Job done.'

Well, almost. Clough still had to do his television interview for the BBC and in those moments, stood beneath the floodlights with John Motson asking the questions, there was even more defiance than usual in his voice.

The delivery was word-perfect. 'We play with discipline,' Clough said, looking and sounding like a man absolutely in control. 'We don't play with any problems for referees. We try to entertain. And you never know, John, you and your profession just might recognise that we are a good side.'

It was all about that last sentence. The second 'you' was almost a bellow.

Ken Smales had some unfinished business of his own. They like a told-you-so where he was brought up, and on the way out of Anfield he passed the one part of the ground that he knew would still be full. The pressbox was rammed with newspapermen jabbing their fingers into rotary-dial telephones and dictating their match reports to the copytakers at the other end of the line. Smales tapped the *News of the World*'s correspondent on the shoulder.

'Reg,' he said, with a big smile. 'Deepest apologies. I know it wasn't the result you wanted.'

Chapter Eight
Forty-Two Matches Unbeaten

'Nobody had heard of this lad Birtles a week ago.'
*Clive Tyldesley, commentating for Radio City, a Liverpool
radio station*

'Aye, they fucking have now.' *Bill Shankly, Radio City pundit*

Unfortunately for Colin Barrett, the battle for supremacy at the top of English football was not the only drama gripping the nation in September 1978. The first episode of *Dallas* was aired eight days before the tour de force of Barrett's career. His wife, Sue, was hooked and Barrett had a nasty surprise the next time, in a moment of nostalgia, he pushed his tape of the match into his video recorder – no DVD players in those days – and settled back to watch that once-in-a-lifetime goal.

It was Texan accents Barrett could hear rather than Hugh Johns's commentary, and though the storyline centred on a larger-than-life egocentric who apparently thought he was untouchable, it was not one wearing a green sweatshirt. 'It was around the time JR Ewing had been shot,' Barrett recalls. Sue had taped the episode when a record television audience found out who pulled the trigger. And you can probably guess the rest. Barrett reckons it was another ten years before he saw his volley hitting Ray Clemence's net and the victory run where he was getting close to breaking all kinds of sprinting records before Viv Anderson finally managed to catch him.

Yet football can be brutal sometimes. Barrett never properly recovered from a bang he took, in a challenge with Middlesbrough's John Mahoney, ten days after the Liverpool game. His knee ligaments had been ruptured and, after that, Barrett found himself in the demoralising cycle of long rehabilitation periods, then making his comebacks only for his knee to give way again. Every time he returned to the team, the same happened again. Every time he thought he had cracked it, it finished with him back at square one. Barrett had been playing superbly, on the brink of a possible England call-up, but there just wasn't the medical know-how in those days to fix the problem properly.

The long grind of hope, desperation and crushing disappointment lasted twenty months before Forest had to accept there was no way back and gave him a free transfer. There was an unhappy year at Swindon in the Third Division but Barrett's knee carried on failing him and, after that, the phone stopped ringing. 'Nobody wanted me,' he says. 'And that was it, end of story, finished at the age of twenty-nine.' There was no insurance payout. Nobody from the Professional Footballers' Association got in touch and there was none of the wealth and security that meant a modern-day player in that position would be set up for life.

He and Sue moved back to Southwell, ten miles outside Nottingham, figuring that was where they had been happiest, and he took a job pulling pints at his local pub, the Crown Hotel. For a while, he worked for a business making and selling snooker tables. He had a short stint in the commercial department at Forest, on Clough's recommendation, but he found it difficult making the transition into an office job. Sue eventually went back to work as a teacher while her husband looked after their three young children at home. Then one day he was painting the outside of his house and someone walking by asked if he could do the same for him. Barrett said yes and word got around. His new life, with his own painting and decorating business, took off from there.

Barrett was an unlikely hero but, in another sense, they all were. Seven of the Forest players waiting to get their passports stamped in the next round of the European Cup had been taking on York City in the Second Division three seasons earlier. Clough had 'dragged in recruits from all corners, nooks and crannies and the occasional dog track'. Many had been drifting almost unnoticed through the game. Several had apparently reached dead ends in their careers and, astonishingly, five of the players with championship medals had been there since Clough's first day. That side, Clough reminisced, couldn't have 'beaten a team from *Come Dancing*'.

Clough had put together the most attractive and disciplined side in the country and he had done it at a club where only a few years earlier there were signs on the walls reminding people to turn the lights off to save on electricity. As Clough put it: 'We took one sugar in our tea instead of two, we used margarine rather than butter and we drank Tizer instead of Scotch because we got thruppence back on the empty bottle.'

What had happened since was nothing short of a miracle. There had never been a more dramatic rise to the top and it was reflected in the way attendances had shot up. In 1972–73, Forest's first season after dropping out of the First Division, their average was 9,995 and some of the gates were desperate: Cardiff, 6,414; Carlisle, 6,886; Hull, 7,711. The average, pre-Clough, during the first half of the 1974–75 season was 11,630. That rose to 16,670 once he was appointed and the average in 1977–78 was 32,500. Clough thought it should be more, and frequently criticised the Nottingham public for not turning out in greater numbers, but there was nowhere else where the crowds had multiplied at the same rate. In five years, it was roughly a 320 per cent rise.

A phone-in on Merseyside radio, meanwhile, asked Liverpool supporters what they would choose if they could have one wish, and the most popular answer had nothing to do with beating Everton or Manchester United, their traditional rivals. They craved something different in Liverpool now: a goal against Forest. They hadn't managed one in their last five attempts and it was becoming an obsession. Not that Everton's record versus Forest was a great deal better. When Forest won 3–2 at Goodison Park to knock Gordon Lee's team out of the League Cup, that made it ten games in fifteen months against the two Merseyside clubs without losing. Peter Taylor was sitting on the bus afterwards when someone knocked on the window and, thinking it was an autograph-hunter, he pulled it open. It was an Evertonian, and he was shouting: 'I hate your fucking club.'

Forest were the scourge of Merseyside and there were even signs that the man Clough referred to as 'dear old Bill' was beginning to tire of hearing his friend on television. 'He's worse than the rain in Manchester,' Shankly remarked. 'At least God stops that occasionally.'

By early October, Forest had overhauled Leeds's record of thirty-four games unbeaten in the First Division. They hadn't lost at the City Ground since being promoted and suddenly a team that didn't know how to find the back of the net rattled in thirteen goals in four straight wins. Birtles, the new golden boy, had called time on the Withe debate. Woodcock had rediscovered his best form and the other JR – John Robertson – was playing so well his team-mates were wondering if there was any other footballer in Europe with greater mastery of the ball. 'You could write a number on every panel of the ball,' Kenny Burns used to say. 'If you then said: "Number four please, John," he'd swing the ball over and you'd get the number four landing on your head.'

As for the manager, he was graduating ever more skilfully into a league of his own. Clough's success had reinforced his already impregnable belief that he had the right to say what he liked when he liked and, at Forest, nobody dared take him on. One story summed it up. Clough was asked to deliver his annual report to the committee and it consisted of nothing more than two photographs: the First Division trophy and the League Cup.

In one sense, it still felt slightly preposterous that a club with Forest's modest stature could be seriously thinking about winning the European Cup, when two years earlier they were playing in the Anglo-Scottish Cup and their opponents included Kilmarnock, Ayr and Orient. In another sense, the confidence was contagious when two men with the assured belief of Clough and Taylor were fronting everything up. 'We'd knocked out the European champions – sorry, the double European champions,' John McGovern says. 'Liverpool were the kings of Europe and then this team of upstarts, a team from nowhere called Nottingham Forest, had done them again. Could we actually win it? After that, we were bound to think we had a chance.'

At the same time, Forest knew their second-round tie against AEK Athens would not be straightforward. Clough's men had played at the Philadelphia stadium, a primitive concrete bowl, in pre-season and the lingering memory was of the Greek fans setting fire to piles of litter. 'It made us think,' Bowyer says, 'if they could do that in a pre-season friendly, what would they do when we went there in the European Cup – set fire to the whole ground?'

The team were staying in a complex of chalets close to the Aegean Sea and Tony Woodcock, who was sharing with Anderson, remembers the air of uncertainty when Archie Gemmill was holding court the night before the match. 'It was all new for us young lads. We'd never played abroad before and the experienced players were telling us what it might be like. "These Greeks," Archie said, "they're a dangerous lot. We'll have to watch it here tonight. They could easily turn up at this hotel, you don't know what they're going to do. All sorts of things happen in Europe."'

Clough had been revving it up himself and offended the Greek journalists by refusing to do a press conference when the plane landed and preferring to go to the beach rather than train at the stadium. That was perceived as a snub and led to headlines such as the *Athletic Echo's* 'Beat the Snobbish British 3–0'. Clough was branded a 'dictator' and he made it clear what he thought of the reporting at the official conference. The atmosphere was souring and Gemmill told his younger team-mates he knew from playing abroad with Derby that everyone had to keep their wits about them. Watch each other's backs, he said. The Greeks did more than just smash plates – sleep with one eye open.

As it turned out, the only problem that night was an electrical storm that caused a power cut as the players sat outside playing cribbage. The hotel was in total darkness as they struggled through the grounds to get some candles from the reception. Yet one of the younger members of the squad was alone in the dark and starting to wonder what the hell was going on. Viv Anderson had left the group early to go back to his room and read a book and now his mind was playing tricks. Gemmill had spooked him. 'I started imagining things,' Anderson says. 'It was pitch black, but I thought I could see someone. I was there for over an hour and I was scared. I remember thinking: "Is Archie right? Are the Greeks coming to get me?" It was stupid, yes, but everyone had been saying how intimidating they were, how they would do anything to beat you, and I'd started thinking they had got into the hotel and they were coming after me.'

Woodcock eventually headed back and when he banged on the door he found his team-mate had barricaded himself into the bathroom. 'All I could hear was Viv shouting frantically: "Who's there? Get back! Keep out!" He was sitting on the toilet, frightened to death, with his feet pressed against the door.'

It might not be entirely accurate therefore to describe Forest as intrepid travellers on their maiden voyage across the seas – 'There was definitely a shadow there,' Anderson still insists – but they put on another stout performance the following night and there was another piece of classic Clough chutzpah before the game. The stadium was a shrieking, whistling, fire-cracking pit of bias, but Clough wanted to show the Greek crowd it didn't bother them and conducted his team-talk in the centre-circle. McGovern's early goal broke the din and the first impromptu bonfires were already visible when Birtles added Forest's second. AEK had to play seventy minutes with only ten men after one of their strikers was daft enough to swing a punch at Burns. They pulled one back with a generous penalty but Forest finished with a 2–1 lead to take back to the City Ground and, for a team largely made up of first-time Euro-travellers, they had kept their nerve admirably in the face of a hostile crowd, some cynical attempts from the AEK players to rough them up and even a brush with the local police.

The traffic in Athens was never kind at the best of times, but it was so clogged up that day Forest's driver took it upon himself to find any way possible through the jams. 'We were going the wrong way down one-way streets,' McGovern says. 'We were overtaking on the inside and outside lanes of the motorway. We nearly crashed at least four or five times and we had three police cars chasing us, sirens wailing, by the time we got to the ground.' But they had made it on time and Forest's own version of *Wacky Races* ended with a collective effort to persuade the police to be lenient. The driver accepted an on-the-spot fine and his passengers made sure he wasn't out of pocket. 'All the lads chipped in,' McGovern says. 'Talk about a nice easy way to prepare for a European tie.'

Athens was certainly an eventful trip, because it was the

next morning that Clough and Lloyd had the most seismic of all their rows. Lloyd had turned up to get the bus to the airport wearing jeans and a casual shirt, when every other player was in Forest's blue blazer and grey trousers. Lloyd knew that might mean trouble, but he had not been told there was a dress code. McGovern confirmed there hadn't been any official guidelines and Lloyd thought he was off the hook when Clough turned up in his tracksuit bottoms and familiar green sweatshirt.

Except Clough then disappeared back inside the hotel for ten minutes and came out again in his own blazer.

'Hey, why are you the odd one out?'

'Nobody, but nobody, told me anything about wearing a blazer,' Lloyd protested.

'Get back and change immediately.'

Three times, Clough demanded Lloyd returned to the hotel and each time the player refused, pointing out his blazer was at the bottom of his case and had been loaded on the bus. The argument quickly escalated and when they were back in England, Clough began his next team meeting, the day before a game at Ipswich, by handing Lloyd a white envelope with a little red Forest motif on the front – the tell-tale sign that it was a fine.

'That's for you, Big Head,' he said. 'Don't open it now. You can open it when you go home.'

Lloyd tore it open immediately to find out £100 was being docked from his wages for a breach of club discipline.

Straight away, he was on his feet. 'I'm not paying this. I hadn't been told to wear a blazer, so you can stick this in the fucking bin.'

'That, Lloydie, has just cost you another £100.'

'Okay, let's jump straight to £500, because I've still got plenty to say.'

The two of them went at it hammer and tong for the next ten minutes and, as a snapshot of their relationship, that stand-off probably summed them up perfectly. Lloyd was the alpha male of the group, with a temper that could set off a car alarm. It was built into Lloyd's psyche that he could never back down and always had to have the last word – and Clough, knowing all that, was the one man who never let him have it.

Clough eventually went to the team-list that had already gone up on the wall and casually rubbed off Lloyd's name. 'Then £500 it is,' he said, inserting Needham's name instead.

Lloyd stewed on it over the weekend then went in the following Monday to hand in a transfer request, only to find that Clough had gone on one of his mid-season trips to Majorca. Over the next week, Lloyd's temperature eventually came down from boiling point to simmering. Stuart Dryden persuaded him to withdraw the request and Clough, perhaps realising he had gone a little too far, later sent Lloyd's wife a bouquet of flowers. She sent them back with a note telling him exactly where to stick them. But Lloyd did pay a £100 fine. 'I knew I wasn't going to beat him,' he reflects now. 'I tried. But nobody could beat Clough.'

Only a small number even attempted it. Martin O'Neill was one who did try to stand his ground, but he had his own issues with Clough around that time and, like Lloyd, his fingers were burned more times than he could possibly remember.

Clough stopped a training session on one occasion because

he knew O'Neill was in a mood with him. O'Neill was full of professional pride: it hit him like a sledgehammer if Clough ever left him out and the Irishman, by his own admission, had a tendency to sulk.

Clough told O'Neill he didn't like self-pity or miserable faces and they weren't going to start training again until everyone knew what was bothering him. O'Neill refused, so Clough announced that no one would be leaving until he had spat it out.

'Fine,' O'Neill said, 'I want to know why I'm in the second team.'

'I can answer that,' Clough replied jauntily, and he was walking off even before he had even finished his reply. 'Because you're too good for the third team.'

Another time, O'Neill went to see Clough to ask if he could play a more central role rather than being used on the right. Forest had become a lopsided team, with its heavy slant towards Robertson on the left, and O'Neill was starting to think he had the graveyard shift out on the other side. 'What do you think you can do that Archie Gemmill can't do?' Clough asked him. O'Neill persevered and Clough eventually concluded that his player could have the choice of two shirt numbers for the next match. 'The first option,' he said, 'is to carry on as the number seven and play on the right. The second is to wear the number twelve jersey and sit on the bench. Your choice, young man.'

There were many stories of that nature over the years, but what really bugged O'Neill was the nagging sense that Clough did not see him as an essential part of the team. The Irishman was a regular target for Clough's putdowns. He was rarely given credit and he always felt, for all Clough's qualities, that if he had received more encouragement it might have brought another 20 per cent improvement out of him on the pitch. 'I felt as if I was always trying to prove him wrong, whereas some of the other players were trying to prove him right,' O'Neill says. 'Some people, like John Robertson, played the game to prove Clough right that he was a great player. I always felt I had to prove him wrong and because of that I was always looking over my shoulder. I always had this thing in my mind that he was just waiting for the right moment to oust me. It was a constant battle.'

In reality, Clough clearly had a high regard for O'Neill when he was involved so regularly and part of the original Gang of Five, with Robertson, Bowyer, Anderson and Woodcock, who had been there since day one. 'I'm quite proud of that,' O'Neill says. 'I lived through it, from the very first day he walked through the door. I survived all the threats to send me back to university – or sometimes Siberia, depending on how he felt.'

Their relationship was particularly strained during the first half of the 1978–79 season and O'Neill was convinced it started during a pre-season game when Clough made a comment about how he was playing and O'Neill deliberately looked the other way. Players simply didn't get away with that kind of stroppy behaviour when Clough was manager. 'The following week was the Charity Shield against Ipswich,' O'Neill says. 'I bent the ball round the goalkeeper for the first goal. Brilliant. We were leading 1–0 and I was playing very well indeed. We got the score to 3–0 and then I had another chance. Robertson crossed from the left, I chested it down and volleyed it in. I was absolutely delighted. I'd scored twice and there was plenty of time to get myself a Wembley hat-trick.

'Then I looked across to the touchline and I could see David Needham was coming on – and it was my number that had gone up. David Needham? A centre-half? For me? I knew immediately that was all to do with the argument before. I'd ignored Clough and that had really irritated him. He was saying something to me and, honestly, I should have known better. I lost count of the number of times John Robertson said to me: "Don't do it, don't get involved with him, just stay calm," but I found it hard sometimes. I always wanted the final word and there was only one person having the final word. I'd played well that day at Wembley, whatever he said, and to be replaced by a centre-half was just an insult. So as I went past him, I couldn't help myself. "Scared in case I get the hat-trick?" I asked. "Stop yapping," he replied.'

The following Monday the team were flying out to Spain for a friendly against Celta Vigo. O'Neill was still hurting badly. 'He said to me when we were getting on the plane: "If you want to know why I took you off, come and see me at the hotel." I said okay, but I never did.'

O'Neill certainly had a hard time but he was smart enough to know he was on to a good thing. The friction hurt him sometimes – frequently, indeed – but he never lost sight of the fact that Clough, as maddening as he was, was special. Clough fascinated him – even the little things, like his instructions to the team at half-time. 'He would pick up on things you might not even have remembered yourself,' O'Neill says, 'and even if you did remember you certainly wouldn't think he or anyone else would. He knew the game inside out. He never took us out on the training field and did a three-hour coaching session, but he did like to coach during the course of the game. He was sharp, clear in his messages. He spoke with great authority. I know now he had the greatest charisma of any manager in the twentieth century. I just have to admit I didn't always appreciate it at the time.'

The usual routine would be to hold a meeting with the players on the day before games. Sometimes Clough would not say anything about the match whatsoever and, daft as it sounds, even that left the players feeling good about them-selves, as though he wasn't concerned in the slightest about what was going to happen. At other times, a few clipped sentences were often enough. 'He would pick out two or three players and let them know, very clearly, that if the opposition were going to get the better of them, he was going to be falling out with them,' O'Neill says. 'Sometimes it would be the midfielders – Gemmill, myself, McGovern and Bowyer. "If they are going to run the show on my pitch, I'm going to fall out with you and you and you and you. Okay? See you tomorrow." And, God almighty, you left that room knowing you had to be on your mettle.'

Clough also had the knack of making his players feel like they were unbeatable, often with just one sentence. 'You didn't even spit the wrong way,' Clough told Lloyd after one performance. Others would get the little hand sign. A player who was out of form might be told he was the first name on the team-sheet the following week. Frank Clark had been feeling his age earlier in the season, seriously thinking about quitting and contemplating an offer from Derby to become their new reserve-team manager. Imagine how he felt when he came back into the team and picked up the newspapers after one game. 'If that was an England trial,' Clough had said, 'my left-back would be getting a cap.'

Psycho-analysing Clough was never easy but the bottom line was simple: whatever he was doing was working. His players would walk through a pit of snakes for him, never mind a field of nettles, and every time a new situation threw up a different bunch of problems he came up with an answer, and just about always the correct one.

In Athens, for example, Clough detected a few of his players might be a little uptight about their first competitive game abroad. 'Most clubs would have gone to the stadium for some training,' Kenny Burns says. 'When we arrived the gaffer said: "Put your bags down, get changed and I'll see you in twenty minutes, we're going to the beach." This was the day before the game. We went down there thinking we were going to have a bit of five-a-side. But he had other plans. "Right, we're going to have a game of rugby." Big Larry was puffing out his chest, thinking: "I'll have a bit of this, a proper man's game." The first time he got the ball he went running down the wing and tripped up in the sand. Within seconds, there were fifteen or sixteen players kicking sand all over him. Elbows, knees, boots, the lot. He got a battering.'

AEK were managed by Ferenc Puskas and Forest's players watched the Greek side train on the City Ground pitch the night before the return leg. Puskas didn't mind them standing on the touchline – something that would never be allowed in UEFA's modern rulebook – and even at the age of fifty-one, squeezed into his tracksuit, the Hungarian showed his

211

exceptional qualities. 'He was hitting shots from the edge of the box and every one was flying into the top corner,' Peter Shilton says. 'He'd put on weight but his shooting power was incredible. He was showing off a little bit. The poor goalkeeper couldn't get near any of them. I'm not sure what it did for the goalkeeper's confidence, but it wasn't what I would have wanted the night before a game.'

Unfortunately for Puskas, his players could not show the same accuracy the following night and his goalkeeper was beaten another five times. Anderson's goal was the pick of the bunch, struck from twenty-five yards with the outside of his right boot. Needham opened the scoring with a near-post header. Birtles added two more to his collection and Robertson put in the other one. Clough made Lloyd captain for the night and it finished 5–1 with a sixteen-year-old Gary Mills coming on as a substitute. Forest were through 7–2 on aggregate and the results had fallen nicely. Bruges, finallists from the previous season, had already gone out. Juventus had been eliminated. Cologne, the German champions, were still there along with Glasgow Rangers, Grasshoppers Zurich, Austria Vienna, Dynamo Dresden, Wisla Krakow and Malmo. Taylor made no bones about it: 'It's there for the taking.'

Ron Greenwood had been at the match and later that month Viv Anderson became the first black footballer to play for England. He was the youngest Forest player to win a full cap, aged twenty-two, and made his debut in a team that had Woodcock playing in attack and Shilton in goal. Forest now had ten full internationals and Shilton was playing with such high consistency by that stage Sir Matt Busby described him as one of the four greatest goalkeepers he had ever seen, with Frank Swift, Bert Trautmann and Gordon Banks.

The oddity was that Shilton had to alternate with Ray Clemence in the England team because Greenwood could not choose between the two. Clough used to say it was 'absolutely barmy' when Shilton was so flawless and he rarely spoke about one of his players with so much admiration. Lloyd can remember falling out with Shilton during one pre-season friendly and 'grabbing him round the windpipe' at half-time after he had been blamed for giving away a penalty. 'I half-throttled him, but guess what happened next? Cloughie took me off because I'd dared to touch the great Shilts.'

Shilton used to be absolutely meticulous in his preparations, training like a demon and always wanting to improve himself in any small way. His fame was spreading off the pitch as well. One of his many awards in 1978 was for 'Head of the Year', when he and Angela Rippon were presented with trophies for their immaculately kept hair. There were no signs of that head getting too big, but Clough made sure it stayed that way. It was because of Shilton that he started wearing the green sweatshirt – 'there's only one number one around here,' he explained – and Clough, always needing to be on top, had other ways to get under his skin.

'We'd be playing a big game against Arsenal or Manchester United and I'd walk in about two o'clock,' Shilton remembers. 'I would be focused, getting into the zone, but Clough would play squash before games on Saturdays. He would have a bath and he would time it perfectly so that when I got there, he would get out and start towelling himself down in my spot. He'd push all my kit out of the way. He'd leave a big

213

pool of water on the floor and say, "Hold on a minute, Peter," while he finished drying off.

'He'd put on his rugby top, his shorts and his scruffy trainers and as he walked past me he'd give me a little nudge as if to say, "I hope you didn't mind me using your space," knowing I was annoyed because he had left all the water on the floor and I would have to clear it up myself. On a big match-day, it was the last thing I wanted. He said to me once he did it deliberately to annoy me, because I was playing that well he couldn't think of anything else to get under my skin. It was just one of his little tricks and it worked because things like that did keep your feet on the floor. I wasn't too big to clear up after him.'

Clough had all sorts of ways to keep his players grounded and Trevor Francis did not get any special dispensation when he joined the club, in February 1979, in the £1 million deal that announced to the football world that Forest could now compete financially with any of their rivals. Francis was ordered to brew the tea for the other players at half-time. Clough berated him for bringing his own soap and towel into training and when Francis played his first game without wearing shin pads he was informed very matter-of-factly at half-time that Forest had spent an awful lot of money on those legs so he had better find himself a pair straight away.

Francis had already been given a taster of life under Clough when he won the ATV Midlands player of the year award in

1977. Clough had been asked to present the trophy and admonished the Birmingham City striker for coming to the stage with his hands in his pockets. Clough delivered the line in the way of a Victorian schoolmaster ticking off an errant pupil. 'Yes sir,' Francis replied meekly, as if to illustrate the point.

Nonetheless, Clough's appeal was still enough for Francis to turn down a more lucrative offer from Coventry to sign for Forest. He wasn't even put off when he arrived at the City Ground to start negotiations only to be shown to an empty room and informed Clough had popped out for an hour for a game of squash. For Francis, that was just the first of many surprises. 'When he eventually turned up, I had already made up my mind that as long as they gave me a fair deal, I would be happy to sign. I also wanted Brian Clough to know the importance of what it meant for me to play for him, so I asked him to include a clause in the contract that stipulated if he ever left the club I would be allowed to leave too. Peter Shilton had asked for the same, he explained, but the FA wouldn't sanction it.

'Then the chairman popped his head in to ask Brian how the negotiations were going. The response was: "Mr Chairman, when I have something to tell you I will let you know – now get out." I can just remember thinking: "Wow, he's pretty strong," because that was quite something to hear a manager talk to his chairman like that.'

Francis had been a prolific scorer at Birmingham, scoring fifteen goals in his first fifteen matches before he had even turned seventeen. Four of them had come in one match against Bolton and the hype surrounding football's 'Superboy' was summed up by the headlines on BBC's *Sports Report* one night: 'And Trevor Francis did not score today!'

He came from Plymouth originally and in his early days at Birmingham his father Roy, a shift foreman for the South West Gas Board, would drive from Devon to get to St Andrew's and his mother, Phyllis, raised petrol money by doing sewing and tailoring locally, at six shillings an hour. Francis was an ordinary boy with an extraordinary talent. *Woman's Own* ran a feature on him at one stage, telling the story of how he met his wife Helen on holiday – a romantic mini-novel in which he lost her number, could remember only that she worked as a hairdresser in Llanelli and systematically rang every salon in the telephone book until he found her on the fifteenth call.

Francis was twenty-four when he signed, a brilliantly sharp and agile striker who could leave his markers standing by his speed and turning ability. He was doubling the previous transfer record but Clough quickly made it clear there would be no preferential treatment, telling him to turn up the next morning because Forest had an A-team match against Notts County in the Midlands Youth League. Francis had been injured for the previous couple of weeks. Forest's first-team game had been called off because of a frozen pitch and Clough wanted to see his new man in action. 'I'd like to see you in the A team tomorrow,' he told Francis. 'And I'm not asking you to play, I'm telling you.'

The venue was Grove Farm, a windswept set of communal park pitches close to the Trent, and if Francis was surprised to be making his debut in such modest surroundings try to imagine the shock of his opponents when Forest's bus rolled up and English football's man-of-the-moment jumped off.

The County team that day was largely made up of schoolboy trialists but also included a centre-half by the name of David McVay who was coming to the end of his time with the club and helping to make up the numbers. What McVay hadn't expected was that he would be the first player to waft his size-elevens in the direction of the man whose transfer had made it on to the national six o'clock news.

McVay went on to become a celebrated writer, author of the critically acclaimed *Steak Diana Ross: Diary of a Football Nobody*, and tells the story about how he spent the previous night swaying at the bar of the Flying Horse Hotel, one of Nottingham's oldest watering holes, blissfully unaware about what was awaiting him in the morning.

He does not remember exactly how many pints he had sunk, other than it was double figures and topped off with a visit to 'one of the less salubrious curry houses down Arkwright Street'. But he can vividly recall the sudden wave of nausea when he realised through his bleary eyes and a monstrous hangover what was going on.

'It wasn't until a man in green turned up that the penny dropped,' McVay says. 'Clough, patrolling the touchline and barking orders, had actually sent his million-pounds man into football's version of the Wall of Death. Was he insured for injury? No one was quite sure. Was it legal to hand him his debut in this way? Again, pass. And was physical contact allowed should he enter our radar? No one dared ask. Had anyone before, or has anyone since, contrived such a debut for their most expensive signing? Of course not. And could it happen today, given that not one national newspaper or, heaven forbid, television camera turned up to witness it? Not a chance.'

Francis does not have such a good memory of what he was doing on the night of 9 February 1979, but it was fair to say it did not involve soaking up copious amounts of alcohol with a vindaloo. He does, though, remember there was a 'maximum twenty people' watching the two sides play out a 2–2 draw. 'It was a strange way to start my Forest career,' he says. 'I certainly wasn't expecting it to be that way.'

He can also recall what happened to one of the spectators who shouted 'Got to do better than that, Francis' when he missed an early chance.

Clough jogged halfway round the pitch to wag a finger at the heckler. 'His name is *Trevor.*'

Francis made his league debut at Ipswich and it was then he realised his price tag had affected him more than he had realised. 'There was a lot of pressure on me. I tried not to let it get to me, but I remember getting terrible stick from the Ipswich fans chanting "What a waste of money." I did my best to block it out, but every time there was a stoppage it felt like the same chants were going round the ground, over and over again. All the focus had been on me. I was familiar with the back-page headlines, but this transfer was front-page news. It was the biggest day in my football career and we had broken the transfer record. Plus there was an added pressure because Clough was such a great goal-scorer himself he set extremely high standards for his forwards. According to him, any chance in the penalty area was a good chance.

'With five minutes to go, we were drawing 1–1 and a cross

came in. I knew I couldn't reach it with my head but I could get to it with my fist and I punched it into the back of the net. I was hoping I would get away with it, but the referee saw what had happened and gave a free-kick. The game finished 1–1 and when we came in afterwards Clough ripped into me like you could not believe. "Listen," he said. "You play for Nottingham Forest now, we play fair at this club, get yourself changed and in the bath and don't ever let that happen again." That was my first lecture, the full force of his tongue, and he could be quite brutal. He didn't spend an unnecessary amount of time trying to make the point and it hit home.'

Francis had not got on with Burns when they played together at Birmingham. There was friction and Burns felt envious back then about the amount of praise and publicity lavished on his younger team-mate, as well as the fact 'he was driving a TR6 while I had an Austin 1100.' Clough had already squared it with Burns on the day he turned up at his wedding and the two players made their peace.

There was, however, one outstanding problem. Forest had followed up the League Cup win at Everton by knocking out Brighton in the quarter-finals, then beating Watford 3–1 over a two-legged semi-final, but Francis was cup-tied and would not be able to feature in the final against Southampton. He had also signed too late to play in the European Cup unless Forest went all the way to the final, so he was back on tea-making duties when they took on Grasshopper Zurich in the quarter-final.

'It was a bit of an eye-opener for Trevor,' Burns says. 'I walked past the dressing-room table at half-time and started getting a cup of tea. Cloughie walked in with Trevor behind him. "What are you doing?" he said. "Put that back." Then he turned to Trevor and said: "Trevor, you get the cups of tea because, unlike him, you've done bugger all in the first forty-five minutes."'

Grasshoppers had already knocked out a Real Madrid team featuring Uli Stielike, Vicente Del Bosque and Juanito, but Larry Lloyd can remember going into that match thinking Forest would have no problems getting into the semi-finals. 'We were expecting to beat Grasshoppers,' he says. 'Grasshoppers? They're the little green things that jump around your garden, aren't they? No, they didn't worry us.'

Forest's crowd were also getting cocky. Against AEK, they had sung 'There's only one team in Europe' and 'Are you watching, Liverpool?', later changing it to 'Are you crying, Liverpool?'

Peter Taylor warned everyone that Grasshoppers were a decent team, but Swiss sides didn't have a great pedigree in Europe and Forest were in danger of doing precisely what other sides had been guilty of against them. Archie Gemmill remembers the attitude being: 'Hey, we're Nottingham Forest, champions of England and conquerors of mighty Liverpool while they were – who exactly?'

Yet Grasshoppers had some talented players. Claudio Sulser was a Swiss international striker who had elevated himself to superstar status with the goals that knocked out Madrid. Sulser had scored nine times in the opening two rounds, including five in one game against the Maltese champions Valletta, and Clough was so impressed with the little player operating slightly further back he ended up signing him a couple of seasons later. Raimondo Ponte was a Swiss-Italian attacking midfielder with an eye for a pass. He rarely impressed when he joined Forest – 'Raimondo spoke a million languages until you told him to work harder,' Ian Bowyer says, 'and then, funnily enough, he didn't understand English' – but Ponte was superb for Grasshoppers when the teams met in the first leg in Nottingham. He caused all sorts of problems and Forest were in danger of looking too complacent early on when Sulser ran clear after ten minutes and clipped his shot past Shilton to leave a sudden, damp silence inside the City Ground.

One-nil down, Forest were facing a new test of nerve and passed with distinction. Garry Birtles changed the game with an equaliser before half-time and the second half showed why it was almost two years since Forest had lost on their own ground. John Robertson made it 2–1 from the penalty spot early in the second half and in the last three minutes Gemmill and Lloyd both added more goals. No team had ever come back from 4–1 down in the first leg of a European Cup quarter-final. It didn't make the second leg a complete formality, but not far off it, and Forest were now virtually in the semi-finals.

'I went to see the boss afterwards,' McGovern says. '"Boss, are we off tomorrow?" But he said he wanted us all in nice and early. "Some of the people who came to see you tonight deserve your support, and we're going to see them tomorrow." The next morning he took us to Carlton Colliery. "We're going down the pit to see the workers on the coalface," he told us. We put on the hard hats, the knee pads and the elbow pads and we went down in the cage, switched our headlamps on, and crawled on our hands and knees to the coal face to meet the miners and say thank you for supporting us.'

Clough always liked to keep it interesting and when it came to the League Cup final in March 1979 there was another demonstration of how he worked in an entirely different way from the other ninety-one managers in the league. His players were expecting to go straight to their beds when they arrived at their hotel the night before the game, but Clough was having none of it, announcing that he wanted to have a drink together. Everyone was told to dump their bags and come back downstairs and when Gemmill didn't arrive, Jimmy Gordon was instructed to ring his room to say Clough was waiting.

'I'm not coming down,' Gemmill, a ten-o'clock-to-bed-man, said. 'Tell him that's me done for the night.'

Two minutes later his phone rang again and it was Clough. 'Get yourself down here now,' came the message, and then the phone went dead.

Clough then took everyone to a partitioned-off room and triumphantly announced that 'no one leaves until we've supped the lot' just as a waiter arrived with a dozen bottles of champagne. When Clough told his players to have a drink it usually meant one or two, not seven or eight. But Clough had thought the players were too quiet on the coach and decided something had to be done to relax them. O'Hare said he was more of a bitter drinker, so Clough ordered twelve pints of bitter. Clough and Taylor then entertained everyone with stories about the old times at Hartlepools and the double act were on such good form it had gone 1am when the players finally staggered away. At least one had to be carried to his room. Very few made it to breakfast and Birtles woke up not just with a sore head but all the skin rubbed off his knees. He had collapsed on the stairs and was 'on all fours' by the time he made it to his room.

The next day, Forest were nursing a collective hangover and, by half-time, they looked in need of smelling salts as well as headache tablets. David Peach had given Southampton the lead and their 1966 World Cup winner, Alan Ball, was doing his best to wind up his groggy opponents. Ball had told a newspaper that morning that he didn't regard Clough highly as a manager and celebrated the goal by running provocatively in front of the Forest dugout. Ball could be a deliberate irritant sometimes. On the way back to the centre-circle, he punched McGovern in the back to get his attention. 'This is Wembley, son,' he shouted gloatingly, 'try to enjoy it while you're here.'

Clough's late-night booze-up was threatening to blow up in his face until he got to work at half-time, telling his players they had had enough time to shake their heads clear and it was time they started taking better care of the ball. 'Don't any of you say that was anything to do with last night,' Clough said. 'How dare you underperform with all your families and all our supporters in the stands?' He then singled out poor old Gemmill for an almighty dressing-down, telling him he was coming off if he didn't wake up soon.

The transformation was remarkable. Forest were at their exhilarating best in the second half, overwhelming their opponents. Birtles's raw knees did not stop him scoring twice – as well as two disallowed goals, one wrongly given as offside – and when Forest took the lead McGovern ran past Ball in the centre-circle, resisted the temptation to give him a whack but pinched his bottom instead. 'This is Wembley, Alan, why don't you start enjoying yourself while you're here?'

Woodcock also scored before Southampton pulled one back with a couple of minutes remaining and the game finished with Clough insisting that he and Lawrie McMenemy broke usual protocol to climb Wembley's thirty-nine steps and collect medals with the players. There were none set aside for them but the Football League's secretary, Alan Hardaker, hastily found two empty boxes and they were handed over as if it was all part of the arrangement. It wasn't, of course, but Clough had a bee in his bonnet because Hardaker and his colleagues had stopped him and Taylor leading out the team together. Clough gave Taylor the pre-match honour but got to take the trophy home, placing it on top of his television while he ate a bag of fish and chips.

Four days later, Forest drew 1–1 with Grasshoppers in Zurich's Hardturm stadium to go through to the European Cup semi-finals 5–2 on aggregate. Briefly, there was a scare when Sulser opened the scoring from the penalty spot, but Birtles set up O'Neill for the equaliser and later that night a small group of victorious players quietly left through a back door of the team hotel to celebrate with a few drinks. 'It was one of the few occasions when we disobeyed Clough's orders,' Woodcock says. 'We thought we'd pop out to see what Zurich was like. A few of us sneaked out and I can remember John Robertson desperately wanting to come but he just couldn't. "He'll find out," he was shouting. "You're all doomed when he finds out." He went to his bedroom and waved from the window but he wouldn't risk it.'

Winning had become a routine and Forest were still chasing Liverpool hard in the league despite the added strain of being involved in the European Cup, with all the League Cup games on top and the kind of misfortune with injuries they had avoided the previous year. Barrett missed six months initially because of his knee injury. Burns needed an operation to repair his knee cartilage and there were five players missing when they went to Anfield at the start of December with their unbeaten league run now standing at forty-two games.

The unbeaten run had hit forty with a 3–1 win at Tottenham. A goalless draw against QPR made it forty-one and a 1–0 win at Bolton was number forty-two. It had reached the point, according to Lloyd, that 'if we drew two games back-to-back it felt like a crisis. We'd have a meeting: "You – have you checked your weight, have you put two pounds on? What's wrong with you?" There was something wrong, we thought, if we didn't win. Twenty games unbeaten, twenty-five games unbeaten, thirty games unbeaten, forty games unbeaten. The numbers just kept going up and up. A lot of people said stuff about us, but it didn't bother us. We were a bloody good side and we never thought we were going to lose.'

Expectations had changed. It was later that season Clough could hear the supporters behind his dugout breaking out into slow hand-clapping because Forest were struggling to break down their opponents. Never mind the fact Forest were playing their fourth game in eight days, or that the opposition was Manchester United. The game was approaching half-time without any goals and the crowd was restless. 'What do these people want?' Ken Smales asked. 'Blood?'

At Christmas, the club's cartoonist, Toz, marked Forest's success with a caricature of Clough at the top of a Christmas tree resplendent with festive parcels showing off their achievements over the previous year: Football League Champions, Manager of the Year, Football League Cup, Record Unbeaten Run, County Cup, Charity Shield, Player of the Year. All that was missing was the European Cup and the FA Cup. Three bottles of Bell's whisky, the traditional manager-of-the-month prize, were lined up round the tree. As for the man himself, he had been superimposed in the fairy's position, wearing a halo and carrying a magic wand.

Yet the forty-third game always looked treacherous. Liverpool were even more hyped up than normal, desperate to get one over on their bogey team, and knowing that if they won it would leave Forest with an almost irretrievable gap to make up at the top of the league. Liverpool already had a six-point lead, albeit having played two games more. They were playing what many observers believed to be the most fluent and overwhelming football of any Liverpool side, before or since, and had led the way since winning ten of their first eleven games. Alan Hansen has since said that team was the finest he ever played in during fourteen years at the club. Graeme Souness says the same about his own time at Anfield, and there are many Liverpool fans who remember that game creating the best atmosphere there had ever been at Anfield for a league match.

In the process, Liverpool managed their first goal against Forest in six attempts, or just over six-and-a-half hours of match-time. It was a penalty scored by Terry McDermott that sparked what Smales later described as 'scenes of near hysteria'. McDermott scored again and no team came back from 2–0 down at Anfield in those days. 'They murdered us,' Clough admitted. 'We didn't get a kick from three o'clock onwards.'

The run had lasted the equivalent of a full league season. It had been a year and twenty days since Forest's last defeat and the scenes at the final whistle showed what it meant to the team that had stopped it going any longer. 'I don't think I have ever seen Liverpool players look as delighted as they were on that day,' Shilton says. 'But I guess they were due one by then.'

Clough later described the record as the greatest achievement of his managerial career and said: 'If that had been any other club apart from Forest, the Royal Mint would have knocked the Queen off the coin to put them on.' Forest's run had incorporated one defeat in sixty-three matches, cup games included, and when Clough left the away dugout at Anfield he did something his players could never remember him doing before. He walked to the edge of the pitch to wait for them to come off. He stood there for a few seconds. He looked at the dejection on the faces of his players – and then he started applauding.

Chapter Nine

Robertson Eats Malmolade

'There's no answer to that.' *Eric Morecambe*

The door was open just far enough to see. Brian Clough was sitting with his players in the boardroom for a team meeting when, one by one, the stars of Cologne started to file in through the main entrance of the City Ground. Toni Schumacher, the heir to Sepp Maier as Germany's international goalkeeper, was first. Dieter Müller, one of the Bundesliga's most feared strikers, came next. Then Bernhard Cullman, Bernd Schuster and the other players, virtually all internationals, who had led *Die Geissbokke* – the 'Billy Goats' – to the German league and cup double.

What they did not realise was that Peter Taylor, voice hushed, was providing a running commentary as they came through and the Forest players were struggling to conceal their laughter. 'That goalkeeper,' Taylor whispered, as the imposing Schumacher marched past. 'Trust me, he couldn't catch a fucking cold, that lad.'

Müller had been the joint leading scorer in Germany, with twenty-four goals, in Cologne's title-winning season. 'He's shot,' came Taylor's verdict. 'No legs.' Schuster was one of the rising young stars of the Bundesliga. 'Nothing to worry about,' Taylor scoffed. Heinze Flohe went through. How, Taylor asked, had a dummy like that won all those German caps? Herbert

Zimmerman was an attacking left-back for club and country. Roger van Gool was a Belgian international winger. Yasuhiko Okudera had won Japanese player of the year. Taylor took them all down. 'It's a Midland League side,' he whispered. 'Doncaster Pork Butchers.'

It was the day before the first leg of the European Cup semi-final and Cologne were there to train on the pitch. Some of their players waved politely. A couple nodded. Mostly, they just stared ahead impassively, not giving anything away. They were a formidable sight. 'A Midland League side?' Martin O'Neill says. 'I can remember thinking: "Hang on, haven't Cologne won the league and cup double in Germany?"'

Cologne were in their seventeenth year of competing in Europe. They had beaten Bayern Munich, home and away, on the way to winning the 1977–78 championship and survived a wild and eccentric final day of the season when the defending champions Borussia Moenchengladbach, in second place on goal difference, scored twelve times without reply against Borussia Dortmund to set a new Bundesliga record (and spark an inquiry by the German football federation). Cologne beat the bottom club, St Pauli, 5–0 on the same day, which was enough to win the league by virtue of having conceded three fewer goals. Otto Rehhagel, Dortmund's coach, was sacked the next day and the club fined the players 2,500 Deutsche Marks for their shoddy performance. There were allegations of match-fixing and, though there was always an element of comedic exaggeration with Taylor, he had been over to Cologne's Müngersdorfer stadium and came back with the genuine impression there was nothing to fear. 'Have double steak,' he told everyone when they met for their pre-match meal the next day. 'Get yourself some pudding if you fancy it. We'll beat this lot by five, no problems.'

'He was absolutely adamant,' O'Neill remembers. 'He said: "There are two things I look for: can they head the ball? No. Are they quick? No. They have got no pace and we'll murder them, so get yourself double helpings. And just wait until they see the state of our pitch." Well, I remembered those words when the game started. They were two-nil up in nineteen minutes. They were the quickest team we had ever played and the pitch hadn't bothered them one jot. We were getting a chasing and I think we all gave a collective look over to Taylor in the dugout as if to say: "What in hell's name were you talking about?"'

Forest's dream of becoming the most unlikely team to reach a European Cup final looked dead and buried in those moments. Van Gool had fired in the opening goal. He also created the second, slicing open the home defence to leave Müller with an open goal, and Cologne did not seem in the slightest bit bothered that the past eight months of football had taken its toll on Forest's pitch. The few remaining blades of grass were dotted around the corner flags and two days of heavy rain had created a layer of mud reminiscent of the Glastonbury music festival after a rain-lashed weekend. Except Cologne were knocking the ball around as if they were playing on a bowling green. Just before half-time, Van Gool ran clear again. His shot grazed the outside of the post and the loudest and most raucous crowd at the City Ground in memory almost shrieked its relief. A third goal at that stage and even Taylor might have had to admit Doncaster Pork Butchers looked odds on to reach the final.

Instead, Forest found an inner resolve. It took a while for them to shake their heads clear, but it gradually became clear that there was going to be no meek surrender and that, if they were being shown the exit door, they would not simply be fetching their coats and politely ushering themselves out. The acoustics of the City Ground had never sounded better and from that point onwards they played with the commitment and esprit de corps of a team that was going to give absolutely everything to rescue themselves.

The drama was unremitting: the champions of England versus the champions of Germany, slugging it out on a pitch that looked like it might cause an epidemic of trench foot. The shirt numbers were almost obliterated by the mud as both sides went for all-out attack. It was an epic, throbbing battle and by the time it was all done, among all the different emotions of what David Lacey described in the *Guardian* as a 'harrowing night' for Forest, there was also the overwhelming sense that the City Ground had witnessed something truly special. 'One of those nights,' O'Neill says, 'when you knew what Puskas, Di Stefano and all those other great players felt. It felt like everything football should be. I came off the pitch thinking I had played in the most atmospheric game imaginable.'

Forest, of course, did not have a Puskas or Di Stefano. Their heroes went by names such as 'Bomber' and 'Robbo' and could remember getting the run-around from Carlisle, never mind Cologne. Ian Bowyer, Clough used to say, was 'one of the most genuine pros I ever worked with'. He wore every shirt number, from one to eleven, in his time at the club and played in every single position. He even had a couple of stints as an emergency goalkeeper, including a remarkable game against Oxford in

1975 when John Middleton broke his nose just before half-time and Bowyer kept out everything before George Lyall scored a late Forest winner. Bowyer was a Clough stalwart – 'the man of many parts', Hugh Johns called him – and the player the *Manchester Evening News* called a 'Manchester City reject' did not have it in his nature to believe Forest's position, 2–0 down against big-time opponents, was irretrievable. It was Bowyer's effort shortly afterwards that hit the crossbar to lift the crowd and make them believe there was maybe still time for a feat of escapology. Garry Birtles pulled one back shortly before Van Gool's missed chance and it was Bowyer, with his habit of scoring important goals, who brought Forest level early in the second half with a thumping shot.

As for John Robertson, it was difficult to overstate his contribution that night, other than to say it went beyond the fact it was his diving header that gave Forest a spectacular third goal to put them in the lead. The only other time Robertson scored with a header came in a miserable 2–1 home defeat against Hull in 1975 when he missed two penalties, with his family down to watch him from Scotland, and the first one came back to him to nod in the rebound. The second didn't, and Robertson was so mortified he had a year off penalties.

That apart, it was such a rarity for Robertson to get his head on the ball that the manager once decided to do something about it. Clough made everyone form a circle in training and put Robertson in the middle with Bert Bowery while the other players threw the ball up into the air for them to challenge each other. Bowery was over six foot and as wide as a wardrobe. Robertson did not win one.

His goal against Cologne was certainly a collectors' item but there was another element to the story, and it said a lot about Robertson that he was involved in the first place. The previous Saturday, he had gone out for a few drinks after getting back from a 3–1 win at Chelsea. It was two in the morning when he got home, but his phone was ringing and the voice at the other end of the line told him there had been a car crash. His brother, Hughie, had been killed. Another car coming in the opposite direction had gone across the central reservation of a dual carriageway on the outskirts of Glasgow. Hughie's wife, Isobel, was killed instantly. Hughie was cut free from the wreckage but died in hospital later that night. The only survivor was their eight-year-old daughter, Jillian, who had been sitting in the back seat and suffered serious internal injuries.

Against that kind of tragic backdrop, it was a wonder Robertson could even find the strength to play. It was the Monday morning when he got in contact with Clough, two days before the Cologne game, and he has never forgotten his manager's compassion. 'He couldn't have been any kinder or more supportive. He told me to take as long as I wanted, not to worry about the game and to come back only when I was ready.' The funeral was due to take place the day after the game, but Robertson returned to play the hardest match of his life, then travelled straight back to Scotland to be at the service. His family had told him that if he was able to play, it was what Hughie would have wanted, so he was there because he felt it was the right thing. 'And when I scored,' he says, 'I said to myself that one was for my brother.'

It would have been some way to win the match, but there

234

was still one more late and dramatic twist. Forest had looked vulnerable all night defensively. Kenny Burns was injured, Viv Anderson was suspended and Peter Shilton had chosen a bad night to show the world that even a goalkeeper of his distinction was not immune to the pressures of his industry.

Okudera was brought on in the eightieth minute and barely had time to get a scuff of dirt on his pristine white kit when he tried his luck from twenty yards. His shot dipped in front of Shilton but it hadn't been struck with great power and in that split-second there were 40,000 people in that crowd thinking he would have to do better than that to beat a goalkeeper of Shilton's expertise.

Shilton's approach to football was meticulously well ordered. With him in goal, it gave everyone confidence. Except something had malfunctioned. 'I was in a daze that night,' he remembers. 'I felt tired. We'd gone 2–0 down and it was unheard of for us to let in two goals at home, let alone in the first twenty minutes. I felt a bit dazed, a bit jaded. I was expecting the ball to skid in the mud, but the pitch had dried out a little bit by that stage. It didn't hit the deck and come up at me as I was expecting. Instead it kept low.'

The shot squeezed under his body, in front of the Trent End, skidded through the mud and nestled in the bottom corner of his net. There followed that sudden, awful silence when the crowd realised what had just happened, and who had been at fault, and there was the tinny, surprised roar from the away fans. Cologne's players were celebrating in a mud-splattered, ecstatic scrum. The game finished 3–3 and Shilton's state of depression was not helped the next day when he saw the newspapers. One headline roared: 'Japanese Sub sinks Shilton'.

It was a desperate disappointment and the only consolation was that, having conceded those two early goals, the outcome could easily have been much worse. 'Although Forest's prospects of survival look slim indeed, they are far better than they were at eight o'clock,' Donald Saunders pointed out in the *Daily Telegraph*. 'Cologne were deprived of a virtual walkover by Forest's undying spirit, the commendable skill of Robertson and Bowyer's power and determination.' Nonetheless, Saunders concluded his report with a prediction. 'I have little doubt that when battle is resumed Cologne will add one or two more to the healthy bag of goals.'

That fell in line with the view of most of Fleet Street, but there wasn't a trace of self-doubt from Clough. 'You might think he would be annoyed,' Birtles says. 'You might imagine he was going to throw the tea around the dressing room and give us a real rollicking. But there was no rollicking. He was calm. He told us straight away: "You're better than them, they think they are through but we are going out there to win." There was no problem, no panic, no histrionics. He didn't say anything to play on your mind and leave you thinking: "Could I have done that better?" No, it was 3–3, we're going to win this game, you're better than them and we're going through to the final, as simple as that. Everyone else thought we were out of it and yet, strange as it sounds, he made us feel like a million dollars.'

It was a triumph in psychology, and Clough's post-match television interview with Gary Newbon was another masterpiece. He was disappointed, he said, that they did not have a lead to take into the second leg, but he pointed out that the way Cologne had defended 'didn't overly impress us either'. He also reminded everyone there was still another game to play. 'Let's see how valuable Cologne's three away goals turn out to be when we go over there.'

Then Clough looked straight into the camera to deliver the killer line. He held that gaze expertly, just for the right amount of time to make sure he could not be misunderstood, and when he spoke it felt like he was challenging the entire nation to dare to disagree with him. 'I do hope nobody is stupid enough to write us off,' he said, with the unmistakable air of someone who knew better.

That interview had the effect of balm on his players. They all saw it. Either Clough was an even greater showman than they had already thought, or he genuinely believed they could pull it out of the bag. The consensus was that it was the latter. 'It was that lingering stare into the camera just to make sure everyone had got it,' McGovern says. 'After that, we started believing it ourselves.'

No team had ever reached the final of the European Cup when they needed to win the away leg of the semi-final. The only other way for Forest to go through was a 4–4 or 5–5 draw but, realistically, that was never going to happen. Forest had to win and when they arrived in Germany they found a city already preparing for the final. Cologne had printed their tickets and had them ready to go on sale as soon as the final whistle sounded. Travel companies had hired teams of local youngsters to hand out leaflets advertising their packages. Flyers were stuck under car windscreen wipers to 'see our team in Munich'.

A story had already appeared in the *Nottingham Evening Post* that the Cologne players had been drinking champagne on the flight home from the first leg. 'It transpired Cologne had booked hotels for the final too,' Birtles says. 'Talk about putting your towels out on the sunbeds. Their arrogance was breathtaking and that was just an added incentive. We wanted to ram it down their throats.'

What Forest did have in their favour was the knowledge that the home leg was a one-off and it was inconceivable they could ever defend so sloppily again. Burns was fit. Anderson was back from suspension. That gave Forest their first-choice defence again and, psychologically, something had changed during the intervening two weeks. Clough and Taylor had made sure of it. Clough had predicted Cologne wouldn't score in the second leg and Taylor had been to the bookmakers to lump £1,000 on a Forest win. Cologne had also been on the wrong end of a 5–1 thrashing by Bayern Munich. Taylor had stopped calling them a Midland League side, but he still wasn't impressed. They wouldn't finish in the top half of the First Division, he said.

Forest also knew what they had to do, whereas Cologne didn't have to win and a team in that position can find it unsettling sometimes. Tactically, it is not easy finding the balance between attack and defence. 'After twenty-five minutes, I started to get the sense that Cologne weren't exactly sure how to deal with it,' O'Neill says. 'Should they go forward when that meant they could get caught on the break? Or did they play safe when they needed only a draw? I'm not sure they knew what to do themselves and I think we sensed that uncertainty about them.'

Forest did as they had been instructed, stifling their opponents until half-time, and playing with more confidence than might have been expected for a team in their position. 'Robbo told me after the game that I'd done something after fifteen minutes he'd never seen me do on the field before,' Larry Lloyd said. 'I was running back towards our goal with a German forward. The ball was bouncing. My job was to pass it back to Shilts or clear my lines – boot it clear. But I flicked it over my head, turned and pushed it upfield. I'd never done it before and I never did it in a game afterwards. Yes, we were confident.'

Müller had put an early chance wide, but Cologne's main striker did not even last half an hour after taking the full force of one of Lloyd's bone-jarring challenges. 'Müller had been spouting off before the game about how they were almost home and dry,' Birtles says. 'I think that was part of Larry's game-plan.'

The onus was still on Forest to find a goal and after an hour there were still no clear-cut chances. Barry Davies, commentating for the BBC, was urging them to be more adventurous. 'They have to gamble,' Davies said. Tony Woodcock picked up the ball midway inside the Cologne half. Zimmermann closed him down and as the two players came together the ball spun twenty yards off Zimmerman's boot and went out of play. It gave Forest a corner and a chance to see if the one set-piece routine they practised in training might work.

Robertson floated the ball over. Birtles let it flick off the top of his head and at that precise moment, sixty-four minutes into the second leg of a European Cup semi-final, there was one man in the six-yard area who was already in position, anticipating where the ball might come and bracing his neck muscles. The first header from Birtles was deft. The follow-up from Bowyer was twisting, instinctive and, for Forest, historic. The cross, the flick-on and the finish. 'And we were on our way to the European Cup final,' Bowyer says, 'when two or three seasons before we were in the Second Division. A club that had been mid-table in the Second Division, with crowds of 12,000. It was just unheard of – fairytale stuff.'

There was still time for a late, desperate Cologne rally but that was the point when Shilton reminded everyone there had never been another goalkeeper who chased perfection more assiduously. Shilton treasured his save from the full-back Harald Konopka in the last minute almost as much as he did the one from Mick Ferguson at Coventry virtually a year to the day. The final whistle shrilled shortly afterwards and all sorts of people were suddenly running across the pitch. A committee member by the name of Fred Reacher made a beeline for Shilton. 'He jumped up and gave me the biggest kiss,' Shilton says. 'I couldn't get out of the way.' John McGovern was also taken by surprise. 'The first person I saw at the final whistle was our commercial manager, running on the pitch with his hands in the air, like a mad-man. "How's he got on the pitch?" I thought.'

Photographers were swarming around Bowyer for a picture of the hero. He had his arm round O'Neill and the Irishman's hand was pouring with blood. O'Neill was completely oblivious to it until he got back to the dressing room. 'They had a midfield player called Herbert Neumann and – I don't think he meant it – he had bitten into my hand. God almighty, it was a mess, but I was so into the game I couldn't possibly have noticed.'

As for Clough, it was the culmination of some of his greatest work. Clough had reminded everyone over the two legs of his most alluring qualities. He hadn't let his players' confidence drop. He had made them believe they were the superior team and, ultimately, he had called it spot on. Woodcock used to wonder sometimes whether Clough was lucky or touched by genius. The manager's team-talk was so prescient it helped make up Woodcock's mind. 'He said: "It's going to be a tough one, all right. Clean sheet, as usual, keep it nice and tight. If we get the chance to put the ball in the net we won't say no but we're going to take 0–0 at half-time, come out in the second half, go 1–0 ahead and then we'll close the door again and get off out of here." So what happened? Exactly that.'

It is also worth considering what happened late in the match, with Cologne desperately pressing forward, when the ball ran out of play close to where Clough and Taylor had pulled up a couple of plastic chairs to watch by the touchline (the Müngersdorfer didn't have orthodox dugouts). As the ball came their way, Clough jumped from his chair, ran to pick it up and handed it to one of the Cologne players, telling him it was his throw-in. How many other managers of that era would have been so sportsmanlike when the stakes were so high?

Clough explained later he 'couldn't be small-minded enough to let the ball run by' and was simply doing his job, just like he was the following week when Liverpool visited the City Ground and the man who had scored the goal to take Forest into the European Cup final found himself out of the team. Bowyer wasn't dropped because Clough wanted to keep him grounded; there was never any danger of Forest's match-winner getting too full of himself. It was simply that there was a million-pound signing to accommodate. 'No complaints,' Bowyer said, typically gracious. 'Trevor Francis is a better player than me and we want to beat Liverpool.'

By that stage, Forest had to win virtually all their remaining games to have any realistic hope of navigating a way back to the top of the league. There was no hint of a Liverpool collapse and Bob Paisley's team did to Forest that day what had happened the other way round earlier in the season: playing with control and stoicism and frustrating the home crowd. It finished goalless and when Forest lost their next game at Wolves that was effectively it. There was no way they would catch Liverpool from that position.

The disappointment was profound but, in another sense, it was still an achievement to finish with sixty points in a season when Forest, with all the cup ties totted up, ended up playing eleven more games than the team they were chasing. Forest had finished with four points fewer than the previous season, but their total would have been enough to win the league in five of the previous six years. It was also seven points higher than Dave Mackay's title-winning Derby side managed in 1975, and two more than Clough's Derby in 1972. Liverpool won the league with fifty-seven points in 1977 and Forest would also have finished ahead of the Merseyside club on goal difference if they had posted the same results in Paisley's first title year, 1976, and Shankly's last, 1973. The only team to accumulate a higher total in that period was the one Clough inherited from Revie – Leeds winning the league in 1974 with sixty-two points. No other side did it again before football moved to three points for a win in the 1981–82 season.

Liverpool, like all great champions, had dug in after losing their place at the top of English football and used as motivation the stabbing reminders from Clough that there had been a shift in power. 'Liverpool aren't the best club in the country,' Clough used to say, 'we are.' Clough often talked up Liverpool but, as he saw it, they had a patronising attitude towards Forest. They thought 'we were a group of country bumpkins who didn't deserve to be on the same pitch as them. That lot had enjoyed everything their own way for so long, they couldn't handle someone else pushing them out of the way to collect a trophy or two. They hated us for it.'

Liverpool had certainly been playing with a lot of pent-up frustration. They finished with sixty-eight points, a record under the two-points-for-a-win system, and conceded an all-time low of sixteen goals. Only four of those goals came at Anfield, where they scored fifty-one times. They also equalled Arsenal's 1935 record with a goal difference of plus sixty-nine and, in addition, matched two other records by winning nineteen games and taking forty points at home. Forest had finished in the second highest position in their history and it had needed one of the all-time performances to prevent them defending their title.

Clough's thoughts now turned to the European Cup final at Munich's Olympiastadion and facing a team that was trying to complete a miracle of their own. Malmo were unexpected opponents: a tall, physical team that Birtles later described as 'land of the giants'. Every single one of their players had been born within sixty miles of Malmo and their spirit of togetherness was supplemented with a parsimonious defence. Malmo had kept a clean sheet in six of their eight European ties, knocking out Monaco, Dynamo Kiev, Wisla Kraków and Austria Vienna in the process. Similar to Forest, they also gave the impression they were getting a thrill from the fact that nobody had given them a cat in hell's chance to get that far. Their manager, Bobby Houghton, was formerly Bobby Robson's assistant at Ipswich and had previously been player-manager at Maidstone in the Southern League, playing in defence alongside a young Roy Hodgson. One newspaper described Houghton as 'not even a household name in his own house'.

Forest knew from their own experience how much pleasure could be taken from making journalists eat their words, but when Taylor went to see Malmo they impressed him even less than Cologne. The Swedish side had not progressed beyond the second round of the European Cup in seven previous attempts. They had finished fourth in the *Allsvenskan* and were heavily reliant on set-pieces and a regimented offside trap.

Clough was not there when the team boarded St Eugene, their regular Aer Lingus plane, because he had already taken Barbara and the children on holiday to Crete, leaving Houghton to say he was amazed a manager could get away with that during the season, let alone in the run-up to such a monumental game.

At Forest, it was just the norm. The previous season, Clough missed not only a key First Division game against Norwich but also an FA Cup fifth-round replay at home to QPR. The second replay was arranged for a Thursday night three days later. Clough arrived five minutes before kickoff. 'There he was tanned and healthy but with a face like thunder,' Lloyd says. "You fucking bastards," he shouted. "You've dragged me back from Majorca to get you through this FA Cup tie against a load of shit from London." That was Clough's team-talk. We went out and beat QPR three-one.'

In fairness to Houghton, opposition managers often looked at the way Clough worked and found it slightly bewildering that the formula was so successful. In Cologne, the team had stayed at the Queen's Hotel, overlooking the Kahnweiher boating lake, and in the two days before the game it never really got any more onerous than hiring pedalos on the water. 'We didn't do any training,' Woodcock recalls. 'We didn't even go to the stadium until the night of the match. "We don't need to go to the stadium," Clough said. "It's only another stadium." We just went for a walk around a park. Cloughie loved a walk, of course. Then we got a room in the evening for a game of cards and it was a case of "Anyone for a glass of wine?" And, of course, Clough and Taylor would stand up to tell their stories, like they were Morecambe and Wise.'

When Woodcock played for Cologne later in his career they put him up at the same hotel while he was trying to find a house. 'I got chatting to the staff and they told me Cologne had printed posters asking their fans to go to Munich. "We were going," they said. "We saw your team come into the hotel. You didn't train, you just went for a walk. You didn't even go to the stadium. You stayed up late every night playing cards and drinking. We thought you had no chance. In fact, we were so convinced we put all our month's money on Cologne to beat you all." So they bet a fortune against us – and lost every penny.'

The hotel in Munich was on the road out to Augsburg and, again, there was the same philosophy in place: treat every trip like a mini-holiday. Taylor took them on a walk. They went out for a couple of nights, sank a few beers and found a bar with a jukebox that played Robertson's favourite Roxy Music. There were no curfews, no deadlines and no booze restrictions, as long as they had a good lie-in to sleep off any hangover and didn't bother the management with their bad heads. A freshly tanned Clough did not arrive until the day before the game, with his family in tow, and the team spent his first night sampling the local Piesporter and investigating whether it was true, as Mark Twain once said, that the only way to tell German wine from vinegar was by the label.

Clough had some key decisions the next day, though, because three of his players – Gemmill, O'Neill and Clark – were coming back from injuries.

Gemmill had been touch and go ever since he chased after Van Gool and was turned 'this way, that way and this again, to the extent I was spinning like a top when I felt my groin tear'. That was six weeks ago but Gemmill had been working like a demon to get fit and, a week before the final, he had played half an hour of the Nottinghamshire County Cup final against Mansfield without any soreness. 'Clough had made a promise to me. He said: "If you get fit, son, you will play in the final." It was fantastic for me. I thought to myself: "That's it now, I'm playing in the final." I'd played every match up until the semi-final and, as far as I was concerned, I was fine.'

Clark had been struggling with hamstring issues, while O'Neill was having intensive treatment after taking a whack on his thigh in a game against Manchester City. Frank Wignall, a Forest player from the 1960s, had put O'Neill in touch with a specialist who realised the bang had caused a haematoma. 'The doctor said he thought he could get me fit, but there were two things,' O'Neill says. 'One, it would need a series of injections and, two, he was so busy the only time he could see me was at five every morning. I hated injections but I had to do it. I was so desperate I went to see him for seven consecutive days at five in the morning. He injected my thigh and when he started working on my leg the pain was untrue. But finally we got to the stage where the doctor told me all I needed was a couple of days' rest and that I would be able to train when the team headed out to Germany.'

When Clough joined the team in Munich, he kept everyone guessing apart from one man. 'I was made up,' Bowyer says. 'He walked past me and quietly said: "I was going to play you at tennis today but I can't – you're in the team tomorrow." He just said it quietly so only I would hear.'

Trevor Francis did not have any assurances and was starting to fret. His first few months at the club had been frustrating at times, because of the number of games where he had been cup-tied. Most people had concluded, as difficult as it was to second-guess Clough, there was no way even the most unorthodox manager could leave out the most expensive footballer in history, but Francis could not take it for granted.

'I was sharing a room with McGovern on the day before the game and I can remember asking him if he had heard anything. "John, come on, you must know what the team is, the boss must have confided in you." John said he didn't have a clue. I spent the rest of the day reflecting on it and I worked out that nine players knew they were going to be playing. There were just a couple of doubts. Would O'Neill and Gemmill play if they were fit, or would Bowyer and myself play? I had friends and family who were anxious to know, asking whether they should make the long trip to Munich, but I couldn't say because I didn't know myself.

'We had dinner at seven o'clock and a meeting at eight o'clock. I thought: "At last, this is the moment." Instead we sat around drinking Liebfraumilch. We had a few glasses and Brian and Peter, as a partnership, were brilliant comedy. They just wanted to relax. Archie stood up and said: "Boss, can I go to bed?" Brian said: "I will let you know when you can go to bed, now sit down." We stayed up until 10.15pm – and still we didn't know the team.'

Clough put him out of his misery at eleven o'clock in the morning: Francis was in.

For the others, the tension was getting unbearable. 'The three of us were training,' Clark recalls, 'and we were all looking at each other because we knew that one or two of us were probably going to be disappointed. We knew deep down that Trevor was going to play. That was the first game in Europe in which he was eligible, so there was no doubt in our minds that he was going to play. But that left the three of us. I was thinking I could play left-back and Bowyer would be in midfield with Trevor on the right. Martin was thinking he could play in midfield and Bowyer would play left-back if I was out – and I was only 90 per cent. Archie was thinking the same. It was spinning in our heads and Clough left it literally until the morning of the game before he sat everyone down.'

Squatting on a football, Clough turned to O'Neill. 'You first – do you think you are fit?'

'Right as rain, gaffer,' O'Neill replied.

Clark said the same and then it was Gemmill's turn. 'Sure, boss, I can play – absolutely perfect.'

'Smashing,' Clough said. 'I'm delighted. But you are all lying and I can risk only one of you.'

He pointed at Clark. 'You're playing, Frank.'

Clark asked Clough a few years later how he had come to that decision when the left-back was probably the least fit of everyone. 'He told me that out of the three of us he thought I was the least likely to tell him lies. Basically, his decision said: "I can't trust you, Martin, or you, Archie, but I can trust you, Frank. I was delighted but the two of them were devastated – I mean, out of it, bitter.'

Gemmill was on his feet straight away. 'You must be fucking joking,' he shouted at Clough, in front of everyone.

O'Neill, not usually short of a word or two, had been stunned into silence, but Gemmill's reaction was of a man who believed Clough had reneged on a gentleman's agreement in the worst possible way. 'I exploded,' he remembers. 'It was a serious falling-out and a lot of things were said.'

Taylor eventually took him to one side and started trying to explain what a difficult decision it had been and how, in time, Gemmill would understand why they had to do it that way. That didn't work either. 'Don't give me all that bollocks,' Gemmill shouted. 'You and your mate are shitting on me.'

The argument raged on and off all day. Gemmill was

convinced he had been betrayed and there was a sour mood at the team hotel completely out of kilter with the ambience a few miles away in central Munich, where supporters were already splashing in the Wittelsbach fountain and getting stuck into the *helles* and *weizen* at the city's bierkellers.

Around 25,000 fans had made their way to Bavaria, the largest-ever following at that time for an English team abroad. Special flights had been laid on. Eight trains had been arranged and numerous coach trips. Birtles had one mate who raised the money for his trip by doing tricks in each bar. 'He stood on his head in one, drank a pint and ate a can of dog food. It sounds daft, and he's daft as a brush this lad, but they were desperate. They ended up sleeping outside the ground.'

Others had hitch-hiked, sticking out their thumbs on the A453, on the way out to the motorway, and holding up pieces of cardboard saying: 'Munich.' ATV filmed two fans setting off on a couple of Raleigh racing bikes that had been decorated in Forest regalia for the 1,700-mile round trip.

One guy who had gone on the run was a soldier who had been reported AWOL after going in search of a ticket. 'The soldier had deserted the army,' McGovern says. 'He didn't care about being arrested after the game, he just wanted to get to the final and see us win.' Then there was the story of Lloyd's brother, Ivan, and the kind of ingenuity that was needed in the days before players could whisk their families away in private jets and seven-star luxury. Ivan lived in Bristol. He worked for Rolls Royce at Filton Aerodrome and was struggling to afford the flight costs. 'He jumped a cargo plane,' Lloyd explains, with a proud smile. Ivan sat at the back of the plane, among the boxes of freight, getting a free ride to see his sibling in the biggest club match of them all.

At the team hotel, there was tension. The argument with Gemmill had not been a good start. O'Neill was in a daze, emotionally on the floor, and there were more harsh words before the bus set off for the ground. 'We were sitting outside on the terrace, ready to go, and Garry had a couple of days' growth on his face,' Woodcock recalls. 'Clough came down and straight away: "You've not shaven." Garry tried to explain. "When I sweat during games," he said, "I get a really sore rash if I have shaven and it distracts me." But Clough wasn't having any of it: "If you haven't shaved and you're not back down here within five minutes, you're not playing." Off Garry went. He was back within five minutes, but with cuts everywhere and little pieces of tissue paper soaking up all the blood. He was lucky he hadn't cut his throat.'

It sounds like a typical piece of Clough discipline, but Birtles believes there was more to it. 'I was more nervous that day than any other moment in my life apart from the birth of my kids,' he says. 'Clough told me he had some after-shave in his room and I could use that. Chris Woods had a razor in his bag. So, just before the biggest game of my life, I was running to the gaffer's room to find his shaving kit. I look back now and wonder what it was all about and I'm sure it was because he could see I was nervous. That was his way to take my mind off it and it was great man-management. I had no idea why he was so bothered, but taking me away from everything for a few minutes and providing that distraction did calm me down.'

Gemmill, however, was still raging and struggling to keep

251

his anger to himself. He was the last to get on board and occasionally his temper flared up again. O'Neill was lost in his own thoughts and the other players mostly sat in silence. It was a quiet journey – too quiet, for Clough's liking.

'Brian came down the bus,' Woodcock says. 'He had a bottle of beer in his hand. "Come on, lads, who wants a beer? Larry, have a swig of this." Larry wasn't keen. "No boss, not right now." We were unusually quiet, but then we saw these German fans giving us rude signs on the side of the road. One of them was concentrating so much on us he was walking, walking and then, bang, he had walked straight into a lamp post and knocked himself over. That broke the silence.'

Several crates of beer had been loaded on the coach and it was fortunate for Forest that UEFA did not operate a policy of breathalysers. Clough said later they would have been arrested if they had been fans travelling to a football ground with that much alcohol on board. 'Get stuck in, lads,' was the message from the front of the bus, 'but get rid of the bottles when we're near to the ground.'

But it didn't entirely shift the mood. Forest had thrived for so long on proving everyone wrong it suddenly felt odd and a bit unsettling that everybody now expected them to win. They ought to have been disposing of Malmo easily, but it was exactly that knowledge that created anxiety.

Clough used to preach that a player's first touch set the standard and even some of his more reliable men seemed uptight. Burns began with a jittery header that was meant to go back to Shilton but landed instead on the foot of the Malmo striker Jon Olav Kindrall, who was taken by surprise and made a mess of the shot. Burns, Clough used to say, was as cocksure playing Liverpool as he would be Lincoln – 'he didn't give a toss about anybody or anything.' But that night was possibly the first time an occasion got to Burns. 'I'm from Glasgow, I grew up playing in the streets,' he says. 'Never in my lifetime did I think I would play in a European Cup final.'

After that, Malmo rarely ventured forward, preferring instead to defend in numbers and stifle Forest's creativity, then sporadically trying to hit them on the break. Forest never looked in any danger again, but they were finding it difficult to get through. Every time Robertson had the ball, there were two opposition players in close proximity. It had been a long, hard season and, friendlies included, Forest had played in over seventy games. It was a warm, sticky evening and the match, as so often happened in European Cup finals, was struggling for any real spark.

The ignition came just before half-time. Bowyer had the ball in the centre-circle and, instinctively, he knew to go to the left. Robertson was in his usual spot and that was the first time that he had a couple of yards of space. 'It nearly went out of play, I nearly didn't keep it in. It was the first time a ball had come to me from over five or ten yards. Then I thought: "Well, this is my chance, I'll have a little go here." And, of course, the greyhound was coming up on the other side.'

That greyhound was wearing a red shirt emblazoned with the number seven and desperate to justify his place in the team. 'The world was watching,' Francis says. 'I felt under a lot of pressure that night. Brian Clough had made what he would consider a big decision leaving out Martin O'Neill but, for me, it was a huge decision. I knew I had to justify my selection that night by playing at an extra level.'

Clough used to keep a framed photograph in his study to capture, in a few seconds of frozen time, what happened next. That picture, he used to say, did not just show his finest hour. It also captured both ends of his managerial spectrum. 'One player who had been nursed, cajoled, sometimes bullied but mostly encouraged to the top of his profession, and another who was a thoroughbred even before he came under our influence.'

Robertson's two nearest opponents tried to gang up on him. The first one was the full-back Roland Andersson and immediately he was gesturing for his team-mate Robert Prytz to back him up. Robertson shifted to come inside, where Bowyer was surging forward. He went to go on his right foot and the Malmo players tried to hold him up. But it was a deception. Robertson came back on his left. He was going round the outside and that half-ambling, half-shuffling approach had turned into a surprising change of speed close to the corner flag.

To Robertson's right, every Forest attacker was on the move, anticipating the cross even before he had beaten his men. 'I was probably a good forty or fifty yards from goal when he took possession,' Francis says. 'It was always drummed into me that when the ball was on the left, and particularly when Robertson had possession, it was my responsibility to get to the far post. I knew I had to start sprinting the moment he got the ball, and I had to get into that box because if he went past the full-back, which there was a good chance he would, and delivered the ball when I wasn't there, we were only a minute away from half-time. It hadn't been a great first half. I would have been going in to get another dressing-down from Brian Clough, and you didn't need too many of them.'

McGovern was another ten yards back and had seen Robertson do that trick so many times before. 'It was his usual shimmy – he went one way, the two defenders went the same way and, all of a sudden, he was going the other way. The two defenders were very close together. They fell for it in tandem and then the player we always wanted on the ball had half a yard.'

That was all Robertson needed and that was the moment, on the opposite side of the pitch, Taylor tensed in his seat and grabbed hold of Clough's arm, as if he knew instinctively that something special was about to happen. Birtles was in the penalty area. Woodcock was making up ground to get in there. Francis was coming up on the right and there was one thing about Robertson they all knew: he rarely wasted a cross.

The trajectory was perfect, the ball whipped over by Robertson's left foot to the far post, and for a moment it was tantalising enough for Birtles to think about going for it. 'It was the last second when I realised the ball was just too high for me. I caught a flash of red in my eye. And I knew I had to hang back a little bit.'

The flash of colour was Francis and that was the moment, in the biggest game of his life, the first million-pound footballer on the planet repaid every single penny. Nobody had picked up his run. Malmo had six players back in the penalty area against three attackers. But the left-back Ingemar Erlandsson was young and inexperienced and had lost his man and, in the commentary positions, Barry Davies's voice had gone up an octave. 'Well, that's what I wanted to see Robertson do . . .'

The rest of the story could be told in different noises: the thud of ball against forehead, the wonderful zip of ball hitting net and then the crowd, gathering in what they had seen, with a great, euphoric roar. Francis had never taken his eyes off the ball. He landed on the shot-putters' circle where seven years earlier Geoff Capes had been heaving one of those metal balls skywards in the Olympics. The next time Francis looked up there were team-mates running towards him from various directions. The ball was in the net. The miracle had happened and 25,000 people holding up their home-made banners for 'Forest Mash Swedes' and 'Robertson Eats Malmolade' were in the vortex of one of the greatest moments of their lives.

Chapter Ten
Clough's Bionic Bubble

'Look at the Swedes of Malmo. They were not even a Third
Division side in England but if their forwards had been
anything at all they would have cashed in on a terrible mistake
by Kenny Burns. The outcome may have been something
different from Nottingham Forest's dreary 1–0 win.'
Emlyn Hughes

Brian Clough wasn't there when the open-top bus parade set
off on the journey to the Old Market Square in Nottingham.
Clough had flown back to Crete to resume his holiday. Peter
Taylor wasn't around either, but the more troubling part for
the players was that, a mile into the journey, they hadn't seen
a single supporter and were starting to suspect the whole thing
might be a terrible let-down. 'This is bloody embarrassing,' Larry
Lloyd announced, looking at the empty streets. There was
nobody around the next corner either and the pavements were
so deserted Lloyd and John Robertson sneaked downstairs at
the next traffic lights, jumped off and ran a hundred yards
down the road without anyone seeing. When the bus caught
up, they launched into a chant of 'We won the cup' from the
side of the road. What a photograph that would have been:
two players from a European Cup-winning side pretending to
be supporters because nobody else had shown up.

As it turned out, the team hadn't been stood up. They had
set off from Holme Pierrepont, four miles outside the city,

and the television cameras caught the moment when the crowds came into view. 'There's people,' Lloyd started shouting, 'People!' Lots of people, in fact. They reckon the turnout that day was over a quarter of a million, in a city with a 300,000 population. People had scaled lamp posts, spires and every other possible vantage point. They were hanging out of balconies and branches. They threw scarves, flags, flowers and even the occasional item of underwear at the group of men waving from the top deck. Amplifiers had been positioned by open windows to blast out the Paper Lace song. Passing drivers sounded their horns to create another soundtrack: one, two; one, two, three; one, two, three, four – Forest! Policemen wore rosettes. A convoy of joggers, cyclists and motorbikes, even a few roller-skaters, followed the bus across Trent Bridge and when it finally inched its way into the square the sea of red went back as far as the eye could see. Lloyd looked close to tears. 'I didn't know there were that many people in Nottingham,' he said.

A now-familiar banner – 'Clough's Bionic Bubble Will Never Burst' – had been attached to the walls of the Council House, the building that dominates the square. Other banners were held up by the crowd. 'Martin O'Neill is Magic', one read, and he waved appreciatively from the double-decker with the registration plate 'Nottingham Forest FC'. O'Neill was still full of raw emotion. The previous forty-eight hours had been difficult for him, but he had made an effort to snap out of his depression. Those were the moments, seeing close-up the euphoria of the city, when he started to feel a part of it again. 'I'd seen footage of Aston Villa winning the FA Cup back in 1957 and taking the trophy back to Birmingham. I remembered the great Tottenham Hotspur sides having these parades. I used to think they happened only to other people. That particular night, when it happened to us, all I could think was: "This is what it's all about. We've won promotion, we've won the championship and we've won the European Cup. We're not two-bit players any more, we're big news." If you had seen me by the time we got to the city centre, you might have thought I had scored a hat-trick in the final.'

Nottingham had become the smallest city ever to win the European Cup and it was starting to feel like a trick of the mind that it was only two years and thirty-five days earlier, on 23 April 1977, that Forest had lost 1–0 at home to Cardiff City in the Second Division. Some of those fans had been there at Hull and Carlisle and York, when Clough and Forest were beaten every time, or the numerous occasions when the City Ground rang with moans and groans and it felt like all the fun was happening elsewhere.

Forest weren't even the best side in Nottingham when Clough took the job. Could it possibly be true that in his first season at the club they had lost 4–2 to a Bristol Rovers team who were second bottom in the Second Division? Or that six months later, they went back to the run-down Eastville stadium in Bristol and lost by the same score again? What odds could a punter have obtained back then that John McGovern, the number four for Forest in both those games, would be carrying the European Cup around the Olympic stadium in Munich four years later?

The whole landscape of English football had shifted and the knock-on effect had polished up the crown for the city known as the Queen of the Midlands. In the space of a few years, a football team had brought glamour and vibrancy to Nottingham in a way that had never been seen before. 'The city had changed with the team,' Lloyd says, and the players were having to acquire new tastes because of that change. Lloyd sums it up rather nicely: 'Instead of buying you a pint of lager, like they did at the start, they were buying you a vodka and coke.'

Nottingham was no longer just the city of Robin Hood, DH Lawrence, Raleigh bikes, John Player's cigarettes and Boots the Chemist. It had a new badge to wear and, in the process, it felt like an entire city had grown in stature. Football hadn't given Nottingham much in the previous century but, corny as it sounds, that was precisely why the homecoming was so special. The world and his wife had turned up to see the European Cup – seventy-four centimetres tall, eleven kilogrammes in weight and, in the words of John Robertson, 'bloody heavy' – and every one of those supporters who had travelled across Europe to follow their team had a story to tell on the back of it.

One fan, Barry Whiting, was so overcome by emotion in Munich that when the final whistle sounded he dropped down to one knee and proposed to his girlfriend, Lynne.

'So many miles we travelled for it, and so many memories,' another supporter, Margaret Leyden, wrote in a programme article that neatly summed up the adventures. 'Athens, where we expected aggro and found friendliness and hospitality, where the air was full of Greek music and there was that sudden magical glimpse of the Acropolis. Zurich, crisp and clear, with its cobbled streets, cow bells and Alpine horns. Cologne, where we went into the soaring perfection of the cathedral and found it full of Trent Enders, all behaving impeccably. Munich, that perfect day, and the finish so reminiscent of the Olympic games, with a seemingly endless conga made up of Forest and Malmo supporters. And Anfield, where we had a brick through our window.'

For McGovern, it was a long cry from those days at Leeds when he was convinced his team-mates were deliberately underhitting passes to him or, going even further back, the times at Hartlepools on the bottom rung of the football ladder, earning £18 a week at a club where any season where they didn't have to apply for re-election, or concede over a hundred goals, was thought of as a golden age.

'People asked me after I lifted the trophy why I wasn't smiling,' McGovern says. 'I was smiling, but I was also thinking about my dad. My dad died when I was eleven and never saw me play football. That was the first thing that came into my head: "I wish my dad was here, he might have been proud of me." My mum was there to share the glory but I loved my dad, as all boys do, and I just had that thought in my head. Plus I was also thinking: "What am I doing here?"'

That last line is not McGovern being flippant. As he went to collect the trophy from UEFA's president Artemio Franchi he genuinely did not know what to do. 'I just wanted to get my hands on it as quickly as possible. I reached for it but then I pulled my hands back, because I didn't want to be rude. I mean, what is the protocol? He went to give me it and then he changed his mind as well. We did a little dance and then eventually I got it. People ask me: "Was it heavy?" You could have put an elephant in it, I would still have lifted it.'

McGovern was still thinking clearly enough to turn the

trophy around to 'show our supporters the UEFA badge and do it the right way' and, as handovers go, it was smoother than when he was injured for the League Cup final against Liverpool and the honour fell to Kenny Burns, the stand-in skipper. Burns always kept his dentures in a piece of tissue and asked whoever was substitute to look after them on the bench. On that night at Old Trafford, they went missing. It was a classic Burns story: the first major trophy of Clough's reign and the man holding the silverware was posing with wild, longish hair and no front teeth, looking like Shane MacGowan after a particularly rough night.

Andrew Longmore, the distinguished *Times* correspondent, called Forest the 'Dirty Dozen' because of the way Clough, taking the role of Lee Marvin, had somehow – by good fortune, genius, an act of God, call it what you will – turned a group of mavericks, renegades and novices into a crack fighting unit. 'Forest had their share of misfits. All were strong characters, none had reputations for being ideal club men. They also had their share of raw recruits. They were led by a man whose idea of discipline was to make a man play for forty-five minutes with a suspected broken foot and whose idea of punishment was to send his entire first-team squad through a field of nettles. Above all, like the Dirty Dozen, they developed the street-fighting mentality of the perpetual underdog. Nothing was expected of them so they had nothing to lose.'

They were certainly the most unpretentious bunch of European Cup winners there had ever been, even if nobody was driving around with a Shipstone's Brown Ales beer mat as a tax disc any longer. Robertson had developed a taste for

Martini and lemonades – 'with an umbrella,' Burns says, disdainfully – but the team still travelled to some away games on the same train as their fans and on the way home the usual suspects often sneaked down to the rowdier carriages for a crafty swig from the coke or lemonade bottles that had been topped up with various spirits.

Clough also insisted they walked to and from the ground if wherever they were playing was not too far away from the train station. It did almost backfire one day at Southampton when some of the local hooligans turned up looking for a ruck, but Forest had some formidable characters among their support and chased them off. 'Get the bastards,' one of the players shouted, as all hell broke loose.

Peter Shilton, meanwhile, was never allowed to forget the time everyone went out for dinner at one of Nottingham's finer restaurants and he was given the menu to order first. Shilton wasn't feeling that hungry. 'I'll have some of the hors,' he told the waiter, 'but none of the d'oeuvre.'

A new stand was slowly taking shape; so slowly, in fact, the disgruntled builders waited to have it out with Clough after he complained publicly about 'the steel erectors being slower than my back four'. The new construction had executive boxes, polished tables and lucrative advertising space and, as a little piece of trivia, it was the first stand in English football where the relevant team's name was spelt out in the seat colours.

A new trophy cabinet was also being installed because, as Ken Smales explained, there had 'hardly been an inch to spare' for the sudden influx of silverware. The old one didn't contain much aside from a smallish replica of the FA Cup and a framed copy of the cheque representing Forest's share of the Wembley gate receipts: £11,402 6d, dated 11 June 1959 and drawn at Barclays Bank, Pall Mall. There was a ball signed by the Busby Babes, various old programmes and pennants and a photograph of Forest's first FA Cup-winning team, from 1898, proudly showing off the trophy even though they were wearing Derby County shirts.

It's a wonderful story. The photographer that day, for reasons that are unclear, had asked both teams to pose with the cup before the match so there would be a suitable picture whatever the result. Perhaps he had another appointment later in the day or maybe he just didn't want to hang around. Or maybe it was because of nineteenth-century photographic etiquette that the picture should be a formal occasion rather than eleven men in muddy kits. Whatever the explanation, the photographer was concerned that Forest's red tops would not stand out well enough in black-and-white, so he arranged for them to borrow Derby's white shirts. So Forest's first great moment of triumph was captured for posterity before a ball had even been kicked and with them wearing the colours of the enemy. It's no wonder they do not look very happy.

Forest had been revolutionised on the pitch. And yet, the champions of Europe still did not have a designated training ground, or even a gymnasium, and were turfed off their usual practice area more than once when it was being prepared for various junior tournaments. 'After that, we just had to set off walking and find where we could,' McGovern recalls. The players were even known to relocate sometimes to RAF Newton, ten miles away, to use an airfield where there was once a bomber base and training school for the Second World War.

Meanwhile Ginger the cat had been spending too much time with one of the local strays and was due to have a litter, meaning the rodent numbers were rising again, as were mice droppings on the terraces.

As for Forest's idea of sports science, it was nothing more refined than standing on the scales every Friday morning while Jimmy Gordon jotted down the different weights to keep track of each player. If someone went up two or three pounds, it might get back to Clough. If it was a smaller increase – one pound or below – the player would normally get away it. 'That's just a good shit,' Lloyd used to say.

The challenge for Forest in the 1979–80 season, the silver jubilee of the European Cup, was whether they could have some more of – to use Gordon's favourite saying – the 'good-to-be-alive days' and show it was no fluke by joining the exclusive band of half a dozen clubs who had successfully defended the trophy. Liverpool had been the last to do it and the other five were Bayern Munich, Ajax, Internazionale, Benfica and Real Madrid.

Nottingham felt like a happy place, but there was one passenger on that open-top bus who was suffering badly and struggling, even for one night, to fake a smile. Archie Gemmill had felt so betrayed he hadn't even bothered with the celebrations and trophy presentation in Munich. Gemmill went down the tunnel at the final whistle and when he was back in the dressing room he let rip at Clough one more time. He never played for Forest again.

'We came into pre-season and that was it,' Gemmill says. 'Peter Taylor took me into the office and said: "You're finished here." The boss was on holiday, so I didn't even get the chance to speak to him. It was just a case of "You're off." It was short, sharp and to the point. They showed me who was boss. But I could see their point of view. It was a serious falling-out. I had made it pretty plain what I thought and they had the ultimate say.'

Gemmill moved to Birmingham City, dropping down to the Second Division, and it was a sadly unsatisfactory way to sour everything he had achieved in Forest's colours. Asa Hartford arrived from Manchester City for £500,000, more than three times the amount Birmingham paid for Gemmill, but it quickly become apparent to Clough and Taylor that the signing was a mistake and they didn't hang around rectifying it. Hartford lasted sixty-three days in total. Forest did recoup most of their money when he signed for Everton, but it left them with a gap in midfield and when Clough tried to fix the problem it was too late.

'I'd been at Birmingham five or six weeks when, one Sunday morning, the phone rang,' Gemmill says. 'My wife picked it up and shouted to me: "The boss is on the phone for you." I couldn't work out why Jim Smith was phoning me. But it was Clough. "I've made a mistake, son. I want you back here and I'll double your money to make it happen." I said to him: "You've shit on me once, you ain't going to do it again." He said: "Is that how you genuinely feel?" And I said "Yeah." I could have gone back to play in another European Cup but I had to make a stance.'

Football can be a hard-faced business sometimes but the

two men did eventually make their peace, even if it was another eight years before they came across one another at a charity match and Clough casually invited Gemmill to join Forest's coaching staff, as if there had never been an issue. In later years, they even became friends. Clough wrote the foreword to Gemmill's autobiography, overlooking the fact the thirteenth chapter was called 'Humiliation by Clough', and went about as close as he ever got to a sniff of an apology. 'Perhaps I'm trying to make amends for some of the rotten things I did to him,' Clough wrote, 'but anyway, he's still here, sitting in my front room, having a cup of tea.'

Gemmill became a pivotal player in Birmingham's promotion season with that scurrying, selfless style of his and the quick, size-six feet that will always be feted in Scotland because of that never-forgotten moment in the 1978 World Cup when he picked up a loose ball on the right of the Dutch penalty area, came inside Wim Jansen's lunge, beat Ruud Krol on the outside, pushed the ball between Jan Poortvliet's legs and lifted it over the advancing goalkeeper Jan Jongbloed for a goal of such beauty that, twenty years later, it was turned into a ballet.

John O'Hare had already been converted into a central midfielder and Forest did, of course, have Ian Bowyer to assume Gemmill's role alongside McGovern. Bowyer was a popular figure among the other players, who had nicknamed him 'Cheshire champion' for having the temerity to give Clough a good thrashing at tennis one day. Clough stormed off the court in a fit of pique but, deep down, admired his player's nerve, and his opinion of Bowyer was so high that a few years later he made him captain for one game against

Chelsea even though he was only a substitute. Bowyer duly went out to the middle, swapped pennants with the opposition captain and then trotted back to the bench.

Bowyer scored both goals when Forest began their European Cup defence in September 1979 against another Swedish side, Oesters Växjo, taking a 2–0 lead into the return leg and safely getting through to the second round, even though there was a period during the return leg when they were losing 1–0 and looking slightly vulnerable. Woodcock's equaliser effectively settled it and Forest returned to their dressing room with a 3–1 aggregate win to find out that, once again, they were England's last representatives in the competition. Liverpool had been drawn against Dinamo Tbilisi and nobody could have imagined what an ordeal it would become. They won the first leg 2–1 at Anfield, but the 3–0 defeat in Georgia sent reverberations throughout Europe. Forest's supporters could belt out their 'One team in Europe' song for another season and Clough, magnificently thick-skinned and convinced of his own greatness, was even more full of himself than usual. 'Success hasn't changed Peter and I,' he said. 'We were arrogant at the bottom of the league and we are arrogant at the top – and that is consistency.'

They were drawn against Arges Pitesti in the second round and two up inside fifteen minutes, courtesy of Woodcock and Birtles, with other chances to win by more after one of the Romanians was sent off. One of the banners in the return leg, deep in Dracula country, showed Vlad the Impaler looking suitably menacing, with the message 'Sorry for you Nottingham', but goals from Bowyer and Birtles secured a 4–1 aggregate win. Forest had now gone thirteen games unbeaten in Europe, breaking the record set in the late 1950s by the Real Madrid side of Di Stefano, Puskas and Gento.

There was also the small matter of testing themselves against another of Europe's genuine superpowers in the Super Cup. Barcelona had just signed Allan Simonsen, the former European footballer of the year, and had won the European Cup Winners' Cup by beating Fortuna Dusseldorf 4–3 in the final. They brought a cast of category-A stars to the City Ground for the first leg but maybe didn't know what they were letting themselves in for when they asked to use Forest's training pitch on the day before the match. When the bus carrying Barcelona's team pulled up, Clough's players had just finished their own warm-up and were making their way off. The sight of their opponents gingerly tiptoeing their way through the nettles caused much amusement. 'I don't speak much Spanish,' Shilton remembers, 'but from the expressions on their faces I reckon they were surprised a team that had won the European Cup trained in a public park watched by people walking their dogs.'

The following night, there was a photograph of Clough and Taylor on the front of the programme surrounded by Forest's new trophy collection and emptying bottles of champagne into the European Cup. Forest won 1–0 and the scorer was Charlie George, which has become a pub-quiz question over the years given that most people have forgotten, or never knew, that the man who scored Arsenal's winner in the 1971 FA Cup final ever played for Clough.

George was on a month-long loan from Southampton and in his four games for Forest there were only glimpses of his mercurial talent, or indeed the rebellious streak that once saw him headbutt Kevin Keegan during a game against Liverpool and flick a V-sign at Derby's fans at the Baseball Ground (with Clough and Taylor in the home dugout). He took his goal nicely, though, and it certainly gave Forest a spicy edge to have him in the same team as Stan Bowles, another player who would walk straight into the top ten of talented yet temperamental 1970s football mavericks. Bowles, once voted QPR's best-ever player, had a reputation for gambling and disorder and had fallen out with their new manager, Tommy Docherty, famously declaring that 'I'd rather trust my chickens with Colonel Sanders' than trust the former Derby boss. He cost Forest £250,000 and Clough had so much autonomy within the club at that point that when Bowles arrived in Nottingham for talks, it quickly became apparent to him that nobody on the committee had the foggiest idea why he was there.

The vice-chairman Geoffrey MacPherson – a man Clough called Dame Margaret Rutherford, because of the way he shared her 'spaniel jowls' – arrived at one point and Bowles remembers Clough turning up two hours late. 'The first thing he said to MacPherson was: "We're trying to sign Stan Bowles." MacPherson's head seemed to drop back against the wall and he went as white as a sheet. He muttered: "Oh, my good God." I thought he was going to have a heart attack.'

Bowles quickly established he had joined an excellent passing side and won the only medal of his career at Forest. Carlos Roberto's penalty put Barcelona ahead in the Super Cup second leg, levelling the final 1–1 on aggregate for a team with a reported bonus of £1,750 a man to win. Forest couldn't afford any bonuses at all, but what price the prestige of out-passing Barcelona on their own ground? Robertson, so nerveless usually from the penalty spot, had a rare miss after the referee pointed to the spot in the second half, but a Burns header was the reward for Forest's superior play and another trophy was added to the collection.

There were 90,000 fans inside Camp Nou and, by the end, a good number of them had resorted to the *panolada*, the in-stadium protest where fans wave white handkerchiefs to signify they don't like what they are seeing. They weren't used to seeing another team lifting a trophy on their pitch and when the Forest players left the stadium in the early hours a crowd of locals was waiting outside.

McGovern feared the worst. 'There were two rows of Barcelona fans, about eight deep, all the way from the exit to our coach. They were all very quiet and I thought: "We could be in trouble here." It was then they started clapping. We walked to our coach and they clapped us all the way. Not a Forest fan in sight, all Barcelona fans. Clapping us out of their own stadium.'

McGovern had also received a compliment of sorts from Clough that night. 'I'd done pretty well. I could tell he was going to say something and I was thinking it had to be praise. "McGovern" – and as soon as he said that I knew it wasn't a good sign. If it was "skipper" I was okay. But "McGovern" was a warning sign. "McGovern, you were our fourth best player tonight." He didn't say who the other three were. He just left it at that and I sat there thinking: "Thanks boss, you really know how to make me feel brilliant."'

By that point, another trophy had come Forest's way in the form of the European Inter-Club Cup, otherwise known as 'Le Challenge Européen', the competition France Football set up to go with the Ballon d'Or to nominate Europe's team of the year. Clough could not attend the presentation at the Paris Lido because Forest had a League Cup tie against Middlesbrough, so it was left to various members of the committee. 'Isn't it sickening receiving all those trophies?' Smales asked in the next programme, before answering his own question. 'Like John Wayne used to say: "The hell it is."'

Forest had won twenty-seven points from the judges, with Ajax in second on twenty-one and Liverpool, the previous winners, on seventeen, one ahead of Barcelona. Garry Birtles, the first player in history to go from Sunday league to winning the European Cup, had been named footballer of the year by the Union of European Journalists, but it was perplexing that none of Forest's players was on the shortlist for the Ballon d'Or. Birtles, for instance, finished his first season of regular top-flight football with twenty-five goals to go with the medal bearing the words 'Coupe Des Clubs Champions Européens', whereas it always mystified Clough and everyone else at Forest that Robertson was never appreciated more widely. At least the Forest supporters knew what they had. On their way to one game the team's coach was overtaken by a minibus of hardcore Reds. The message daubed on their minibus was: 'Robbo lays on more balls than Fiona Richmond'.

Forest had eased into the last eight of the European Cup and the City Ground had become such a fortress it felt almost implausible that it was bottom-of-the-table Brighton who finally reminded them what it was like to lose a league game at home. Forest had gone two years and seven months without experiencing that feeling. The run was remarkable: fifty-one games incorporating thirty-four wins and seventeen draws, with ninety-one goals scored and only twenty-three going in at the other end. Brighton's 1–0 win was a sensation.

It did, however, accompany a run of six away matches in the league when Forest lost their way and were beaten every time, including a 4–1 defeat at Southampton and even worse, the same again at fourth-from-bottom Derby. That was the period Cologne came in for Tony Woodcock, signing him for £650,000 and trebling his wages to £75,000 a year, and for the first time in a long while there was uncertainty. The results had been erratic and Forest were such a tightly knit group it was unsettling for the other players to see one of their own leaving.

Frank Clark had gone at the start of the season, moving to Sunderland as assistant manager, and taking a European Cup medal to remind him he probably made the right choice not going to Doncaster Rovers four years earlier. Clark had made a nonsense of Newcastle's decision to push him out of St James' Park and left Forest after 117 appearances with the honour of being, indisputably, the best free transfer in the history of the club.

Frank Gray was brought in from Leeds to replace him at left-back and, though the changes were not wholesale, it was not a seamless process. Asa Hartford played only three games before he was shipped out. Gemmill was missed and it didn't help that Trevor Francis had a pre-existing agreement to play in the NASL for Detroit Express during the summer and suffered a groin injury while he was out there.

Midway through the season, there was also an attempt to make Martin O'Neill the £250,000 makeweight in a £750,000 deal to sign Mick Ferguson from Coventry. O'Neill went as far as signing the transfer form, only for Clough and Taylor to get cold feet for reasons that were never properly explained and send Ferguson home again. O'Neill was kept on, but the episode reinforced his view that Clough would shift him out without even a backward glance.

As for Stan Bowles, he had won the only medal of his career and made his debut in one of the biggest games of club football but it took only a couple of months before his relationship with Clough had deteriorated to the point of collapse. After one game, Clough was asked how Bowles had played and replied: 'Was Stanley out there today?' Bowles was not the kind to accept Clough's putdowns and he wasn't hugely impressed either to discover his role in the team was to play in central midfield, as opposed to his favoured right-sided position, with the main purpose of getting the ball to Robertson. He and Robertson had become friends, but Bowles didn't appreciate being 'the monkey to Robbo's organ grinder' and knew it was pointless trying to change Clough's mind. 'Cloughie, like some of the great but misguided Roman emperors, thought he was God. No, he *knew* he was God. You had to make an appointment through his secretary's secretary to see him. He would sign players without the chairman's knowledge. No one seemed to mind. In short, he did what he bloody well liked.'

The same could be said of Bowles given the circumstances

that eventually persuaded Clough to cut his losses and move him out at the end of the season, but, to give the player his due, he was not the only one who would have been taken aback by the daily routines employed by the newly crowned European champions.

'I was surprised to find there was very little opportunity to practise tactical moves,' Bowles says. 'In fact, there were no tactics at Forest. Training consisted of walking along the Trent three times a week to a public park, where we had a warm-up game and then an eight-a-side match which was occasionally attended by Clough and Taylor, usually when Peter wanted to take his dog for a walk. The dog, Bess, also attended team meetings. Kenny Burns used to stand on it when Taylor wasn't looking and make it yelp.'

Forest won their opening four league games, including a 4–1 defeat of Coventry and a 5–1 win at West Brom, as well as beating Liverpool in their first meeting of the season. After that, though, their league form tailed off and it was a considerable disappointment to drop as low as fifth by the end of the season. Their long unbeaten run in the League Cup also came to an end, even if the competition did give them another chance to needle Liverpool. Forest had beaten Blackburn, Middlesbrough, Bristol City and West Ham to reach the semi-finals, where they were drawn against the league champions. Robertson's last-minute penalty gave Forest a 1–0 lead to take into the away leg. Robertson then scored another penalty at Anfield and David Fairclough's consolation effort came so late it was little more than an afterthought. Forest had reached their third successful final in the competition and when the two sides met at Anfield in the league Robertson, cocky as it gets, warmed up in front of the Kop by walking up to the penalty spot and miming another successful kick and celebration.

Liverpool won that game 2–0 and also knocked Forest out of the FA Cup by the same score, but the *Daily Telegraph* was slightly off-beam when its correspondent predicted it was only a matter of time before the Merseyside club scored 'a bagful' in one of those fixtures. That was another one for Smales's cuttings book. The reality was that from Boxing Day 1977 to 22 January 1980, Liverpool failed to score in eight of their ten meetings against Forest.

Forest played Wolves in the League Cup final and Clough was put out to discover that their opponents had got in first to book the hotel where his team usually stayed. Clough saw the opportunity to play some mind games and John Barnwell, the Wolves manager, told the story later about how on the morning of the match he was idly looking out of the lounge window when a bus pulled up and the wives and children of the Forest players spilled out, informing the concierge they had a group booking in the restaurant. 'Cloughie had sent them there to disconcert me,' Barnwell said. 'He knew that I'd want peace and quiet for my players, not a bunch of kids screaming in the foyer. I went berserk. He'd disturbed me and he would have known I'd be thrown off my job.'

A few hours later, Barnwell tried to get his own back by leaving Clough waiting in the tunnel before kickoff. When the bell went to signal it was time for the players to line up, Barnwell kept everyone back. 'At the third time of asking, I led my players out of the dressing room into the tunnel and I went to the head, looking for Cloughie. Blow me, he'd done me again – Jimmy Gordon was leading out Forest and Cloughie was already sitting on the bench by the halfway line.'

Forest had gone twenty-five matches unbeaten in the competition, going back three and a half years, but it came to an end that day because of a collision between Shilton and Needham that left Andy Gray with a tap-in for the game's only goal. Lloyd had been Forest's outstanding player in the first six months of the season, but he had gone over the disciplinary points and lost his appeal against the suspension. Needham was an accomplished deputy, but he and Shilton crashed into each other going for a high ball and it was a wretched way to lose a final.

From then on, Europe became the priority and a pattern was now established whereby each trip was regarded as a city-break – very often, one of near stag-do proportions – and a group of mostly twenty-something men set about preparing for some of the biggest matches in the football calendar with some enthusiastic drinking and the mentality to expect anything.

The quarter-finals pitted Forest against Dynamo Berlin and they travelled into the Eastern Bloc with some trepidation. Their first view of Schoenefeld airport was a shock, with its Russian aircraft and at least twenty field guns pointing skywards. Smales was then interrogated at passport control, because the visa officials had expected one more player (Burns was injured and stayed at home), but the real commotion was when Robertson ambled through with his bag over his shoulder and a book under his arm. Robertson, a bookworm, always liked to learn about the countries he was visiting. On this occasion, his choice of reading – a history book with a large blood-red swastika on the front – was probably not the wisest. Robertson was grilled for thirty minutes in an interview room before the East German authorities decided he could go. The book, however, was *verboten*.

It was not the only thing Robertson lost on that trip, either. His insistence on wearing his favourite pair of orange-brown loafers had been a standing joke for years. Those shoes had clocked up thousands of miles. The suede had virtually all rubbed off, leaving them with a greasy sheen, and yet he had hung on to them like a dear old friend. 'Those hush puppies had soaked up rivers of liquid, notably rainwater, beer and piss during their loyal service,' Bowles remembers. 'Eventually Peter Taylor got so fed up he wrenched them off Robbo and lobbed them high over the Berlin Wall. As the lads watched them sail over, we half-expected them to be tossed straight back by a dissatisfied German tramp. As they didn't return, we can only assume they contributed to the collapse of Communism.' Bowles, presumably, heard this story from the other players; he hadn't turned up himself at the airport, explaining later that he was terrified of flying but not thinking to let Clough know in advance.

Forest had lost the home leg 1–0 to spark the same kind of inquests that assumed they were dead and buried against Cologne. Again, they put on a brilliant performance in the away leg. It was a bitterly cold night in Berlin and Clough told his players to leave the dressing room with deliberate uprightness, straight-backed and unconcerned by the Arctic temperatures. Dynamo's players, in contrast, had warmed up in gloves and tights. Taylor had already been outside to snoop on Forest's opponents, reporting back that they looked frightened, and Clough wanted to get into their heads some more.

Forest put three goals past the six-foot-seven goalkeeper Bodo Rudwaleit inside the first half, Francis scoring two of them and Robertson adding a penalty, and Clough opted for a different tack when his players came in, euphoric, at the interval. 'Sit down and none of you say a word,' he instructed. For the next ten minutes there was absolute silence, punctuated only by Francis giggling under his breath at the silliness of it all. Dynamo pulled one back early in the second half with a penalty of their own, but Forest held out against some concerted late pressure to leave with an exceptional result.

To others, Forest's preparations might seem barmy sometimes. On the day before they played Ajax in the first leg of the semi-final, Clough gave everyone a day off to go shopping or to the races. Clough had a day at home and Taylor went to Scarborough. Forest won 2–0 with another goal from Francis and another Robertson penalty, and when the team arrived in Amsterdam for the second leg they spent the night before the match on a tour of the red-light district. Taylor went through the charade of trying to negotiate a group booking for one of the shows – 'there's seventeen of us, you know' – and Clough ordered the eighteen-year-old Gary Mills, the youngest member of the squad, to approach one window and find out how much everything cost.

Clough gave the embarrassed teenager a pen and piece of paper, ordering him to jot everything down, and there was lots more banter and levity until a group of Ajax fans, all worse for wear, on the other side of the street recognised Clough and started hurling insults.

Most managers would have ignored it and walked on. Clough marched over and started telling them they should be ashamed of the language they were using to guests of their city and that Ajax and their supporters had not encountered anything like that when they were in Nottingham.

The hostility continued and at one point Shilton, Burns and Lloyd exchanged looks and started crossing the street to back up their manager. 'Hold your horses,' Taylor told them. The players then watched Clough carry on remonstrating with the Ajax fans until they held up their hands, accepted they had been out of order and apologised to everyone.

The drama over, Forest's players found a seedy little bar opposite all the brothel windows, ordered several rounds of beers, listened to the jukebox and spent an hour chatting to the locals and sex tourists.

'Here we are, out enjoying a beer the night before a European Cup semi-final,' O'Neill said, looking at his watch. 'It's five past ten, the Ajax players will all be in bed now.'

'Aye,' Clough said, 'but none of them will be getting any sleep.'

In the modern day, when alcohol is anathema to most managers, it would be a scandal splashed all over the newspapers, accompanied by long, scolding columns asking whether they had lost the plot and calling for resignations. Back then, people just shrugged and acknowledged this strangely successful club made a habit of knocking back a few drinks on the nights before games and that it hadn't done them much harm so far.

The one time it seriously threatened to blow up in Clough's face was against Southampton in the League Cup final and, that apart, there was only one other occasion when one of his players can remember it backfiring.

That was in Pitesti, the town Clough described as Middlesbrough without the glamour, where Taylor was so unimpressed with the landscape he abandoned the usual match-day walk after a hundred yards. There was a booze-up the night before that game too and John O'Hare, after all his years with Clough, had come to think of it as the norm. 'The problem was it wasn't very nice beer, so I drank some of the other lads' beers for them,' he says. 'I ended up putting away four or five pints because I didn't think I would be playing. It was bad beer. Then the next day we got to the ground and I found out I was in the team. It was an afternoon kickoff, because they didn't have floodlights, and I was feeling so rotten at half-time it was the only time in my life I had to fake an injury. I went into the dressing room and said to Jimmy Gordon: "My hamstring's gone." I'd never pulled a hamstring before, but I felt that bad because of the beer the previous night. I had to go off – the only time I bottled it in my life.'

A banner appeared at the City Ground during the first leg saying 'Nottingham Forest wipe the floor with Ajax'. Forest did just that, but Ajax had an even better home record than Liverpool in European competitions, unbeaten at De Meer Stadion since 1959, with only one defeat in forty-six games. Their sweeper, Rudi Krol, had been part of Ajax's formidable success in the early 1970s. The goalkeeper, Piet Schrijvers, had played in some of Holland's 1978 World Cup games and Frank Arnesen was the Dutch player of the year. Soren Lerby's header midway through the second half gave Ajax hope and a different side to Forest could conceivably have wilted. Clough's men dug in. They had worked out a way to subdue Krol, with Francis dropping back on him, and Burns in particular was magnificent in the face of a late onslaught.

All of which brought Forest to another of those moments in time when the dreamers became dream-makers once again, and it became a little easier to understand why Lloyd, when he went into the after-dinner speaking circuit, used to open his routine with one of his favourite lines. 'Brian Clough was supposed to be here with me tonight – but unfortunately he's doing a sponsored walk from Dover to Calais.'

The date was 30 May 1980. Ian Curtis, frontman for Joy Division, had just been buried. Henry Hill, the mobster whose story inspired *Goodfellas*, was signing up to become an informant for the FBI. *The Empire Strikes Back* was in its first week at the cinemas. Jack Nicholson was peering through the hole he had just created with an axe in a bathroom door. Pacman had just been released, Alton Towers had opened and Seve Ballesteros had won the US Masters, his second major, at the age of twenty-three. Robert Mugabe was the new president of Zimbabwe and Ronald Reagan was plotting how to remove Jimmy Carter from the White House. South Africa had banned Pink Floyd's 'Another Brick in the Wall' and Johnny Logan was number one in the UK with 'What's Another Year?' Sebastian Coe and Steve Ovett were preparing to race in the Moscow Olympics and on a balmy May evening at the Santiago Bernabeu, Madrid, at approximately 8.25pm local time, two football teams were lining up in the tunnel and a broken-nosed old centre-half by the name of Kenneth Burns was removing his false teeth.

That, unfortunately for Kevin Keegan, was precisely the moment the European footballer of the year happened to turn around from the line of Hamburg players and look directly at the man who would be marking him that evening. Burns returned his gaze with the slightly mad stare of someone who should be wearing a stocking mask. 'That was when I saw my chance with Kevin,' Lloyd says. 'I shook his hand and whispered in his ear: "Look, Kev, we've known each other a long time. I like you and I will be straight with you. Kenny Burns is planning to kick the shit out of you tonight. He says you are a dead man. Just look at him, if you don't believe me." Kevin's face was a picture. Kenny had just stuck some pink chewing gum in his mouth and, I swear, for the life of me it looked like he was eating raw flesh.'

The story goes that Keegan started as a striker that day but ended up playing as a sweeper, so desperate was he to avoid the gap-toothed Glaswegian. It has been exaggerated over time and the record books show there were only two fouls on him throughout the opening forty-five minutes – though, admittedly, nobody ever kept stats for what happened off the ball. What cannot be denied, though, is that Hamburg were not happy with Forest's tactics. It was never reported at the time but they even returned the pennant that McGovern had handed to Hamburg's captain Peter Nogly at the coin-toss. 'Keep it,' came the message. 'We don't want anything to remember you by.'

That might have had something to do with the provocative

283

comments Taylor made beforehand when he predicted a 1–0 Forest win, identifying the various weaknesses of Hamburg's players. Taylor, as always, envisaged no problems, insisting that the goalkeeper Rudi Kargus 'isn't worth two bob' and that Horst Hrubesch was so useless with the ball at his feet he 'needs half an hour to turn round'. Taylor also pointed out that Manny Kaltz, Hamburg's vaunted right-back, was not comfortable when opponents ran at him and, privately, he also told his players that Keegan was tiring 'as he always does at this time of the season'.

Again, Forest's players were tempted to suspect Taylor was over-egging the truth and reminded themselves that he once described Juventus, Derby's opponents in the 1973 semi-final, as 'a mid-table Third Division team'. Hamburg had beaten Real Madrid, spectacularly, in the semi-finals, losing the first leg 2–0 in the Bernabeu before thrashing the Spanish champions 5–1 at Volksparkstadion. Before that, they had knocked out Hajduk Split in the quarter-finals and in the second round Keegan scored in both legs as they won 6–3 on aggregate against the Dynamo Tbilisi side that had eliminated Liverpool. Hamburg were clear favourites. Keegan, tiring or not, was one of the players Clough regarded the highest and Kaltz was a West Germany international renowned for his overlapping runs and *bananenflanken*, the 'banana crosses' he whipped into his team's forwards. Hrubesch was known as *Das Kopfball-Ungeheuer* – the header-monster – in the Bundesliga and often benefited from Kaltz's deliveries, explaining their routine in its simplest terms as 'Manny banana, I head, goal.'

Clough had prepared for the final by taking his players back to Cala Millor for a week, where he insisted they did 'absolutely bugger all' bearing in mind they had already played sixty-four games that season. 'I told the players there would be no training, no formalities,' he explained. 'It was a case of get your shorts on and into your flip-flops and get down the beach. And at night have a few drinks – but if you've got a bad head in the morning don't come complaining to me. The players came and went as they pleased. And if they weren't in till two in the morning they slept till eleven. Busy doing nothing, soaking up the sunshine and San Miguels in Majorca was the best preparation any team ever underwent prior to a European Cup final.'

Viv Anderson has a memory of 'walking down the main street in Cala Millor and hearing some holiday-makers saying: "They can't be playing in the European Cup in a week's time . . . all they do is drink,"' while Robertson, having been introduced to Tia Maria for the first time, was involved in a comedic scene at the airport on the way home when, still half-cut, some loose change spilled out of his top pocket. Every time he bent down to pick up the coins, more fell out of his pocket. Two or three times it happened, leaving him scrabbling around on the floor in full view of everyone. Robertson was carrying a bottle of Tia Maria in a brown paper bag, Rab C Nesbitt-style, but even then Clough let it go.

There was, however, one member of the squad who was getting withdrawal symptoms. All the lounging about wasn't good enough for Peter Shilton, who liked to train every day, and it didn't help his state of mind that when he went off to find somewhere suitable, walking up and down the seafront and exploring various hotel grounds, he couldn't find a single piece of available grass in the entire resort.

'I was panicking,' he says. 'I said to Peter Taylor, who

understood because he used to be a goalkeeper himself: "Look, I need to do some diving around, I need to handle the ball, I have to do something." Peter said: "Don't worry about it, when we get to Madrid we're staying in the mountains and it's a lush training pitch." So I just did some running. I tried to do a bit of ball work on a bit of grass I found beside one hotel, but the owner came out and told us to clear off. Otherwise, the only bit of diving around I could do was on the beach, surrounded by all the holidaymakers.

'I wasn't fully prepared and when we arrived in Madrid the training ground was like a hard tennis court, baked in the sun and as hard as concrete. Diving was out of the question, unless I wanted an injury. I was panic-stricken and I went to see Peter again: "I thought it was grass!" Clough strolled over to find out what the problem was. "Well, you better go and find whatever you can," he said. I went off with Jimmy Gordon and the only bit of grass we could find was a traffic island, fifty yards in diameter with two trees on, in the middle of a busy dual-carriageway. I did two fifteen-minute training sessions, a little bit of diving around, and Jimmy put down a couple of tracksuit tops as makeshift goalposts and threw a few balls in the air. So that was my preparation for a European Cup final, on the middle of a roundabout with all the traffic tooting their horns.'

As it turned out, Hrubesch was carrying an ankle injury and started on the bench, but that blow for Hamburg had to be put in context next to Forest's own problems. Trevor Francis had shown the full range of his attacking qualities in the previous two rounds, but in the penultimate home game of the season he found out the hard way what a brutal business professional sport can be sometimes. Forest were four up against Crystal Palace, with ten minutes to go, and Francis was looking for his hat-trick goal when he chased after the ball and suddenly collapsed to the ground. 'My first thought, and I mean this, was that someone in the crowd had shot me,' he says. His Achilles tendon had snapped and Francis did not even join the travelling party in Madrid. Clough had told him to stay away because he felt, psychologically, that the sight of their match-winner the previous year on crutches would have a negative effect on everyone.

That told only part of the story, though. Stan Bowles had blown any chance of playing by not turning up for the trip to Majorca and throwing a tantrum when he was left out of the team when Forest staged a testimonial match to mark Robertson's long service. 'Bowles would have had a chance of playing in the final,' Clough said. 'He won't be involved now unless he is in the box with the cup.'

Forest were down to the bare bones and, incredibly, about to become the only side in the history of the European Cup who could not even fill their bench for the final – naming four substitutes instead of the permitted five. One was Jim Montgomery, Sunderland's goalkeeper in the 1973 FA Cup final, who had been drafted in from Birmingham when Chris Woods, seeing no chance of getting past Shilton, moved to QPR. O'Hare was another substitute, approaching his thirty-sixth birthday. Needham was on the bench and Bryn Gunn had been drafted in as back-up for Frank Gray because the left-back was carrying an injury. Gunn came from Kettering and had broken into the team at the start of the 1975–76 season, at the age of seventeen, but virtually disappeared ever since.

To add to Forest's problems, Shilton needed a painkilling injection because of a shoulder injury and Lloyd, who had just been voted as the club's player of the season, had damaged his ankle on his return to the England team for a game against Wales. Shilton was suffering so badly that Montgomery, who was now thirty-six, was on standby to make his debut, while Lloyd had to endure an unorthodox fitness test before Clough let him play.

'On the morning of the match we had a five-a-side. My ankle was strapped up and Clough had that look on his face. He decided he was going to get involved and for twenty minutes he followed me around, repeatedly kicking my ankle. I was in bits. If I went left, he went left. If I went right, he did the same. Tap, tap, tap. "Do you feel that?" I'd say: "No, not at all, gaffer." My ankle was the size of a football. I got back to my hotel room, screamed in agony, and called down for the biggest bucket of ice you've ever seen.'

The injury to Francis also meant Mills taking over from Brian Kidd of Manchester United as the youngest player ever to start a European Cup final. Mills was quick and lively. He had run in the All England Schools 100m final and been capped at schoolboy level at both football and rugby but, plainly, it wasn't a good sign that Clough was having to bring in fringe players, or that he had to improvise so early in the match. Mills initially lined up with Birtles in attack, but Forest were so over-run in the opening exchanges Clough instructed the teenager to forget everything that had been planned and drop back into his usual midfield position. It might not sound like a huge change but it was the first time Forest had abandoned the 4-4-2 formation that had served them so well and it left them with an unusual system for the age. 'Managers nowadays all play 4-5-1,' Lloyd says, 'but in 1980 nobody did.'

The onus was on Birtles to lead the line on his own and he ran himself into a frazzle. 'I've never seen a lad cover as much ground, willingly and unselfishly, as Birtles did that night,' Clough later said. 'Honestly, I've never seen a more exhausted footballer in all my time in the game.'

Birtles finished the game with his socks round his ankles, his shin pads discarded and scarcely able to jog let alone run. But his tackling back, holding up of the ball and scrapping for possession set the example for everyone. Nobody kept statistics back then of how far each player ran, but Clough was pretty sure it would have been a record. Birtles, he said, had done more miles than Emil Zatopek.

Shilton said afterwards he had never played in another game – not even the European Cup tie against Liverpool – where the opponents had put so much pressure on his goal. Hamburg swarmed all over Forest from the start and had no choice but to drive forward again after that moment, twenty-one minutes in, when Robertson had his first chance to take on Kaltz and establish whether Taylor was right.

His body swerve and change of direction took Kaltz out of the game in an instant. Robertson had come inside then knocked the ball into Birtles and kept on running, left to right, towards the 'D' of the German penalty box. Birtles had his back to goal and Nogly right behind him. The striker was knocked off balance, but as he went down he still managed to extend his left leg to get the next touch. And then the ball was back with Robertson, the mercurial Robertson, and he was away from Keegan next and drawing back his right foot.

'I was stretching but I caught it with the outside of my boot. I saw it sail towards the corner and I thought: "It's got a chance." And then I thought: "Wow, it's going in, it's actually going in." And then I suddenly felt very tired. You see other guys running to the supporters or doing somersaults when they score. I must have been in a state of shock. Or maybe I was just knackered – it had been a long run by my standards. I stood rooted to the spot, put my hands in the air and thought: "Whoa, I've just scored in a European Cup final." When I was a kid I thought the European Cup was for Puskas, Di Stefano, legends like that. And then I was mobbed, of course.'

That was the moment of Robertson's football immortality. It wasn't the most powerful shot, a low right-foot drive that bounced a couple of times across the turf. The ball went to the left of Kargus. It clipped the inside of the post and Robertson's arms were up in the air. His team-mates were running to him from every angle. And Shilton was already bellowing to his defenders to concentrate, to keep tight and not to switch off even for a fraction of a second.

The rest of the night was a blur that left the Forest players on their knees with exhaustion. They had to give everything to hold on to that lead and their backs-to-the-wall operation in the second half did not appeal to every football connoisseur. Brian Glanville, in the *Sunday Times*, accused Clough of 'tactical cowardice' and lamented the lack of adventure. 'Having acknowledged the excellence of Shilton, the prowess of Lloyd, Burns, O'Neill, Birtles and Robertson, it must still be said that their second-half strategy was a craven one,' he wrote. The Spanish football writers called it 'soulless'. The German press denounced it as 'Blitzkrieg' football.

Yet Forest were on their last legs, running on empty with an experimental team that had only one recognised striker in their entire squad. Could they really be blamed for sitting back, absorbing the pressure and then trying to hit their opponents on the counter-attack? Clough brought on O'Hare to try to calm everything down and in the last quarter of an hour it was obvious the limping Gray could not last any longer. Gunn was the only option. 'I remember taking my tracksuit off,' Gunn says. 'Peter Taylor turned to Cloughie and said: "Oh Christ, we're in the shit now." That wasn't much of a confidence booster, to be honest.'

Birtles was so exhausted that when he ran clear late in the match he couldn't even get his shot away. 'My legs felt like treacle. It was like being on the end of a fishing line and being pulled back.' Yet he still found the strength a few minutes later to take the ball to the corner flag as Keegan came over to challenge him. 'I did a couple of little circles and he ended up giving away a free-kick. Keegan was so frustrated he picked up the corner flag and threw it to the floor. I enjoyed that.'

Keegan's mood extended to the airport the following day when he was flying back to England at the same time as the winners and complained to Clough about Forest's refusal to open the game up. He also decided not to wish the Forest players well at the traditional winners' banquet. 'I am a bad loser and I was too gutted by the defeat,' he explained. 'Neither was I a lover of Nottingham Forest.'

The memory of those sour grapes would make Clough's eyes twinkle in later years. Clough came into the press conference after the match, gave the Hamburg coach Branko Zebec a kiss on the cheek and almost floated out of the room. 'I've not seen a team apply itself better for many years,' he said. 'Shilton, Burns, Lloyd spring to mind, but it's pointless naming names because everybody concerned with Nottingham Forest has won the European Cup. We gave Hamburg a lesson in application, determination, dedication and pride, all the good things we don't hear enough about and that are taken for granted in English football. We had no option but to defend and if you have to defend then you must do it well. We did it well. We weren't lucky, we were good.'

McGovern had been reacquainted with UEFA's dignitaries to accept the trophy – 'it's easier the second time around' – and none of the men in suits had any idea that Forest had secretly called in a local firm of silver-makers to patch it up after discovering various bumps from one of its many nights out (sometimes transported in the boot of Taylor's car). Birtles, exhausted, was wearing a red bowler hat. O'Neill no longer had to torture himself about missing out in Munich. Shilton had got through the 'longest night of my life' and the celebrations went on so long inside the stadium the lights eventually went out. Gunn woke the next morning 'cuddling the medal'.

Clough summed it up to the media. 'You win something once and people say it is all down to luck. You win it twice and it shuts the buggers up.'

Forest had defied everyone's predictions again and on the bus journey to the airport Clough leant back in his seat and looked across to the man sitting on the opposite row.

'Pete,' he said, 'tell me what we've won and in how long. What is it, about four years? Two European Cups, a championship, two League Cups – has anyone ever done as much in such a short time?'

Taylor chuckled and reminded Clough that it all started against Orient in the Anglo-Scottish Cup. 'We've won so much,' he said, 'I can't remember everything, except that we've been in five finals and won four of them.'

It was later that he realised he had miscalculated. Forest had played in seven finals; winning six. The full list of achievements started on 15 December 1976 when Forest won the Anglo-Scottish Cup, even if the rest of football scarcely took a blind bit of notice. That was followed, in order, by promotion in the 1976–77 season, the League Cup and the championship in 1977–78, the Charity Shield, the League Cup and European Cup in 1979, the Super Cup in 1980 and, lastly, the European Cup again. Forest had played finals against Orient, Liverpool, Southampton, Malmo, Barcelona, Wolves and Hamburg, losing only to Wolves. In the process, they had broken countless long-standing records and beaten the champions of England, Greece, Switzerland, West Germany, Sweden (twice), Romania, East Germany, Holland and West Germany again. And, of course, Barcelona.

All of that had been done at a club where turmoil was once a normal state of being. That club had been on its sickbed, thirteenth in the Second Division, five points off the bottom three, when Clough landed his coat on the peg for the first time. Derby, champions-in-waiting at the time, were now a Second Division team, relegated three days after Forest had seen off Ajax. Chelsea, one of the clubs promoted with Forest in 1977, had dropped back into the second tier within two years – albeit with newly decorated dressing rooms.

Yet the most incredible part, perhaps, is that if it had not been for a mercifully foggy night against Southampton on 16 February 1977, Forest may not even have won promotion and their history would never have been marked out in those defining moments: the demolition of Manchester United at Old Trafford, Roberton's penalty in the replayed League Cup final, Shilton's save at Coventry, Barrett's volley against Liverpool, Bowyer's header in Cologne, Francis in Munich and, finally, Robertson in Madrid.

Twenty years later, a German author tried to sum up the fairytale: 'In the whole history of football, there has never been a team that can compare with Nottingham Forest from 1977 to 1980, and there never will be again. They came literally from nothing and, overnight, became the best club side in England. No one can explain how it happened. Perhaps the same God that gave the world Robin Hood smiled again on the poor of Nottingham. In just two years they rose from near obscurity to the greatest prize in the world of club football. They were football's equivalent of the Napoleon of 1797 and the Beatles of 1963. And they deserve those comparisons. They must surely lay claim to being the most remarkable club team in football history. No team from any country had achieved such a feat before. No team will ever achieve that feat again.'

Birtles sums it up another way. 'Every time I watch Liverpool now, I look for the flags on the Kop because there's a two-year gap in the dates. They go from '77 and '78 to '81. And I always think: that's us, that gap. We did that.'

Whether those players received enough credit is debatable. Forest had played one hundred and eighty-four competitive games in three seasons and lost only twenty-six. They won 78 per cent of their European Cup ties when, to put it into context, the most celebrated of Sir Alex Ferguson's Manchester

United sides won 68 per cent of theirs in 1997 to 2000. Over those three-year periods, Forest won seven major trophies to United's five. Yet when the debates start about the greatest football teams in history, one of those sides barely gets a mention.

Clough, of course, was hailed as a genius. Yet did the players get the praise they deserved? On a scale of one to ten, Burns gives his old manager a rating of nine. 'As good as he was, the team was better – ten out of ten,' he insists.

Just consider the BBC Sports Personality of the Year awards in 1979 – with a disgruntled Ken Smales sitting in the audience – when Forest were beaten to the team award by the British show-jumping team. 'Our Forest team won the European Cup and League Cup,' Smales grizzled later on, 'yet the team award was won by four horses!'

Equally, take a look at the different teams that have been honoured in the National Football Museum's hall of fame. Manchester United's European Cup-winning side from 1968 is there. So is the Liverpool side of 1978 that Forest deposed as First Division champions and knocked out of Europe. The Busby Babes of the 1950s were inducted a few years back, as was the Manchester City side that won the league, the FA Cup and European Cup Winners' Cup from 1968 to 1970. Aston Villa, European Cup winners in 1982, are honoured, as are England's 1966 World Cup winners and the Preston 'Invincibles' of 1888–89. The criterion is that the side must have played at least twenty-five years before. Yet the Forest team that won the European Cup back to back, as well as two League Cups, the Super Cup and all those other records, have never been nominated.

'What pisses us off more than anything is that we were never appreciated and never properly recognised for what we achieved,' Birtles says. 'We beat Malmo and everybody thought, "Oh, it's only Malmo." Well, they had beaten some bloody good sides to get to the final, and so had we. We played the European Cup when it was the champions of every country. It's now the champions and also-rans of every country. We beat Hamburg with Kevin Keegan and Ajax with Rudi Krol. But it was all Liverpool this, Liverpool that and Liverpool sodding everything in the media. Aston Villa won the European Cup once and are in the hall of fame at the National Football Museum. We're not. Yet we won the damn thing twice, back to back.'

In Madrid, waiting to fly back from the final, some of the players gave an impromptu press conference at the airport. 'One of the questions narked Robbo,' Birtles recalls. 'He got a bit annoyed with the journalists and said: "You just think we're a bunch of rag-tags because of where we came from." Larry had been at Coventry and nobody gave him a chance. Kenny had his reputation and people had given up on him. Robbo and Martin were in the reserves before Brian came. Viv was a local lad. He and Tony were there before Brian came. We all knew the genius of Clough and Taylor, but the players had to respond to that genius and that was the beauty of that team. They all responded.

'Some players went the other way and didn't make it but the ones who took everything on board went all the way to the top, and they deserve so much praise for doing that, because when you have been used to mediocrity it is so easy to stay in mediocrity. We all resented it a bit that we didn't get more credit.'

Robertson was a case in point. 'When I try to tell people how good he was, it can be difficult because it was over thirty years ago,' McGovern says. 'So what I generally say is: "You know a few years ago there was a guy called Ryan Giggs who played until he was forty and was regarded as one of the best left-wingers of all time? Well, John Robertson was like Ryan Giggs but with two good feet, not one. He had more ability than Ryan Giggs, his ratio of creating goals was better and overall he was the superior footballer." Giggs had the longevity – but Robertson, in a short space of time, was the better player.'

It is high praise, but they all say the same at Forest. 'I often get asked to name the best player I ever played with,' Lloyd says. 'Well, I played with the likes of Kevin Keegan, John Toshack, Steve Heighway and Tommy Smith at Liverpool. But I always say that little chubby left-winger at Forest was the best. He was an absolute magician on the ball.'

O'Neill is equally effusive. 'John always hates me talking about him. He's very modest, but I actually enjoy it because John was one of the first players I met in October 1971 and I always felt he and I were interlinked. John was a central midfielder back then and he could pass it, either foot, all over the park. But if you had told me on that cold January morning of 1975, sitting in the dressing room waiting for Clough to arrive, that John would be the scourge of Europe and probably the most influential outfield player in the game for three years – and I include a lot of Liverpool players in that – and he would do it from a position of outside-left, I might have laughed for about a month.'

Robertson had played in every game for three years and left his influence on two European Cup finals – scoring one winning goal, and setting up another. 'Over the years,' Taylor wrote in Robertson's testimonial programme, 'I've seen any number of left-wingers, including the likes of Gento, the famous Real Madrid player who everyone used to rave about. Well, you can have the lot for me – in terms of productivity nobody compares with John.'

Jimmy Gordon wrote: 'I saw a lot of Tom Finney and Stan Matthews in my time and it was very difficult to choose between them. But when you look at what Finney and Matthews had to offer, John has a bit of both – and something extra on top.'

Robertson's brilliance on the wing was one of the primary reasons why Luiz Felipe Scolari, the former Brazil national team manager, once said he had 'fallen in love' with Clough's Forest team and developed such a soft spot for that side he always thought of them as his favourite English club.

Yet when does Robertson's name get mentioned among the greats of European football? He was never shortlisted for the European footballer of the year award and the average modern-day player would probably have to stick his name into Google judging by a line in Craig Bellamy's 2013 autobiography. Bellamy played for Norwich when O'Neill was manager and Robertson was on the coaching staff. Yet he had never heard of Robertson. 'Someone told me he had been a proper player once. I know that now. I know that people thought he was a genius, that he was Brian Clough's favourite player at Nottingham Forest, that he won European Cups. But back then, I'd look at him with bandages round his knees, puffing on a cigarette and think: "No chance."'

Some of Robertson's old team-mates have a theory he does not get more acclaim because he is Scottish, but that was never a problem for Jim Baxter or Kenny Dalglish. More likely, it was because he didn't play for one of the traditional elite clubs and there was someone else at Forest who hogged most of the publicity; or maybe it was because Robertson, with his ropey dress sense and throaty nicotine-laced chuckle, did not look like the classic superstar. Bowles might not have been at Forest long but he had a wonderful way to describe his team-mate. 'Robbo was one of those blokes who could never look smart,' he said. 'No matter what you did with him he always looked like an unmade bed.'

All that can really be said for certain is that there had never been another team with so much gloriously swift achievement. They were the titans of their day, the boys who reminded everyone that if you wanted something enough there might just be ways and means of getting it. There had never been a more unusual movement at the top of their sport and it left the entire football world scratching their heads.

'Who is this McGovern?' a perplexed Günter Netzer, the German midfield legend, asked after Forest had won in Cologne. 'I have never heard of him, yet he ran the game in the second half.'

Then there was the chief football correspondent from the Dutch newspaper *De Telegraaf* who interviewed Shilton after the same game and told Forest's goalkeeper: 'Out of your entire team, your name is the only one that is familiar to me.'

'Well, you'll know us all now,' Shilton replied.

Forest's rise to the top, lest it be forgotten, also took place when only the champions of each country and holders could compete in the European Cup. There was no safety net of multiple group stages to guard against the occasional defeat here and there and the legacy, thirty-five years on, is that Nottingham has won the competition more times than London, Paris, Berlin, Moscow and Rome – with a combined population of 30.4 million – altogether. It took Manchester United, champions in 1968, another thirty-one years to win the European Cup for a second time – Ferguson's win in 1999 coming at his fifth attempt – and it was 2012 when Chelsea finally notched up one for London. Arsenal, Tottenham and all the others are still on the waiting list.

'All of a sudden, Nottingham didn't just have Robin Hood,' McGovern says. 'We had Robin Hood, Brian Clough and Nottingham Forest. Everybody recognises Nottingham Forest throughout the whole of Europe now. Go to any country and say you're from Nottingham – "Aah, Nottingham Forest." They were adventurous days. They were unorthodox days because we had an unorthodox manager and his partner. I've never heard of another side, for example, preparing for a European Cup semi-final by visiting the red-light district in Amsterdam and negotiating with a pimp for a team discount. But it worked.

'In five years, a football team from out of nowhere won promotion. They were cheeky enough to win the league by seven points. They beat Liverpool to win the League Cup the same season. That was cheeky enough but then they won the European Cup at the first attempt. They won the League Cup again, then the following year they won the European Cup again, just to prove it wasn't a fluke. I mean, that was right cheeky. According to the media, they were a one-hit wonder who would never do it again. But that team showed they could compete on equal terms with anyone in Europe, and they were the only team you would fancy to beat Liverpool. And they did beat Liverpool.'

All this, remember, from a manager who lasted forty-four days in his previous job. 'Don Revie said to Brian Clough: "You couldn't do it better than I did," pointing out he had lost only four league games,' McGovern continues. 'But Nottingham Forest lost three. Brian did it better and then he won two European Cups. So, sorry Don, he did it a lot better, in less time.'

McGovern was once described as Forest's water-carrier. Well, someone had to carry the water if Clough was going to walk on it and he didn't do too badly. Franz Beckenbauer is the only man who has lifted the European Cup more times and it was the faithful McGovern who instigated the decisive move on that sweet-scented night at the Bernabeu.

McGovern won possession near the halfway line. Bowyer was involved. O'Neill fed it to Gray. Mills had a touch. Then it was Robertson versus Kaltz.

'We've got a little fat guy who will turn him inside out,' Clough had told Gary Newbon the day before the match.

'John Robertson?'

'Oh yes,' Clough said, and now he was laughing. 'A very talented, highly skilled, unbelievable outside-left . . . he will turn him inside out.'

On 1 October 1980, Nottingham Forest lost 1–0 at home to CSKA Sofia, going out of the first round of the European Cup 2–0 on aggregate. They have never been back.

'We were like one of those comets you see flying across the night sky. We burned brightly, but it was all too brief. But, boy, did we burn brightly for a while.'

John McGovern

Acknowledgements

Thank you to my colleagues at the *Guardian*, especially Ian Prior, for allowing me the time to write this book. Matt Appleby, one of my old match-going friends, has been an invaluable help with his encyclopaedic knowledge. José Mourinho was incredibly generous with his time and a delight to speak to. Thanks also to Nigel Clough, plus all the players who appear in this book, in particular John Robertson ('who fired the cannon?'), Colin Barrett, Garry Birtles, Ian Bowyer and Frank Clark, all great company as well as great footballers. At Headline, Jonathan Taylor made it happen at very short notice. Grenville Williams, Andy Hallam, Nigel Roe, Jitz Jani and Kevin Marriott provided some great stories of following the club. Thank you to Zoe and our little boy, James – brought up in Manchester but stubbornly telling his friends at primary school he supports some team called Nottingham Forest (Florence next). Most of all, thank you to the hugely talented Jonny Owen, a friend now as well as a colleague, for inviting me to write the book and creating a masterpiece of a film. If Brian Clough were here, you'd be getting one of those 'perfect' signs.

Daniel Taylor

Firstly, I have to thank my family and Vicky McClure, whose love and encouragement know no bounds. A massive thank you to Daniel Taylor, my favourite football writer and the only person whom I wanted to do the book of the film, for being prepared to do absolutely anything to make it happen. I'd also like to thank Lisa Toogood and Jim Gill at United Agents who contacted Jonathan Taylor at Headline and made all this happen at the drop of a hat. Finally, a special mention to all the players who spent their precious time talking to me and our two other brothers-in-arms, Owen Davies and Matt Appleby. Last but very much not least, everyone at Spool (County Craig and Penny) and of course the best film producer out there, Henry Normal, a Forest fan born and bred, and all his crew at the brilliant Babycow, especially Chloe and her mint 1970s-style graphics. Diolch yn fawr iawn.

Jonny Owen

Bibliography

The Official History of Nottingham Forest, Philip Soar
20 Legends: Nottingham Forest, John Brindley
Forest's Cult Heroes, David McVay
Forest Giants, John McGovern and Rob Jovanovic
Forest – The 1979 Season, John Lawson
Forest 1865–1978, John Lawson
Nottingham Forest Champions 1977–78, John Shipley
Clough, Tony Francis
Nobody Ever Says Thank You, Jonathan Wilson
Clough, The Autobiography, Brian Clough
With Clough By Taylor, Peter Taylor
150BC, Dave Armitage
The Life of Brian, Tim Crane
Forest Rambles, Richard Pulk
Kicking With Both Feet, Frank Clark
His Way, Patrick Murphy
Both Sides of the Border, Archie Gemmill
My Magic Carpet Ride, Garry Birtles
Super Tramp, John Robertson
Viv Anderson, Andrew Longmore
Stan Bowles, The Autobiography, Stan Bowles
Hard Man, Hard Game, Larry Lloyd
Peter Shilton, The Autobiography, Peter Shilton
From Bo'Ness to the Bernabeu, John McGovern

Picture Credits

Action Images: 2 top left;

Associated Newspapers/Solo Syndication: 4 top;

Getty Images: 3 bottom (Bob Thomas), 4 centre (Chris Smith/ Popperfoto), 7 bottom (Bob Thomas);

Press Association: 1 top (PA Archive), 1 bottom (PA Archive), 2 bottom (S&G and Barratts/EMPICS Sport), 3 top (PA Archive), 4 bottom (PA Archive), 6 bottom (Peter Robinson/ EMPICS Sport).

All other photographs courtesy of the *Nottingham Post*.

Index

311

DANIEL TAYLOR

Dwight, Roy 140
Dynamo Berlin 277–9

Edwards, Maurice 86
Eintracht Frankfurt 193
Elliott, Steve 167, 169, 177
Enderby Town 174
England (national team) vii, xii, 10,
   34, 41, 51, 65, 70, 78, 88, 102, 111,
   113, 114–17, 139, 146, 150, 155,
   157, 184, 198, 211, 212, 213, 288,
   295
Eriksson, Sven-Goran xi
European Championship: 1996 vii
European Cup:
   1969–70 16
   1972–3 16
   1978–9 vii, ix, 165, 169–95, 201–6,
      211–12, 219–21, 224–5,
      229–41, 243–62, 293
   1979–80 268–9, 272, 277–301
   1980–1 303
European Cup Winners' Cup:
   1968–9 295
   1969–70 295
   1978–9 269
European Inter-Club Cup: 1979 271–2
European Super Cup: 1980 269,
   270–1, 293, 295
Everton 18, 88, 90–3, 94, 103, 113,
   121, 124, 129, 158, 162, 171, 200,
   219, 266

FA Cup:
   1897–8 21, 264
   1956–7 258–9
   1958–9 3, 17, 21, 139–40, 263–4
   1966–7 19
   1970–1 69, 269
   1972–3 287
   1973–4 18

   1974–5 23, 29, 42, 44–6, 50
   1975–6 54–5
   1976–7 75, 118
   1977–8 129, 138, 161, 245
   1979–80 276
FA Youth Cup 43
Fairclough, David 275
Ferguson, Mick 159, 240, 274
Ferguson, Sir Alex 7, 186, 294–5, 300
Finney, Tom 161, 298
Flohe, Heinze 229
Football Association (FA) 18, 96, 115,
   116, 117, 144, 215
Football League 224
Football Writers' Association 160
Ford, Tony 162–3
Franchi, Artemio 261
Francis, Helen 216
Francis, Phyllis 216
Francis, Roy 216
Francis, Trevor ix, xv, 214–20, 242,
   247–8, 253, 254–5, 256, 273–4,
   279, 282, 286–7, 288, 294
Frost, David 37, 38
Fulham 29, 50, 56

Gemmell, Tommy 16
Gemmill, Archie ix, 85, 88–9, 98–9,
   102–3, 105, 121, 123, 127, 128,
   132, 133, 134, 138, 158, 161, 188,
   189–90, 202–3, 207, 210, 220, 221,
   222, 223, 246, 248–50, 251–2,
   265–7, 273–4
Gemmill, Betty 88
Gento 269, 298
George, Charlie 269–70
Giggs, Ryan 297
Giles, Johnny 33, 35
Gillies, Matt 15, 16, 23, 49
Glanville, Brian 290
Glasgow Rangers 146, 212